Also by Kathy Kolbe

The Conative Connection

Pure Instinct

PURE INSTINCT

Business' Untapped Resource

KATHY KOLBE

TIMES BOOKS

RANDOM HOUSE

COPYRIGHT AND TRADEMARKS

The terms Kolbe Conative Index®, KCI™, Action Mode®, Kolbe Concept™,
Kolbe FairSelection System™, Natural Advantage™, Kolbe TeamSuccess Program™
are claimed as trademarks. Where those terms appear in this book, they have been
printed in initial capital letters.

Library of Congress Number 93-8571
ISBN 0-8129-2069-4

Manufactured in the United States of America
9 8 7 6 5 4 3 2
First Edition
BOOK DESIGN: GLEN M. EDELSTEIN

To Will

INSTINCT is usually defined as the faculty of acting in such a way as to produce certain ends, without foresight of the ends, and without previous education in the performance.

The animal richest in reason might be also the animal richest in instinctive impulses.

—William James (1890)

CONTENTS

INTRODUCTION

A New York cabbie was driving me to the Random House office for a session with those who would be marketing *Pure Instinct*. Buoyed by an enthusiastic response at a seminar I had just conducted across town for a corporate client, I settled back for one of those fun and enlightening conversations that often come with such taxi rides. His questions were common: "What brings you to town?" "So what's the title of your book?" But his response challenged me. As he slammed on the brakes and began shouting, I thought it might even kill me.

"What?! You've written that people have instincts? You and your kind, you're the ones who make people out to be nothing better than dumb animals." He jerked back into traffic, yelling over his shoulder and punctuating his opinions with punches to the gas pedal or brake. "Hear the music I've got on the radio? It's classical stuff. I'm no sheep. See this book I've got sitting next to me? I'm bettering myself. Yeah, you, I'd be better putting my fingers in my ears than listening to anything *you've* got to say. I wish I were rich enough to buy up all the damn books of yours that they print. People shouldn't suffer through some dame writing about how we're all just a bunch of idiots who go around doing things for no good reason."

I gave him a big tip because he had given me more than just a terrifying ride through New York City. He'd helped put *Pure Instinct* into context for me. Above all, he'd confirmed that this book is a challenge.

It challenges the taxi driver's assumption—which he may have gotten from a modern-psychology textbook—that there are no such things as human instincts. It espouses, and substantiates the following theory: that our best decisions and greatest sense of accomplishment come when we act on instinct. I may never be able to convince the cabbie, however. It takes a certain faith to believe we were all created equal yet with individual strengths that can never be taken from us.

For business executives, the challenge in *Pure Instinct* is to build on the natural abilities of every person in the organization. For employees, it's to commit their innate talents to their work groups and jobs. For all of us, the challenge is to confront unavoidable conflicts without passing judgment on one person's value over another. This book challenges assumptions about the "right" and "wrong" ways to solve problems. And it takes on anyone whose limiting stereotypes interfere with the potential of others. It confronts false notions of what a person of color, or particular gender, or someone in a wheelchair, or an elderly person is able to contribute.

My challenge has been to give you a comprehensive sampling of my theory, experiences, and research as they relate to the workplace. I have forced myself not to stray too deeply into the psychological and educational arenas. As important as they are, this is not the book for a complete analysis of those issues. Nor is it the place for a full statistical review of research studies. I have focused more on anecdotal examples and on case studies. Here the challenge has been to give you sufficient insights without betraying the confidences of my clients, a diverse group that includes international corporations, start-up companies, universities, government groups, and sports teams. Every incident and person in this book is real. However, when I use only a first name, it is not the actual name of the person in the story. When descriptions are incomplete or have been altered, it is to protect people's privacy.

I'd like to pose this challenge for the cabbie: Read *Pure Instinct*, then try to ignore it. Don't let it change the way you view the world.

I'll bet he can't.

Pure Instinct

CHAPTER ONE

STRIVING INSTINCTS

THE FORCE BEHIND PRODUCTIVITY

Whenever you've had to make tough decisions and you've known one course was the "right" way but your instincts told you to go another direction, which route have you usually taken? If you went against your instincts, were you sorry later? Thousands of decision makers in all types of businesses tell me their greatest victories came when they trusted their guts. Then they lament that they're unsure of how to tap into these hidden resources or to maximize their use of this uncanny quality.

When people tell you to trust your instincts, they certainly aren't referring to Sigmund Freud's sex or death impulses, nor to Carl Jung's herd or nutritional drives. They are calling for the use of an executive function of your mind, something that is innate, action-oriented, subconscious, protective, definitely not learned, and clearly a necessity. These instincts are the same influences the media have noted in MOs of athletes, chefs, artists, and politicians. They're the drive behind my starting a business twenty years ago, and being able to dodge disasters over the years. These energy sources within us propel us toward personal productivity. They form the inner self that struggles for freedom, that cries out for self-actualization. Without acting on them, we are condemned to lives of frustration. They are what I call our *Striving Instincts*.

Especially in tough economic times, clients tell me they are burned out, fatigued, and sick of just going through the motions of problem solving. Reorganizations and policy shifts haven't addressed the pent-up stress. The exasperation runs so deep it cannot be "fixed" by superficial makeovers. Our global economy is in trouble because we have lost sight of the very basis of productivity: human beings' capacity to commit the mental energy of their instincts toward shared goals.

OVERTHINKING SOLUTIONS

THE BUSINESS WORLD HAS FOLLOWED THE ACADEMIC COMMUNITY BY DISTRUSTING, even demeaning, human instinct. Instead it has focused on training programs that are meant to develop work *habits* but actually drum out every iota of naturally inspired action, therefore inhibiting workers' best performances. Managers don't trust employees' internal decision-making capacity and try to force them into lock-step procedures, as if there were only one "right" way to seize an opportunity. Corporations often give more credence to computers than to instinctively based common sense.

As those in charge ponder what needs to be done to speed up our economic recovery, they bypass instinct and become paralyzed by cognitive gridlock. Most of us operate in a business environment that overthinks and underdoes. Workers are sent to "feel-good" seminars to get motivated, which ignore the other elements of creativity and do not help companies succeed. One more edict telling personnel how they *have* to perform, one more committee imposing restrictions, one more course teaching the *approved* methodology, one more quantitative analysis of what went wrong—all add up to further congestion of the creative juices. It's time to put our fingers in our ears and start listening once again to our instincts. We won't get unstuck until we do.

Striving Instincts are the restless urges of every would-be contributor. Thwarting them has led to unprecedented high levels of job stress, now the number-one cause of heart attacks. Instead of seeking ways of identifying and using individual strengths, many employers demand conformity to a particular method and reject people they fear will act differently. They do this without any proof that a job can be accomplished only one way.

IMPEDIMENTS TO SUCCESS

GOVERNMENT-IMPOSED REGULATIONS COUPLED WITH BUSINESSES' EMPLOYEE-selection practices often result in a devastating game of red rover. Like the playground invitation to break down a human chain, they limit the potential players who are invited to "come over" and try to succeed. Even those given the opportunity to attempt breaking down barriers face a status quo braced against admitting them to the team. The test they must pass has never proved fair, yet it keeps most would-be participants out of the game.

Is it any wonder we're in trouble? Can we turn our backs on people's instinctive strengths and not expect negative outcomes? The joy in the creative process comes through productive effort. When all hope for attaining the thrill of success is put out of reach, it follows that many people will turn to artificial "highs." History will undoubtedly take note of our era, one in which human beings' instincts to strive have been largely ignored. Substance abuse is rampant, along with crime, suicide, and failed relationships. Self-confidence, the by-product of productivity, has eroded along with the economy.

Despite these gloomy statements, I believe the prognosis is positive. How can I be so sure? Because all the battering and bruising the world imposes cannot still the bubbling in our instinctive caldrons. Eventually we will have to take off the lid and remove the limitations on instinctive action that inhibit productivity.

Philosophers have generally agreed that instincts provide the force that drives natural urges. Striving Instincts are power sources, and they must find outlets. They compel us to be productive. When we function according to them, we fulfill our destinies and make our best decisions. When we act contrary to them, their power works against us. The human spirit is actualized through these instincts. Any attempt to thwart our Striving Instincts is an effort to crush our spirit. The very energy within our striving capacities will battle anything blocking its free expression.

Throughout history, despots have tried to limit instinct-driven action. Dictators have attempted to control freedom of speech, freedom to barter, freedom to work according to natural methods. Sooner or later every society overthrows such forms of oppression. The Chinese entrepreneur risks imprisonment to negotiate deals despite government restrictions on bartering; the writer in a totalitarian society knowingly faces punishment in order to express inner drives by putting pen to paper. All of us have a power within us that forces us to accomplish our purposes through *pure instinct.*

TAKING ACTIONS THAT INCREASE
JOB SATISFACTION

My goal is to help it happen sooner. The pain in our workplaces is too great; the personal rewards are too few. People are suffering a lack of self-esteem, and organizations are not meeting otherwise attainable goals. Even my most financially comfortable clients worry about "losing their touch"; they don't believe they are appreciated for who they are and often lack a sense of personal accomplishment. Financial and other material rewards cannot compensate for being unable to fulfill your potential.

Whether you are directing mental energies toward goals in a professional firm, sales organization, manufacturing firm, home environment, or classroom as student or teacher, you need to fulfill your responsibilities through your natural way of striving. I have chosen to focus on job-related issues because they usually devour the bulk of our striving energy. Often it is through our work that we are known—and most likely come to know ourselves. Yet their jobs are also a source of frustration for most people. According to a 1992 study by Shearson Lehman Brothers, only 18 percent of Americans feel that their vocations are both personally and financially rewarding.

Most jobs are unrewarding because they force people to work against their instinctive grain. One worker fortunate to have a role that allows her to thrive instinctively said, "I find this job so personally rewarding that I would do it even if I were paid half as much." But such sentiments are few and far between in today's workplace.

When you are out of work or have to work in a manner that is out of sync with your instincts, you not only kick the proverbial dog, you want to kick yourself for letting it happen. This book provides action plans that allow you to *do* something about it.

Most of what I've learned about the Striving Instincts has come from managing my own publishing business and helping clients throughout the world increase productivity. Victor, who is now the CEO of a midwestern communications company, exemplifies what can happen when an otherwise top performer begins to work contrary to his instincts. He rose to the top, proving he was not afraid to make tough decisions. He pursued unique leads and developed markets when others thought there was no hope of their succeeding. In fact, he was so successful that he was promoted to the senior management team despite not having a college degree, usually a prerequisite for advancement in his company.

"My not having a degree was so disturbing to the board of directors," he said, "that they had me get an undergraduate degree and an MBA in a crash program paid for by the company." That's when Victor discovered what had made him productive. "I learned what didn't work. I tried acting according to the formulas I had studied, but the more I did things the 'right' way, the worse my productivity. I blew it when it came to closing sales. I wasn't as effective in making budget projections. I lost my touch."

It took Victor a full year to truly understand why his performance had deteriorated. He valued the knowledge he'd acquired. "So I began doing things by the book instead of trusting my instincts," Victor reflected. "Those instincts had always served me well, but I thought I'd become so smart I didn't have to listen to them anymore. It cost me. Big time."

We all pay a price when we don't pay attention to our instincts. Victor eventually fought to reclaim his. He later become CEO of his company because he had the necessary education *and* because he'd found learned methods did not need to interfere with his native talents. Productive effort includes both the ability to reason and the energy of instincts. Victor learned he could not substitute one for the other.

During the time he suppressed his instincts, they never betrayed him. No amount of training or education could erode the force of these innate abilities. Deny them all we want, they remain steadfast, providing the basis for our every action. In our uncertain world, instincts are the only human factor guaranteed to remain constant.

When I first met Victor, he had no words to describe his Striving Instincts or how they function. He didn't know if his instincts differed from others', and what made them unique. Without better understanding of what had gone wrong, he feared he might repeat his mistakes. "It's scary," he said. "I knew I had lost sight of my own strengths and had to go back to listening to my gut reactions. When I use what I've learned *without* letting it overwhelm what my instincts tell me to do, I make my best decisions. But it was tough not to make the same errors all over again when I knew more about statistical methods than I did about my internal modes of operation."

WHY SOME PEOPLE GET MORE DONE

MY WORK, WHICH I DISCUSSED IN MY EARLIER BOOK, *THE CONATIVE CONNECTION*, focused for years on the actions that result from engaging our instincts.

Conative actions are our talents. They are the effect of our channeling the energy of instincts toward intended, or *volitional*, actions. It was gratifying to be able to tell Victor that I had an instrument, the *Kolbe Conative Index*, or KCI (explained in the next chapter), which would pinpoint his individual conative strengths and give him a picture of his unique *modus operandi*, or MO. But these talents are the tip of the iceberg, the observable traits that stem from the subconscious—and therefore hidden—force of instincts. *Pure Instinct* plumbs the greater depths of our abilities, the source that gives Victor and the rest of us the power to create.

I spent a dozen years researching conative talents and their implications for individual and group performances. It was not enough. Victor's KCI result went a long way in revealing how he needed to communicate and what situations caused him stress. They also explained why he succeeded in some roles and failed in others. But it was not until I observed and interviewed thousands of people—whose KCI results I had in hand—that I was able to explain why people with similar results accomplish at different levels. I found that though we all have equal instinctive power, those who are more productive engage that power more fully, focusing its force and reacting within reason. Others fritter away their mental energies, misdirecting efforts or unduly editing their own actions. *Pure Instinct* looks at how you can target your natural talents for the greatest possible impact. It allows you to anticipate your own foibles and to give others' reactions a positive spin.

Victor's KCI result gave him what he termed "the missing link" for completely understanding his potential. Once he learned how to manage instincts in relation to thoughts, feelings, and commitments, he maximized his own and others' efforts. This book will share with you how Victor and other high performers have increased productivity, job satisfaction, and self-confidence by putting their instincts to work within the context of their skills, personalities, and desires.

CHAPTER TWO

ACTING ON INSTINCT

When conducting seminars, I frequently set up a situation in which three or four people work as a team to solve a problem for which they have no experience, training, or educational background. I provide them with a bag of junk and ask them to develop a prototype of a particular product or service. After four minutes of preparation, they have one minute to tell the audience how they have met the goals of the assignment. I call the exercise "Glop Shop."

If participants decide to strive—to accomplish the task I set out for them—they will immediately kick into instinctive behavior. Each person will naturally act in observable ways that reflect his own particular inclinations. One team member may attempt to set priorities and define specific objectives, while another might sort through the glop, categorizing the materials as if taking inventory. A totally different way of contributing could come from a trial-and-error approach, as a participant suggests various alternatives, some of which may not even be practical. A fourth process—one easily separated from the others—is seen as another person quietly picks up some of the materials and begins building a tangible object.

These same behaviors can be found in any problem-solving situation.

They are the actions that result from the unencumbered use of Striving Instincts. Each approach reflects a specific source of energy, a distinguishable Striving Instinct. I have identified these as the Striving Instincts to *probe*, *pattern*, *innovate*, and *demonstrate*.

> The *probing* instinct creates a need to investigate *in depth*.
>
> The *patterning* instinct causes us to seek a sense of *order*.
>
> The *innovating* instinct is the force behind *experimentation*.
>
> The *demonstrating* instinct converts ideas into tangible *form*.

A person who defines specific objectives in Glop Shop is operating from the probing instinct. Categorizing the materials is a sign of patterning. Trial and error signifies the innovation instinct. Building a tangible object engages the instinct to demonstrate. The Striving Instincts can be clouded by learned and preferred behaviors. If I gave the team members the normal tools of their trade, they would know a "correct" way to use them. That knowledge might make them act out of habit rather than use their instincts. For instance, a group of office workers given papers, pencils, and reference books would limit the probability of anyone undertaking a three-dimensional demonstration.

If I told team members they could take as long as they wanted, most would take longer than was necessary to do their best work. While they may prefer a longer preparation period, people usually focus their instinctive energy better when they act without taking time to review everything they know. Adding time for thinking through solutions *after* engaging their instincts would enhance their efforts.

Most Glop Shop participants want to know if there is a "right" way to accomplish the task. They hesitate to begin the problem-solving process because they have so little experience operating on pure instinct. Our striving instincts have been obscured by the fear that we'll look stupid if we don't act the way we are supposed to act. In later chapters I will discuss how cultural and job demands, self-expectations, and team relationships impact whether or not you have free use of your instinctive talent.

OPERATING FROM DIFFERING PERSPECTIVES

THE FOUR STRIVING INSTINCTS ARE EXPRESSED THROUGH THREE POSSIBLE *OPERATING Zones*. These zones form a spectrum of behaviors for each instinct. *An*

Operating Zone indicates the perspective through which a person naturally uses a Striving Instinct.

Operating Zone	*Behavior*
Prevention	Resist
Response	Accommodate
Initiation	Insist

OPERATING ZONES

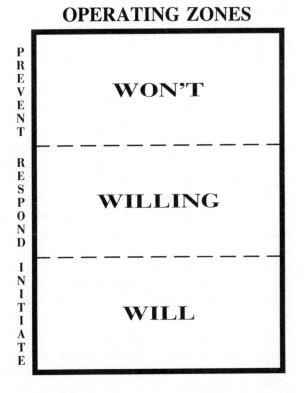

The reason people's actions vary despite everyone having the same Striving Instincts is because they have differing perspectives on each instinct. For example, one person will *initiate* plans in the patterning instinct, while another may *respond* to structure or live within procedures, and a third person will *prevent* overregulating or getting boxed in.

In Glop Shop, each person will gravitate first to any instincts he has in the initiation zone. For instance, people who start by putting all the materials in some order are likely to initiate systems in most problem-solving situations.

Others are more naturally inclined to respond to established procedures or programs. They'll stay with a plan once someone else has put it in force.

The preventative zone—in the case of patterning—gives people the energy to avoid getting bogged down in a process or becoming overly rigid. The preventative zone provides balance. It acts as a resistance, or a force that keeps you focused. If one member of the Glop Shop team lays everything out by size, another person with a resistance to patterning will avoid that effort and move the group toward another solution. The noted psychologist and philosopher Otto Rank referred to resistances as "a self-inhibiting instinct operating in the individual just as vital and genuine as are all other self-persevering and self-expressing instincts."

If a Glop Shop team was made up of people whose instincts for innovation were in the initiation zone, it could well use a person to prevent them from spending the entire preparation time brainstorming chaotically. Perhaps you've worked in situations where no one seemed able to pull the plug on the probing instinct, which allowed "analysis paralysis" to set in. Or you've seen what happens when a group gets caught up in its own grand design, only to discover that its customer base is impatient with what is perceived as repetitious introductions of look-alike products.

Everyone possesses all four Striving Instincts, each with one of the three zones of operation. The combination of these instincts—in their particular zones—make up a person's modus operandi. Your MO reflects the combination of zones in which you function through all the Striving Instincts. Your KCI result identifies your MO.

Recent years of observation have convinced me that it takes the same amount of effort to prevent action as it does to respond to or initiate it. A worker can prevent an accident by avoiding a distraction and can prevent a customer-service problem by resisting the temptation to justify the specifics of a situation. Managers often make the mistake of not rewarding all three Operating Zones equally. Too often kudos are given to those who initiated an activity, and not enough attention is focused on those who kept it going or prevented it from going too far.

While it is possible for an individual to operate in the response zone in three or all four instincts, I have never seen anyone either initiate solutions or prevent problems through all of them. Nature seems to give each of us a balance to our strivings. Those who respond through three or four instincts are the *Facilitators* of the world, who bring opposing perspectives together. When a person insists on certain ways of acting, that energy is offset by abilities to accommodate other methods or resist getting caught up in yet differing approaches.

FREEDOM TO BE YOURSELF

MY DEFINITION OF SUCCESS—*THE FREEDOM TO BE YOURSELF*—IS TIED TO THE Striving Instincts and their Operating Zones. Successful people are those who have found paths that allow them to use their instinctive powers freely, without stepping on others. On the other hand, people who try to (or are required to) perform against their own best instinctive methods inevitably suffer some form of stress that decreases their productivity. Such stress results when they attempt to function outside a natural Operating Zone in one or more of the Striving Instincts. While one employee may thrive in a particular role, the assignment may have to be accomplished in a manner that diminishes another's potential contribution. Our Operating Zones cause us to act, react, and interact differently, which explains why the same job requirements, training programs, "self-help" advice, or diet plans won't work for everyone.

An office manager who naturally initiates innovations may be held back if he is required to prevent change. A staffer whose probing instincts operate in the response zone will work under duress if she is required to initiate research and provide footnoted documents. The diversity of talents among people has no good or bad, right or wrong to them, except that they be unencumbered.

We all make the best use of our instinctive energy when we find a fit between our inclinations and commitments. We fail when we try to accommodate innovation despite our guts telling us it will lead to chaos; or when we agree to initiate procedures even though we're barely able to accommodate them when they already exist. Imagine the disaster if a person whose instinct is to resist mechanical demonstrations tries to fix equipment at a nuclear-power plant.

Later in the book I discuss the specifics of how you can improve team performance by bringing together people with a variety of instinctive perspectives. I also explain why having too many people who achieve through one instinct can be the downfall of a group, just as too little of a necessary ingredient can cause it to self-destruct.

ACTION MODES

ENERGY FROM EACH STRIVING INSTINCT TRIGGERS A DIFFERENT SET OF ACTIONS. These lead to four consistent or characteristic ways of performing; what I term an *Action Mode*. The observable way an Action Mode expresses the subconscious power of a Striving Instinct depends upon its natural Operating Zone. The three zones span a scale from 1 to 10.

Action Modes are the talents over which you have conscious control. As I will explain more thoroughly in Chapter 3, they are the conative abilities that link the internal force of instinct with quantifiable performance. They determine how you will, won't, and are willing to function, based on the necessities of your instinctive makeup. You may *know* you should review your file notes before making a call, yet you usually fail to do so. You *wish* you would keep more organized records, but when you do, you can't find where you put them. What you "should" do will always be overpowered by a conflicting instinct-driven *need*.

Fact Finder Characteristics

Fact Finder is the Action Mode that results from using the instinct to probe. It includes a spectrum of behaviors relating to gathering information. Some people have to define their options and examine possibilities in great depth. They become experts or authorities in specific areas. Others are generalists who attack a broader scope of pursuits. The three Operating Zones put an entirely different spin on the Fact Finder Action Mode.

Operating Zone	*Fact Finder Actions*
Initiating	Details, strategies, research
Responding	With specifics, editing, assessing pros and cons
Preventing	Analysis paralysis, or minutiae

Each zone indicates a differing degree of thoroughness necessary for an individual. Some people simply have to give you every detail of the movie plot. They are the ones who ask questions until they have the last piece of information, who operate with practical strategies based on historical evidence or personal experience.

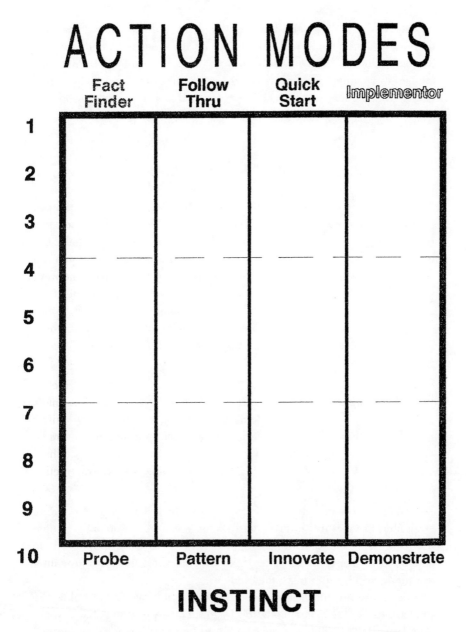

ACTION MODES

	Fact Finder	Follow Thru	Quick Start	Implementor
1				
2				
3				
4				
5				
6				
7				
8				
9				
10	Probe	Pattern	Innovate	Demonstrate

INSTINCT

Other people use information to satisfy someone else, responding with sufficient specificity yet not delving any more deeply than necessary into the details. For instance, they may wonder who is fourth, fifth and sixth in presidential succession. But for all their wondering, they won't search for the answer if they don't know it already. If a debate gets going over the issue, some people will need to cut off the discussion and move on to another topic. These people prevent situations from becoming immersed in specifics. Even if they raised the question—and find it interesting to consider—they'll get frustrated if the discussion gets bogged down in what they consider trivialities.

Follow Thru Behavior

Follow Thru is the Action Mode that results from using the instinct to pattern. It determines how you relate to structure. Its characteristics range from acting sequentially to sporadically. An *insistent*–Follow Thru baseball player goes through a ritualistic pattern or series of sequential steps in preparing for a game. An *accommodating* player tries different systems, occasionally turning to one recommended by a teammate, then switching to another. Routines will be bothersome for a resistant Follow Thru, even when they prove effective. The amount of structure people need is forecasted by their Operating Zone in the Follow Thru Action Mode.

Operating Zone	*Follow Thru Actions*
Initiating	Systems, procedures, design, order
Responding	By adjusting to existing plans, maintaining classifications
Preventing	Getting boxed in, being overly structured

Some people naturally put things into a system. They have an urge to straighten the picture, to flow-chart the options, and to organize people and materials. The first thing they do when faced with a problem is to sort out the possibilities. They take inventory of all the information accumulated by initiating Fact Finders.

Then there are those who will live within the system and follow the procedures. These accommodating Follow Thrus put things back where they belong. They may not need to have phone messages given to them in alphabetical order, but they will maintain such structures.

Those in the preventative zone in Follow Thru rebel when they feel boxed in by schedules or routines. They resist having to stay within the parameters of policies and procedures, and instead create their own alternatives. Sometimes their resistance to filling in the form can lead to open-ended comments that improve productivity.

Recognizing the Quick Start Mode

Quick Start is the Action Mode that results from using the instinct to innovate. It deals with your perspective on risk, and ranges from being highly negotiable to irrevocable. *Insistent* Quick Starts cut deals that are flexible and crammed with options. Yet their estate planners may have the risk-averse approach of irrevocable wills and trusts. These differing perspectives on risk are clearly defined by the following zones in the Quick Start Action Mode:

Operating Zone	*Quick Start Actions*
Initiating	Change, deadlines, uniqueness
Responding	By mediating between the vision and the given
Preventing	Chaos, a crisis atmosphere

People who initiate Quick Start projects create the chaos that others have to clean up. But in the process these change makers add vision and risk to the mix. Always negotiable, they defy the odds and intuit possibilities that would otherwise go untried. Because they instigate the unusual, people who operate in the initiating zone of Quick Start are natural promoters and entrepreneurs.

Accommodating change is no problem for people who respond in Quick Start. For instance, they'll go along if you change your mind at the last minute and want to see a different movie.

Don't expect the same of those who operate in the preventative zone of Quick Start. They keep changes from getting out of hand, trying instead to reach agreement on what will stay the same. What some consider enhancements, they sense could cause a potential crisis. Their resistance to risk can save the day.

Using Implementor

Implementor is the Action Mode that results from using the instinct to demonstrate. It determines how we relate to objects and physical space.

It functions through use of three-dimensional or tangible implements or tools. Its perspectives range from concrete to abstract. A person who views the world through tactile efforts needs to plant a garden in order to find joy in it. A resistant Implementor can find as much fulfillment in writing a poem about a garden, the abstract notion being as important as the tangible reality. The degree to which people have to see something in order to believe it is determined by their Operating Zone in the Implementor Action Mode.

Operating Zone	*Implementor Actions*
Initiating	Constructing, transporting, manipulating, and protecting tangible goods
Responding	By using machinery or implements for either tangible or intangible effort
Preventing	Need for tangible evidence or physical proof

Those who initiate solutions by using tools and implements are the hands-on Implementors. While others discuss the video they just saw, these folks are probably tinkering with the VCR. Their need for physical movement and space keeps them from staying in one place for very long. They tend to build solutions rather than talk about them.

People who respond through the Implementor mode are able to deal with both tangible and intangible solutions. If others need to put together a concrete demonstration they'll help build it, but they don't need to see the prototype in its final form in order to make a decision.

Prevention of Implementor action indicates an ability to create from abstract concepts such as words and numbers without having to use three-dimensional forms and models.

While it is not necessary to complete the KCI to benefit from examples in this book, it is also not advisable to guess your MO. Most people are off considerably when they try to figure out how they would score.

If you are curious about the particulars of your talent, the KCI is available on page 349. It asks for 72 responses to questions regarding how you are most and least likely to take action in a variety of circumstances. The situations given are general enough to apply to almost anyone, and it takes about twenty-five minutes to complete.

KCI results, which will be sent to you (details explained on page 345), include eight pages of individualized information regarding your instinctive talent and how to use it most productively.

It includes suggestions for wise use of time, your best methods of communicating, careers others with your conative abilities have found fulfilling, and ways to reduce stress. The result is summarized on a chart pinpointing where your talent falls among the operating zones for each Action Mode. A KCI result of 5-7-2-6 would denote an accommodation (4-6) in Fact Finder, insistence (7-10) in Follow Thru, resistance (1-3) in Quick Start, and accommodation to Implementor. In addition to printed information, results from the KCI in *Pure Instinct* include an audio cassette of my interpretation of your creative potential.

Only professionals I have trained on the Kolbe Concept may interpret the KCI for others. So businesses may not receive confidential information about employees without a certified Kolbe specialist to handle the process.

TRUE EQUALITY

EVERYONE HAS THE SAME AMOUNT OF INSTINCTIVE POWER—AND AN EQUAL NEED to act freely according to those instincts. Each of us has talent in all four Action Modes. Our particular zones of operation, determined by our instinctive patterns of behavior, are with us from birth. Every possible combination of Operating Zones provides the same potential for achievement.

Our instinct-driven talents are the one way in which we are all created equal. Yet the opportunities to use these talents often differ significantly. Quick Start females and minorities—those with the right instincts to start their own businesses, for example—may well have more difficulty getting bank loans than less well-suited white male candidates for small-business loans. Men with an inclination to initiate designs are often unfairly labeled effeminate because of gender stereotyping of talents. While the distribution of instinctive abilities is the same for males and females, whites and minorities, the young and the elderly, opportunities are rarely so equal.

The data in over 100,000 case studies, including KCI results from every continent and a wide variety of workplaces and educational settings, show that KCI scores are unbiased by age, race, gender, national origin, or disability. Women are as likely as men to initiate action in any mode. As many minorities naturally innovate as do whites. People who prevent rigid structures as youngsters will do the same as they age. Therefore those who limit opportunities for any segment of the population because of false presumptions regarding innate abilities can now be proved wrong. The equal energy of Striving Instincts gives every human being the same potential for productivity. The form that talent takes is differentiated by nothing other than individual differences in Operating Zones.

At long last, the fact that instincts are unbiased makes it possible for us to characterize individual differences without unfair discrimination. When we measure the actions that are based upon instinctive needs, there are no good or bad results. There are only right answers on the KCI because it identifies internal strengths. An insistent Fact Finder is no better or worse than someone who prevents getting bogged down in details. Responding to change doesn't make you a more valuable human being than someone who responds to technical needs.

Once my client Victor understood his instinctive inclinations, he found ways of putting himself in situations that fit his needs. He's a resistant Follow Thru, so he recognized what a waste of energy it was for him to personally design company procedures. Instead he focused on what worked best for him—which happened to be preventing routine methods and initiating new projects through his Quick Start. Pairing his natural talents with appropriate tasks increased his productivity dramatically. Soon he began encouraging others to make similar matches between their instincts and the tasks they undertook.

When Victor introduced the concept of building on employees' natural talents, his company prospered. People were placed in jobs because of what they could accomplish, without reference to their age, gender, or race. Some were given opportunities they'd never expected would become available. A female accounting clerk turned out to have the right instincts to qualify for a marketing position traditionally held by men. A near-retirement employee who initiated through Quick Start was no longer stereotyped as being "too old" to contribute much vision.

The successes at Victor's company have been replicated in hundreds of other situations. Studies conducted by numerous universities and major corporations have concluded that giving people an opportunity to work to their instinctive strengths greatly enhances their ability to achieve measurable goals. On the other hand, working against the instinctive grain has been proved to lead to stress, absenteeism, and high turnover.

Over the centuries, debates raging among philosophers and psychologists have pitted instinct *against* intellect, as if only one of these faculties is involved in decision making. I believe we achieve our best results when we capitalize on both reason and instincts. As you'll see in the next chapter, the creative process is not a fight between reason and instinct, but rather an integration of all the mind's capabilities.

Before Victor discovered the value of using his Striving Instincts, he had become a prisoner of the notion that we can be trained to act the way experts believe we should. He was smart enough to learn those textbook methods—and smart enough later to reject the ones unsuited to him. His mind needed more than to be filled with ideas; it had to strive in its own way. Ideas without effort leave us with unfulfilled dreams. The freedom to operate instinctively makes it possible for us to fulfill our purposes.

CHAPTER THREE

THE CREATIVE PROCESS

S am is a successful small-business owner who started his own printing business several years ago, before the large franchises moved into the quick-print field. He's well organized, initiates plans, and carefully watches his cash flow. If he had his way, little would happen in his shop that wasn't scheduled in advance. Since that's rarely possible, he's constantly having to use his full creative capacity to meet his payroll and keep up with the competition. Sam does what we all have to do in order to reach goals: he cycles through what I call the *Creative Process*.

Many business people tell me they're not creative; especially those who do not initiate in the Quick Start mode. Most people confuse creativity with the instinct to innovate. "I don't come up with unique new products or original presentations," one executive said. "I'm just a meat-and-potatoes plodder who gets the boring part of the work out on time." This guy may not think he's creative, but that's because no one ever explained creativity to him in a way that incorporated his natural strengths.

Most dictionaries define creativity as the ability to bring into being an idea or thing. It is an extension of productivity. It is the highest and best use of our talents. Because we all have the same amount of instinctive power, I believe we were born with an equal capacity to create. The Creative Process, as I define it, is the path that integrates otherwise separate elements of the mind's capacity: the abilities to act with motivation, determination, and reason. We do not all create through the same instinct-based Operating Zones, nor do we have equal levels of motivation, determination, and reason. Differences in these levels allow for an almost infinite variety in how we use the Creative Process.

PRODUCTIVITY CYCLES

FIVE ELEMENTS OF THE MIND ARE INVOLVED IN TAKING A CONCEPT AND MAKING IT a reality. Your productivity is tied to understanding and using all five. It's important to place Striving Instincts within the context of this Creative Process because you manage the energy they produce by controlling the other elements.

Motivation

Motivation is the first essential ingredient in the Creative Process. If Sam doesn't want to solve a problem, it won't be solved. If he's highly motivated, he'll generate the activity necessary to get something done. Motivation is a catalyst for creative power, much as turning a key ignites a car's engine. It represents our desires, preferences, wishes, beliefs, emotions, and all other affective aspects of self. In depicting the Creative Process, I use circles to represent motivation and place them in the starting position.

Sam has several circles of motivation that act as "on" switches for his achievements. They spark the energy that comes from his Striving Instincts, the limited but rechargeable force of his creative power. His engine can operate only according to its specifications—his preset modus operandi—but its power can be activated on multiple occasions. Without motivation as a starting mechanism, the striving resources of the mind will simply languish as unused potential. With motivation, Striving Instincts can propel all of us toward our many goals.

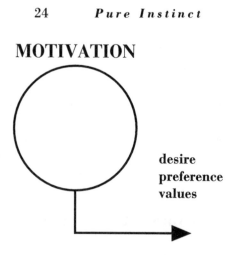

MOTIVATION

desire
preference
values

Striving Instincts

In Sam's case, most of his energy comes from his knack for designing systems. He'll put issues into context before trying to fill in other pieces. Only after he's found a pattern will he use the remaining Striving Instincts to address creative problem-solving situations. Each instinctive urge is like a unit of fuel that adds a specific character to the energy. All the units combine into a mixture that needs to be fully used if the engine is to run smoothly and as far as possible before refueling. I illustrate the combination of Sam's instinct-based talents in a pyramid shape:

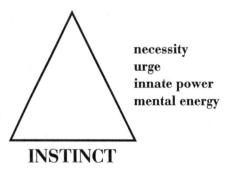

necessity
urge
innate power
mental energy

INSTINCT

No matter how far Sam tries to go or what direction he takes, his instinctive energy will help him arrive at his destination. And it will do so within certain parameters. If he tries to go faster than his instincts allow, he will exhaust his resources and experience mental fatigue. If he is motivated to act contrary to his native abilities, he'll be frustrated and operate with undue stress. Getting where he wants to go is possible with the equipment he was given, but he has to learn how to operate it effectively.

Will

The third element of the Creative Process is your *Will*, the transmission that links your instinct-based power to your actions.

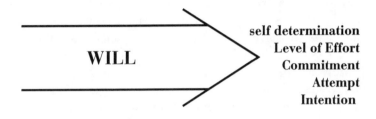

WILL
self determination
Level of Effort
Commitment
Attempt
Intention

Here's the point in the Creative Process where you take control over the *Level of Effort* you apply to particular acts. All Will is free, so you have the choice—or *free will*—to allocate your instinctive powers with varying degrees of self-determination. People are impressed by Sam's drive, which is the apparent result when he is using his Will. It becomes evident when he targets his instinctive energy toward his goals. This freedom to focus his natural talents on his business tasks increases the probability that Sam will succeed in his effort. He's willing, some say, to "throw himself" into the role.

The Will channels the subconscious force of instincts, assigns it, and then transmits it into conscious effort. Much like the gears for your car's engine, the Will controls the amount of available power you use at different times. You can gear up or shift down depending on how many resources you decide to expend while traveling various roads.

There are three Levels of Effort you can assign to any action. These determine the amount of instinctive energy you give an action. *Commitment* is the highest gear, the one Sam uses most of the time in his business. It causes him to focus energy on assigned tasks. *Attempt* is the second level. When operating in this arena, Sam tries to accomplish a goal but doesn't use his full capabilities. The third level is *intention*, which implies minimal effort. For example, it's possible to wish something will happen—to start the Creative Process with motivation—yet never transmit the amount of instinctive energy needed to move toward a goal. This is what happens when people sit idle and waste their innate talents.

An obvious example of the difference between Levels of Effort comes from the following descriptions:

He intended suicide.

He attempted suicide.

He committed suicide.

The meaning also is clear when people intend to call you, attempt to call you, or commit to a time to call you. Sometimes you'll make attempts and they won't work, so you put your energies elsewhere. Your performance on the attempted task wasn't stellar. Had you made a commitment instead, would you have accomplished your personal best? Most likely, though it is essential to have the right cognitive training and attitude to successfully complete the task.

Sam has control over the Level of Effort he gives to each activity that engages his instincts. It's up to him whether he makes a commitment to keep his own financial records or hires someone else to handle the task. He has the instincts necessary to maintain an orderly set of books, but he also needs that talent for the desktop-publishing activities he prefers to do himself. He has to make choices because there is a limit to his instinctive energy. This is when reason intrudes.

Reason

Reason, or thought, is an integral part of the Creative Process. Your Will provides the self-determination that keeps your creativity from becoming aimless, but your intellect helps you assess your options by editing your motives, Striving Instincts, and self-determination.

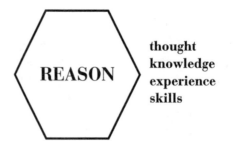

**thought
knowledge
experience
skills**

If Sam did not have this checkpoint in the Creative Process, he might try to do it all and exhaust his energies. Reason intrudes as a warning sign; the light on the dashboard that tells him the engine is being pushed beyond its limits. Ignoring his wisdom would be like not paying attention to hazard signs along the road.

If Sam didn't use reason in his Creative Process, he would strive in ways that were illogical. This would deplete his energy and diminish his results. When his company was faced with competition from franchised quick-print operations, he would have worked harder but continually lost ground to them. Instead he reconsidered his approach, set a new goal, and went back to the creative drawing board. Understanding the obstacles gave him important reasons for taking or not taking certain actions.

The Creative Process, unlike a creative event, can benefit from being stopped midcourse, often at the point of reason, because we're smart enough to reject potentially negative results and put on the brake rather than move further. Reason is the critical point when editing occurs and keeps us from putting too much energy into misguided efforts. The process can then be regenerated with more suitable results.

Conative Actions

The first four elements of the Creative Process result in observable behavior: the conative actions that represent our talents.

ACTION

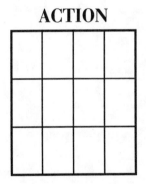

talent
Method of Operation (MO)
performance
conation

People saw Sam create a niche in the marketplace, a specialty shop that allowed him to make productive use of his penchant for design. His motivation and his actions were the only visible signs of Creative Process. Thinking is a conscious activity, but had you taken a snapshot of Sam considering his options, it would have been a picture of a motionless figure. Watching him contemplate would give you no sign of his potential, no clue to the form Sam's actions would ultimately take.

Sam's conative talent is the observable part of the model, the car that can be seen moving down the road. From its speed, consistency, and other factors we can assume certain characteristics regarding its power source and how well it is being utilized. Some people get maximum mileage out of their creative capabilities, and others drive them into the ground. Those who understand how their minds operate are the ones who will most likely use them to reach their destinations.

Creativity is a continuously flowing process. Any motivation can trigger it, and though a lack of Will can diminish or stop the process, the Striving Instincts behind creativity are never depleted or destroyed.

Illustrating the Creative Process using a model is in itself conatively challenging. No single model works for those with differing instinctive perspectives. The way I have drawn the model shows my own perspective.

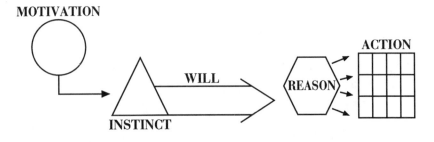

The following models the Creative Process from each Action Mode's insistent point of view.

TRUST, TARGET, AND TEMPER

Thinkers and scholars have had difficulty separating instincts from will because it is impossible to identify or measure Striving Instincts, and because instincts have not been properly placed within a creative process. My consulting work has shown me that even though we all have the power to be productive, we are not equally motivated and do not operate with the same Level of Effort. Often when people become dissatisfied

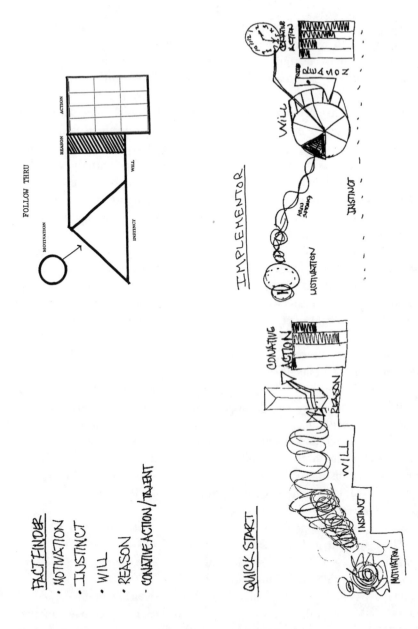

with their performance, they don't know what is causing the problem and therefore lack the tools to fix it.

There are several things we can do to improve performance. First, trust our instincts. Second, target specific goals by giving them the highest Level of Effort, our commitment of mental energy. Third, temper our efforts with reason. Once we have taken these steps, our conative talents—the behavior that combines and integrates motivation, instinctive energy, Will, and reason into productive effort—will reflect our true character.

Because we are usually aware of our motivations and thoughts, it's not surprising that researchers have been able to study them more thoroughly than the Striving Instincts and the Will. Neither instincts nor Will responds easily to empirical study. Instincts are particularly difficult to understand because they operate subconsciously. We are only slightly more aware of our own Will. Some personality tests treat preferences and attitudes as if they are the only behaviors that matter, rather than the ones that ignite us into action.

Motivational speakers can make people *want* to take action, but no salesman ever became a high producer without committing the right instincts to his task. It just doesn't make sense to get everyone revved up to work against his or her own instincts. Motivational approaches backfire when they don't take into account how people need to perform instinctively. At best, many motivational speakers and incentive programs have no lasting effect; at worst, they hinder productivity. Instead of rewarding commitment to a goal, they often punish those who don't conform to the one method of operation that has been chosen as acceptable. Closing a deal by the end of the month might earn a trip to Hawaii, but it doesn't reward the development of a long-term customer relationship.

It takes more than knowing your talents to increase your effectiveness. You also have to target your use of them. You are at your best when you are striving instinctively, when you are "in your zone." When your natural advantage is not effectively employed, the intrinsic qualities you offer go unrecognized.

Unlike instinct, personality depends upon motivation and is not a constant in your makeup. Desires change. Moods can be altered. Personality can cause you to use your talents for a particular purpose, but it is an unreliable basis for predicting actions.

Once psychologists figured out ways of measuring intellect and of statistically comparing people according to IQs, the cognitive function was treated as if it alone ruled the mind. Most modern psychologists claim that only lower forms of animals have instincts and that reason rules our every human action. Yet we all know smart people who don't get the job done and people with average intellect who accomplish great feats.

Knowing that we should do something doesn't mean we will do it. Our knowledge, skills, awareness, and understanding combine as reason. But reason without purpose is unsatisfying. Reason without instincts is powerless. Reason without Will is aimless. And reason without conative action is pointless.

Sam has the same instinctive capacity as all his colleagues, but he has become more productive than most of them. This is not a value judgment of how he has chosen to spend his energy—he could have been just as productive at home raising children—but rather a conclusion based on how much he has accomplished. The Creative Process helps us achieve regardless of our goals. This book will not deal with the moral issues regarding the use of our talents.

If we had only our Striving Instincts, we would be boxed into ways of creating that were imprinted at birth. Our instincts would be oppressive forces. But our Will—tempered by reason—gives us choice in how we use our instinctive energy. With that freedom, we do not have to fear the power within us, but can use it.

Now that we are able to measure our conative talents, we are able to build teams that will work together constructively and cooperatively. We can place the right person in the right job. The KCI measures conative actions derived from instinctive behavior, finally giving us a vocabulary to understand our talents and a way to communicate them with one another. Now we know what we need to do in order to put our creative abilities to productive use.

CHAPTER FOUR

GOAL SETTING

CONTROLLING THE OUTCOMES

Years ago, Eastman Kodak Company executive Kathy Hudson was faced with a major problem. She was the general manager of the instant-photography business unit when Kodak lost a lawsuit to Polaroid that would force her to close down that operation. While Kodak appealed the decision, Kathy was responsible for keeping the troops motivated and working productively. They also had to plan for contingencies in case they won and stayed in business. Her team members worked so effectively during this difficult period that they actually increased profits. Meanwhile Kathy was also negotiating consumers' liability claims in a way that would satisfy the courts and, she said, "represent the values of George Eastman," the company's founder.

Kathy saved her company $1 billion, was recognized as one of *Business Week*'s top fifty businesswomen, and became V.P. and general manager of Kodak's Professional Printing and Publishing Imaging division. The source of her energy was instinct; in her case, an insistence in Quick Start. This compelled her to work against all odds. Many people with her intelligence and Quick Start talents jump from project to project without ever making their mark. They lack Kathy Hudson's Will and commitment.

As she worked with the company's chief legal counsel to prepare a defense for the liability phase of the suit, Kathy's Quick Start spirit developed one of her characteristic slogans. "We had to redefine winning," she explained. "We knew we had lost, so it was a matter of it making a flesh wound, not a mortal wound. We set the goal to keep the loss under a billion dollars, with the slogan, 'Move the decimal point.' "

By committing her talents to specific goals, Kathy channeled her instinctive drive into conative effort. If she had not made these focused demands upon herself, she would have lacked purpose, and her undirected innovative initiatives would have frittered away her energy.

How do high performers channel their instinctive powers to achieve goals? They target their efforts. Front-runners have a single-mindedness that focuses their attention on reaching the goals they set for themselves. The Will controls available instinctive resources, putting them to self-determined uses. Kathy could achieve her goals because she found ways to attain them through her particular talents. She refers to finding "the energy around a problem," which, considering her insistence in Quick Start (her KCI result is 4-1-9-6), means being able to take innovative routes to solving problems. "The best kind of problems," she said, adding Implementor language, "are those with no solutions, for which I have to hammer out agreements." *When objectives are compatible with Striving Instincts, they are likely to be reached.*

"Competition," Kathy said, "is forcing us into a performance culture. We're accepting a wider variation of methods because the issue is, Who's delivering?"

If you are working with others, you have to be sure the goal-setting process itself draws everyone into the action. "Power [to trust instincts] isn't a scarce resource," Kathy explained. "You don't have to keep it to yourself. The more power you give away to the people you work with, the more you get." When people are involved in determining goals, they are more likely to commit their instinctive energy toward reaching them.

Setting goals that channeled her own internal drives and those of her team members helped Kathy control the outcomes. A seemingly impossible job was accomplished. The decimal point was moved below the $1 billion figure.

Kolbe Talent Analysis
KOLBE CONATIVE INDEX® Result

Katherine M. Hudson

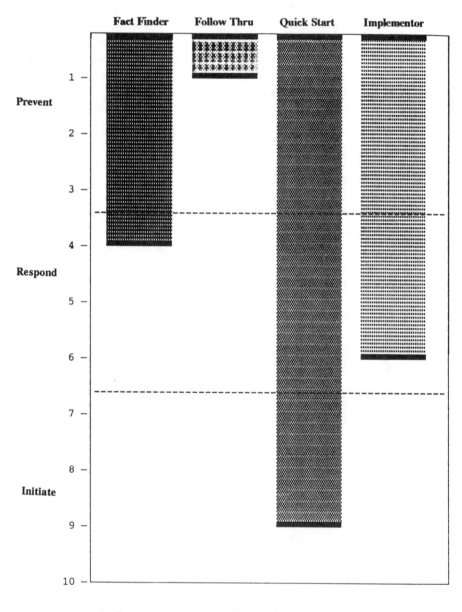

DETERMINING THE DELIVERABLES

GOALS WILL BE REACHED MOST OFTEN WHEN THOSE RESPONSIBLE FOR ACHIEVING them are involved in setting them. Some people have expressed concern that the KCI is deterministic and that it causes them to feel too predictable. However, they alone control the uses of their conative capabilities. No one can force another to contribute instinctive energy. "Personal power," Kathy Hudson commented, "is really the power to be your best. It's all about trusting instincts. Organizations would be more effective if they let go of attempts to control from the top. You can't compete if you restrain the energizing force of creativity. I'm going to be my best when the people on my team are at their best, too." The instinctive strengths of team members will ultimately control outcomes.

Deliverables are goals that we as team members, or as individuals, have the instincts to accomplish *and* the Will to pursue. It is important to set goals, because we have a limited amount of mental energy; it must be managed well so that it will be used effectively. We simply can't do everything. In the Kodak situation, Kathy understood her goals regarding the lawsuit and profitability, and she and her team added value-driven objectives such as maintaining what they believed were the founder's wishes. They had to translate those goals into results. They had to determine the deliverables—those goals they had the instinctive capacity to achieve—then make a commitment to converting them into actions by allocating their Striving Energies among desired outcomes.

Through our Will, we assign instinctive capacities among competing goals. For example, if a go-for-it Quick Start salesperson gets involved in producing a new community musical, he may not do much innovating at work during the show's run. These extra commitments use up his risk-taking juices. He makes a decision between goals. Someone arranging for the care of an ill family member may deplete use of his Follow Thru in that effort, causing an uncharacteristically fragmented approach at work. He makes a choice. He gives at home instead of at the office.

MAKING A COMMITMENT

NO MATTER WHAT OUR GOALS ARE, WE CAN OPERATE ONLY WITHIN THE PARAMETERS of our innate abilities. As a result, we must learn to push the conative buttons for each mode, and that begins with controlling our Level of Effort. Commitments are our unconditional guarantees that we will perform. They are common to high performers, who commit their instinctive power at levels that match the importance of goals. By investing instinctive energy wisely we can ensure our particular contributions of creativity.

A motivation such as loyalty can be a strong factor in productivity, but it alone does not do the job. It can only trigger the Creative Process toward those areas that matter most to us. Commitment is essential, and a lack of it cannot be overcome by desire, personality, working smart, or putting in long hours. For example, a resistant Fact Finder not committed to the task at hand may ask a multitude of specific questions, but she won't really pay attention to the answers. An insistent Implementor who lets the water drip is not tuned in. And the Follow Thru initiator who plans two meetings at the same time isn't making much of an effort.

When there is lots of talk about what needs to be done but little happens, it is clear that only lip service is being paid to goal setting. Such cases never lead to desired results. Vince Lombardi, the great football coach, once said: "The difference between a successful person and others is not a lack of strength, not a lack of knowledge, but rather a lack of will." We must use our Will to channel our instinctive energy into productive activity.

People may have a great deal they *want* to do or they *know* needs to be done, but they still have finite striving capacities. Therefore they have to decide what's most important. And then decisions have to be made about *what* will be initiated, accommodated, and prevented. Kathy Hudson's insistence in Quick Start was captivated by the opportunity to do what was supposedly undoable. Her concern for the company and its future, and her awareness of the problems were *causes* of her action: the reason and motivation. The *effect* was determined conative action. She directed her instincts toward achieving the team's goals.

"WHAT DO WE WANT TO HAVE HAPPEN?"

COMBINING CAUSE AND EFFECT IS POSSIBLE USING A QUESTION I FIRST HEARD POSED by Dr. Maren Mouritsen of Brigham Young University: "What do we want to have happen?" Wanting the best record of customer service is an important motivation, but the goal is to make it happen. It's a good idea for workers to know their company needs to make a profit, but they have to strive in order to make it happen.

If attitudes or social preferences are mistaken as possible substitutes for action, disappointment will follow. "What do we want?" leads to wish lists, not to performance. Phrases like "I want" need to be followed by "therefore I will take action." For instance, the managers of a landscape-design firm set a goal of promoting more minorities from labor-intensive positions to professional roles. But their objectives didn't include any specific ways to accomplish this goal, so it remained unfulfilled.

We also can be disappointed if goals don't take into account the instinctive natures of those responsible for results. For instance, colleagues in a science lab believed they could cut three months off a research project by agreeing with certain hypotheses. But every one of them was insistent in Fact Finder, which made it impossible for the team to carry out a promise of shortening its research. They weren't going to achieve the goal of reducing Fact Finder activity because that would mean performing in ways that were at odds with who they are. We shouldn't embarrass ourselves by making promises we can't keep; we have to recognize the overriding power of Striving Instincts. A statement like "I'll get the forms to you ahead of time next month" is pure fantasy for someone insistent in deadline-driven Quick Start and resistant to Follow Thru planning ahead.

Confusion between motivations and actions (between what we want and how we'll make it happen) can also affect people's attitudes about a work environment. As a small construction firm was pulling out of economic difficulties, it had to deal with the conflict between having a good time and getting things done. When business improved and more time had to be spent filling orders, the employees' on-the-job antics began to decrease. When the owner asked, "What do we want to have happen?" the answer was unanimous. There was more joy for everyone in seeing the company succeed than holding onto what one person labeled "frivolous fun."

The best of intentions cannot substitute for instinct. A Quick Start with only a slight accommodation in Fact Finder information gathering told me four months ago that he would look into a situation and let me know what was going on. "I'll tell you what," he said. "I've got sources that know everything there is to know about that stuff. One of them is probably the world's leading expert. And I've got files of background on it; lots of cases from over the years. I'll see what's in them that can help." If I had taken his intentions as a commitment, I would have been sorely disappointed. False commitments often occur when people offer a talent they don't have. They usually don't mean to deceive you. My friend may have used up all of his Fact Finder energy before he had time to look into the matter, or he may have forgotten he made this commitment. But his heart's in the right place. I suspect someday I'll get a call out of the blue. "It's taken me a while," he may say, "but I've dug up just what I think you need." I'll know he didn't dig it up. It will have popped up in his characteristic Quick Start way.

One frustration of working with highly motivated people is their habit of making promises they won't keep. They want to commit but make the mistake of agreeing to a method rather than a goal. For instance, someone will tell you he'd love to help you plant your garden. He may ask, "Do you want me to bring my tools and do the digging, or would you rather I draw a plan for where things might look best?" When he gets locked into a situation that requires him to work against his grain, avoidance behavior kicks in. "A plan? Really? Don't you think it's nice just to scatter things around? You know, an informal look?" If he's not able to change the commitment to conform to his way of striving, he'll likely pull back on his involvement. "I know I said I'd be there to help with your garden, but I'm not going to be able to make it until later in the day, so I'll bring along some drinks and help with the cleanup if that's okay." He'll probably end up feeling guilty.

A rabbi with an international following had committed his time and effort to a major conference, but he felt disgraced because he hadn't prepared thoroughly. Extensive background papers had been mailed to him months in advance, but this resistant Follow Thru, despite his good intentions, misplaced most of them. "I should have known better," he said. "If I'd only planned ahead, I would have looked for them before it was too late to have them re-sent." He used his Quick Start to skim the replaced material just before the sessions began, but he wasn't satisfied with his contribution.

TRANSLATING IDEAS INTO ACTION

IDEAS ARE THE *WHAT* THAT HAS TO HAPPEN. INVENTIVE RUBE GOLDBERG contraptions don't achieve anything if they stay in the mind's eye. A bright person could think up how one of these might work, but until someone with Implementor talent builds it, nothing creative will have occurred. The thought will not have been translated into productive action. Results are determined by the Level of Effort put into them. Intentions have to be turned into commitments before our full effort is engaged. Kathy Hudson's team had to devote the full force of its striving capacities to continue generating profit while it was closing down the business. It wouldn't have worked if team members had said, "We'll try and see if we can." Or, worse yet: "We intend to move the decimal point—if there's time." They had to commit themselves to the goal.

If you've ever been to a Hard Rock Cafe or to the famous Planet Hollywood in New York City, you've seen the Follow Thru creativity of Charles Daboub. He never planned to make restaurant design a specialty, but he says it came so naturally, "it didn't feel like work." For him "sketching was a daydream," he recalled. "My dad accused me of imagining people would send me checks for my doodling. Sure enough, that's what they do!" He didn't study architectural drawing or interior design in college. In fact, he was selling retail men's clothing when a social acquaintance—former Chicago Bears football coach Mike Ditka— was intrigued enough by his sketching to ask him to do some interior walls in his home, and then in his new restaurant. "I'd never done it before, so I just did it on instinct," Charles said.

"No one ever told me how to do what I do in designing restaurants," he continued. "Instinctively I'm able to sit down and conceptualize a total product before I have to go to a specialist. The electrician guy, sound guy, and kitchen guys never complain that I don't give them the right space." Renowned for his work creating cutting-edge environments throughout the world, this Texan uses his Follow Thru abilities to integrate past, present, and future. "I improve on tradition," he said, "which is more important than coming up with something new. I combine, improve, but hang on to tradition in order to minimize risk. Far-out places confuse customers, and they don't get people to return. I could have done Planet Hollywood with electronic gimmickry and splashes of color, but it would have broken the basic pattern that I find works. I didn't have to be taught how to design a club that is friendly and inviting, one that will last more than twenty years. I just have to have clients who trust me. I can't let go if I have to do what I don't sense will work. Potential clients can tell if I don't believe in how they want to do it." Charles runs his own business and turns down any client who tries to change his modus operandi. "My clients get their return on investment," he said. "And I'm successful because I don't *have* to do what I do."

ACHIEVING WITHOUT COMPROMISING
YOUR TALENTS

WHEN YOU STAY IN CHARGE OF YOUR OWN ACTION YOU CONTROL THE OUTCOMES. In Charles's case, had he tried to satisfy a customer by going against his instincts, it could have been his downfall. Many people have made sales that weren't worth the agony. For instance, Implementors often talk about having had to satisfy a customer by producing something slipshod—and their subsequent regret at having done it.

Robert Miley, an artist whose methods contrast with Charles's, once tried to make his living as a graphic designer. Robert's wonderful Quick Start splashes of color and abstract symbolism were bottled up by his clients' needs to have clean lines and appropriate logos. As his art evolved into an open expression of his creativity, he was able to walk away from the stifling effects (for him) of Follow Thru performance. Now he gets high prices for the treasures he produces, whereas before he was barely eking out a living in his graphic-design business.

When goals are achieved through natural talents, creativity abounds. We are all drawn to productive people. Their attraction is the result of openly communicating their creative forces. Charisma is art on the hoof. Talent that is restrained never produces a masterpiece. Yielding to a customer's perception of how you should function is hypocritical if it forces you to work in a less authentic manner. Placating people by withholding your talent is a lose-lose proposition in which nobody benefits as much as he could. Similar inappropriate compromises of self may occur by succumbing to a boss's wrongheaded demands, a date's unrealistic desires, or a coworker's agenda. It takes incredible energy to fight off all the folks who try to change you or your goals.

Another way you control outcomes is by setting aside energy to work toward them. For example, Jean-Yves Gueguen, the vice-president of strategic planning for American Express, is insistent in Fact Finder and resistant in Quick Start. If he tells me he'll check on something, I know he will provide precise, thorough, and well-documented information. But if he says he'll make a guess, most likely he's neither committed to the issue nor willing to set aside energy. Or he is merely fulfilling a request with an attempt. *Actions taken without committed effort usually fall short of their goals. They lack the determination of Will to contribute either sufficient instinctive energy or the appropriate mode of effort.*

Our Striving Instincts are not unlimited, so we have to use them in ways that will give us the highest possible return on our investment of them. This often includes leaving some energy available for responsibilities that are not necessarily our preferences. For instance, if you use your Striving Instincts without paying attention to goal setting, you may come up short when you or your team needs them the most.

CONATIVE TIME ZONES

OUR INSTINCTIVE CAPABILITIES CAN BE UNLEASHED ONLY WHEN SUFFICIENT TIME IS available to accomplish our goals. The time you need to succeed may be quite different from the time others need. Understanding how we use and value time is key to realistic goal setting. Unlike reason and motivation, actions can be measured in terms of the time we are either expected to or required to take in accomplishing them. We put forth our best efforts when we operate in natural, or conative, time zones. Our MOs determine our perspective on time.

The Past: The Fact Finder's clock is set for the appropriate amount of time, gauged by studying how much time it usually takes to accomplish something. Experience and expertise provide a practical, historical perspective.

The Present: The Implementor's clock stays grounded in the here and now. It requires time to mold today the tangible demonstration of quality efforts that will endure.

The Future: The Quick Start's clock is on deadline, set for a race. It urgently seeks the future, compressing time, seeking shortcuts, and going right to the bottom line.

Integration of Past, Present, and Future: The Follow Thru's clock runs smoothly and efficiently. It doesn't skip a beat as it coordinates with others to complete the cycle at the planned-for moment.

TIMELY DECISIONS

A PERSON'S TIME AND ENERGY NEEDS CAN BE NOTED WITH THE FOUR DIGITS OF HIS or her KCI result. The order in which they are given is always Fact Finder, Follow Thru, Quick Start, Implementor. So my MO of 2-6-8-4 indicates a resistance to spending time justifying with Fact Finder precedent, an accommodation to integrating systems, a strong future orientation, and a responsiveness to present conditions. I will suffer stress if I don't get to the bottom line without being mired in historical evidence. It should come as no surprise that I *intuited* the existence of the Striving Instincts, and needed to place them in the context of my own version of the Creative Process. Only after I discovered the word *conation* was I able to tie behaviors I had observed back to instinct.

Before Dr. Elizabeth Berry, a professor of communications at California State University, Northridge, was accredited in the Kolbe Concept (a training process for professionals in management, human resources, and organizational development), she took time to study its historical underpinnings. Her KCI result is 7-7-5-2. "The first thing I did," she explained later, "was go to the library and take out the only two books that referenced conation and volition. I read them, outlined, and took detailed notes. I'm constantly looking for support material. Then I checked footnotes and bibliographies." *Then* Elizabeth interviewed me to obtain more background and data. She asked copious questions about the history of conative research. "I had to be sure it was grounded in a theory that had existed for a while," she explained later. "I'm uncomfortable with brand-new concepts. I thought the ideas were interesting, but I had to get additional information that made me confident that this was a valid approach. It had to integrate with what I already knew."

After she had read all the available supporting materials, Elizabeth's Fact Finder turned to experts in psychology, philosophy, and education. "Most of them didn't know anything about conation and didn't believe in human instincts," she said, "but they were fascinated and didn't discount this new theory. So I moved on to consideration of my own past experiences and found many of our family dynamics could be explained by interpretation of KCI results. Only then was I ready to become trained so I could do interpretations for other people. Once I had done those, I had the final evidence I needed to begin my research on applications of the Kolbe Concept."

By contrast, Terry Stone, CEO of Bolton Tremblay Funds, Inc., a Toronto-based investment firm, first contacted my office after reading about the Kolbe Concept in *The Wall Street Journal*. A few letters passed between us, and he expressed interest but never followed up with specific questions. Several months later when my husband and I were in Toronto, we stopped by to interpret the KCI results of Terry and his management team. Terry's KCI result was 5-3-8-3.

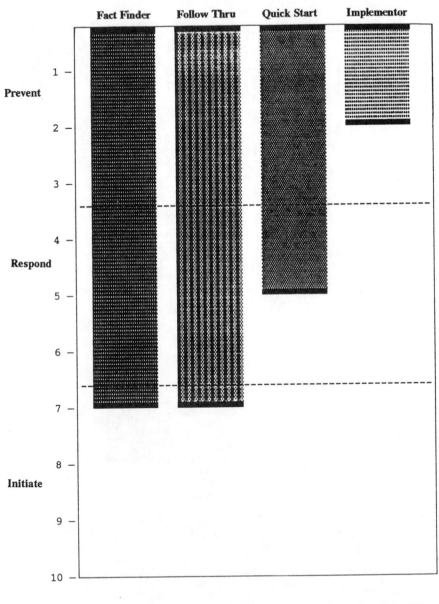

Kolbe Talent Analysis
KOLBE CONATIVE INDEX® Result

Terry Stone

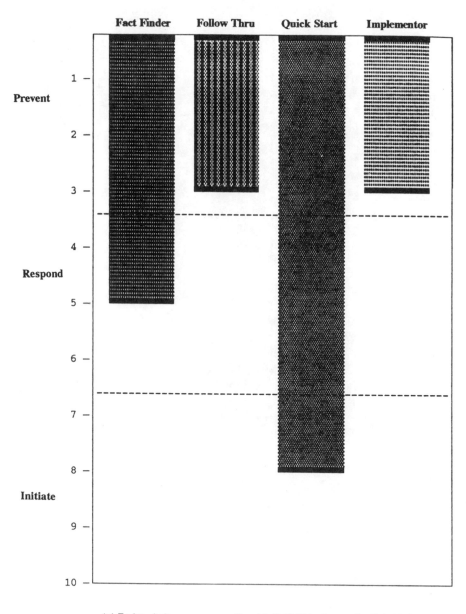

As soon as Terry heard everyone's results, he began brainstorming ideas for future uses of the program. By the time we left only two hours later, Terry had committed to revising his upcoming European convention schedule so I could address his high performers. Furthermore, he had decided to devote his entire convention in Marrakech the following year to the Kolbe Concept, including main platform speeches, break-out sessions, and spousal programs.

When we returned to our hotel room, which was just down the street from Terry's office, the phone was ringing. Buyer's remorse? No, this Quick Start was just wondering if we also had the time to "KCI" his home-office staff and conduct a seminar for them before the European meeting.

Elizabeth and Terry both put time on their side. They operate in sync with their natural inclinations. Elizabeth won't be rushed. Terry won't be kept waiting. She takes time to study. He puts matters aside until he can act with immediacy. Her energy flows when she's gathering historical information. He acts with zest when he's making instantaneous decisions. If either tried to conform to the other's timetable, the resulting strain would limit his or her effectiveness.

Elizabeth is just as decisive as Terry. Once she has all the specifics she needs, she'll take a strong stand. If she ever acts on the spur of the moment, it's because she already has a storehouse of substantiating evidence that allows her to move quickly. Now that she has done her homework on conation, she adeptly "wings it" in Q&A sessions on the topic. Before she completed her research, however, it would have caused her stress.

Marilou von Ferstel, an executive vice-president with Ogilvy Adams & Rinehart, a public relations advertising firm in Chicago, combines Fact Finder and Quick Start with her 7-2-9-2 KCI result. She uses her time to bring in new accounts, anticipate client needs, explore unique concepts, and set priorities for employees. She does not even try such Follow Thru activities as day-to-day scheduling. She doesn't pretend to be the most organized person and told me up front when I planned a seminar for her staff that "the nature of the business" might cause last-minute changes in the schedule. I knew it was *her* nature that would likely lead to changes. Even in the most unsettled environment, an intense systems person would stick with a schedule. Marilou goes with the flow.

ALLOCATING TIME

EFFORT TAKES TIME. COMMITMENT OBLIGES YOU TO USE YOUR TIME. ATTEMPTS COST you something off the clock. When two people who march to totally different conative rhythms work together, it is as disconcerting as a morning person traveling with a night owl. But if responsibilities are negotiated according to each person's instinctive time needs, the trip will be far more productive. For instance, if an insistent Follow Thru were planning a trip for a group, she should include time for Fact Finders to share historical background, freedom for Quick Starts' need for spontaneous adventure, and interludes when Implementors can hang back to check out the quality of goods.

A couple of years ago, my husband and I rambled around Spain in a minibus packed with four of our young-adult kids. It made me wonder how families survive without knowing about Striving Instincts. After a few days, patience wore thin when the insistent Follow Thru slowed us down—again—to be sure he'd seen every single painting in the Prado Art Museum. The Fact Finder–insistent people in our tribe took the time in the bus to read—out loud—every word about the places and things we were to see. They'd get annoyed with me when my resistance to Fact Finder kept me from paying attention, and I would consider it my personal discovery that there were not birds in the plains of La Mancha. "We've wasted our time reading this for you," one complained. "No," I replied, "you haven't, because you did that for yourself. If I had listened, it would have wasted *my* time."

The most classic episode occurred when we discovered that Alan, a resistant Follow Thru who had been studying in Seville, hadn't arranged our dinner reservations in that city on Christmas Eve. At the last minute, his insistence in Quick Start came up with lots of alternatives, none of which he'd taken time to check out (presumably because he had used his Fact Finder for recent school exams). As we walked the empty streets of Seville, we discovered that the local custom dictated all public places close on Christmas Eve. At 11:00 P.M. we found a little Chinese eatery filled with Australians, Germans, and Brits, all of whom had probably left their holiday arrangements in the hands of the resistant Follow Thrus in their groups. The uniqueness of the situation captured the fancy of the Quick Starts among us, but one of the family's Fact Finder–insistent souls dwelled on the inappropriateness of eating egg rolls on Christmas Eve in Spain.

Each of us has a limited amount of striving energy distributed among the conative modes. We have to allocate these abilities according to the zones in which they are available to us. In making restaurant arrangements, Alan used his Quick Start insistence. If we had been eating in his hometown, this would have led to some unusual alternatives. However, in this situation, the task was complex and required more than a casual attempt at fact finding. He learned that unfamiliar circumstances called for a commitment of more time and energy than he had allocated. It was that simple.

SIZING UP OPPORTUNITIES

BEFORE INVESTING TIME AND ENERGY IN AN ACTIVITY, BE SURE YOU HAVE THE appropriate talent to achieve the required result. If, for instance, you are a resistant Implementor, you can be determined to put up shelving, but you'll be wasting your resources in the effort. Beware of saying you will do whatever it takes to get a job done. That may be a great attitude to have, but a caution light should go on when your instincts tell you that you are making commitments you won't be able to fulfill.

If you have made the mistake of committing to do something that goes against your instinctive nature, try to renegotiate your Level of Effort so that it is understood you will instead *attempt* this effort. A customer-service rep for a magazine once tried to convince me that she was going to inject a "sense of urgency" into resolving a long-standing glitch in its change-of-address system. "Don't worry," she told me, "I'll get your subscription rerouted to your new address by the next issue if it kills me." The next month she called with a slightly more realistic approach:

"I've talked with my supervisor, who suggests we cancel your current subscription and reenter an order for you that extends your subscription by the four months you have missed delivery. I'll try to get the paperwork done in time for you to get the next issue, but I can't promise it. Thank you for your patience." As a Quick Start I crave immediate feedback, but I can be as patient as the next person when it comes to not killing the messenger. The first promise was not instinctively consistent. The later response reflected a negotiated attempt that was more honest and acceptable.

When people merely intend to achieve goals, communication problems often occur. Intentions are always conditional. You'll do it if you have time and energy, if the opportunity arises, or if circumstances prove right. If another person perceives that you have made an unconditional promise when you have merely intended to act, the result can be distressing for both parties.

Don't promise that you will make an effort you aren't equipped to give. If you want to make a commitment to do something but are accommodating in the mode necessary to complete the task, your offer must be conditional. The condition is that you will only *respond* to others' initiatives. You ought to clarify that you won't be the one who sets things in motion. For example, it would be false for an accommodating Follow Thru to assure us that she will deliver a meticulously drawn diagram, but we could rely on her to keep her promise to add anything she thinks is missing from our diagram.

A resistance allows you to commit to what you won't do. That's often a very important consideration when people are working together. A little kid who resists Implementor has it easy when asked to promise "not to touch." He isn't irresistibly drawn to touch in order to discover. But his more tactile-minded friend is likely to break that rule. In the workplace, a resistance can remove a liability. "You don't have to worry about Margaret causing chaos on the project," a supervisor says of this resistant Quick Start. Also, you can be certain that a resistant Follow Thru won't mind a distraction. "There's no problem switching things around," a systems-averse person says. "I don't follow the plan anyway." When people are truly committed to their resistances, it can aid their effectiveness. "I won't bother with the details" is an energy-saving device for a resistant Fact Finder. When American Express's Jean-Yves Gueguen guarantees not to shoot from the hip, he is making an unnecessary statement; after all, he is instinctively resistant to risk taking without facts. "Of course he won't!" his wife exclaimed. "If he did, he wouldn't be Jean-Yves."

OVERCOMMITTING

PEOPLE WHO INITIATE QUICK START ACTION OFTEN JUMP IN AT A HIGH LEVEL OF Effort on new projects because they thrive on the risk. "You've got to be kidding," a lawyer says to his Quick Start partner. "You can't just take over the case this close to trial. It's not as if you don't already have too much on your plate. You can't save the whole world all at once, you know." The Quick Start partner knows he won't save the whole world at once, but telling him he can't take over the case this late in the game is like telling a person with an itch not to scratch. As philosopher William James wrote in 1890, instincts are "as fatal as sneezing." Now he's even more determined to prove he can deliver. But his overcommitment may undermine his success. Our instincts sometimes urge an unrealistic level of commitment unless that commitment is edited by reason.

Health factors can also lead to false commitments. Illness and pain interfere with your ability to operate on instinct. Even though your mind supposedly is not affected by an accident or physical disease, the effort required in getting well can tax your mental energy. When Tammie Quick, a PhD in educational administration, and an insistent Fact Finder, was ill, she wouldn't commit to undergoing life-saving emergency surgery until she knew the specialist's educational background. She had difficulty with her recuperation until the specifics of her regimen were justified in great detail. Once her conative needs were satisfied, she could put her energy into healing. However, her sense of appropriateness was frustrated by her lack of energy for writing thank-you notes for flowers and gifts. "It's as if my Fact Finder is still in charge but functioning with a very dim battery," she explained.

Sometimes work can result in real or perceived overcommitments. Workaholics who direct all their energies to work at the expense of the rest of their lives are destructively overcommitted. Just as destructive may be the perception of overcommitment by many who have suffered from the unrequited commitment of losing a job which they gave great effort. The commitment wasn't reciprocated by the company. They may become determined never to get so involved again with their job. Such rejections of their talent may cause workers to withhold such effort in the future. They may become transient workers, hopping from one job to another so they avoid buying into any particular job and being burned once again.

The layoffs of the late 1980s and early 1990s have created this new class of conatively disenfranchised people afraid to commit their Striving Instincts. Simply finding them another paycheck doesn't remove the indelible scar left by what they perceive as unappreciated commitment. They carry their rejection as a contagious ailment, spreading distrust in the workplace. For them to regain their spirit of involvement requires that they be given opportunities to utilize their instincts.

CONATIVE GRIDLOCK

OVERCOMMITMENTS OCCUR WHEN PEOPLE TRY TO DO TOO MUCH. THEY HAPPEN when strategic Fact Finders are faced with pages of unrealistic priorities; when systematic Follow Thrus don't have the time to check everything off their lists; when urgency-oriented Quick Starts are so overwhelmed they miss deadlines; and when quality-conscious Implementors have to stumble through projects, leaving touch-ups for later.

Conative Gridlock happens to people who have lots of determination. The problem is that they make everything they have to do a commitment and then become mired as they spin out of control trying to get it all done. What they have to realize at that point is that the only way to accomplish anything is to decide what *doesn't* have to be done. Outcomes are within their control as long as they'll quit trying to be superman or superwoman. No one can do it all. And those who try usually end up accomplishing very little.

The best defense against Conative Gridlock is to use a resistance, which can help prevent the dilemmas created when an insistence causes you to take on too much. And in situations where we don't have the appropriate resistances to save us, it is wise to turn to team members for help.

Fact Finder resistance prevents gridlock by cutting through information and getting to the heart of issues.

Follow Thru resistance prevents gridlock by bypassing the system and taking shortcuts to solutions.

Quick Start resistance prevents gridlock by identifying the things that can't change and by avoiding distractions.

Implementor resistance prevents gridlock by seeking alternatives that don't require handcrafting solutions.

MERGING CONATIVE CULTURES

THE STRIVING INSTINCTS OF THE PEOPLE WHO MAKE UP AN ORGANIZATION FORM ITS *conative culture*. A company can have an admirable mission statement and reasonable objectives, but it will never attain them if they aren't in line with the Striving Instincts of the people who work there. It's vital to separate an organization's mission or purpose from its overall conative ability to achieve in certain ways. The department-store chain Nordstrom, Inc., may have a published commitment to customer service, but if it hires employees who lack the instinctive Follow Thru to structure such service, the goal will never be achieved.

Father Ray Bucher, a Franciscan priest, is a multistate vicar provincial with a PhD in philosophy. His KCI result is 6-8-4-2. When Father Bucher's God-given talents are stretched by the changing cultures in which he works, he feels stress. His administrative role provides an outlet for his Follow Thru creativity, but not always as much as he needs. "I try to set up structures that allow the guys to live the life they promise," he said. "It's more difficult to do that with old structures gone. Our training is profound, but the follow-up is thin. I try to integrate the friar's past with the future, to get back in touch with the spark that was there." For Father Bucher the structure associated with follow-up and integrating old and new structures is a conative necessity. He spoke of an upcoming sabbatical in typical Follow Thru–insistent terms. He said he planned to take "an internal inventory" and to "reflect, to do things with discipline." Sounds like heaven for a Follow Thru, doesn't it? He hoped he could counter the conative stress imposed by six years of having to work against his grain.

There are times when two or more distinct conative cultures must mix together, and that requires special handling. You can't just throw an entrepreneurial Quick Start–oriented company in with an acquiring–Fact Finder firm and not expect the two cultures to be at cross-purposes. Being aware of the different points of view allows you to integrate them into more broadly based operations, but it won't change the fact that differences exist. The last thing you want to create is a culture of dis-content.

Joe Contadino, whose KCI result is 5-4-8-2, owned an entrepreneurial home-construction business that was acquired by the Del Webb Corp. The conative clash between Joe's company and the publicly traded cor-poration that builds and manages Sun City retirement communities was no secret to anyone involved. The culture at Webb is friendly and enthusiastic; conatively, it is a strategically based group that makes decisions based on practicalities and priorities. At Del Webb, if some-thing can't be proved viable, it won't happen. Joe had entered a Fact Finder world.

But Joe, who is both a CPA and a MBA, leads with Quick Start, and the culture of his group is biased toward that instinctive direction. He's intuitive; his best decisions are gut level. He knows property values and pricing, but he can also sniff out a good deal before it's on anyone's computer. Having to justify his instincts to the resistant Quick Starts at Del Webb almost cost both groups any of the benefits that the differences might have given them.

The corporate word on Joe was that he shot from the hip and didn't substantiate his recommendations for acquisitions. "He's downright scary," one executive said. "I like the guy, but I just don't feel I can go along with his undocumented fantasies." Since the goal of merging these entities was to ultimately build trust, it was fortunate that Joe was able to accommodate Fact Finders. He had to stop using off-the-cuff language in his presentations to the management group and speak to them in their own terminology. His insistent–Follow Thru assistant was there to keep a diary for Joe of the terms frequently used by others in the group. He learned to express ideas in their Fact Finder language.

If two cultures are to merge, both need to be able to communicate without one turning off the other. In Joe's case, this has become a cooperative effort in large part because Del Webb CEO Phil Dion is a classic Mediator. The otherwise jarring differences between the two cultures are bridged by a person in authority who demands consensus. Those involved have committed themselves to finding joint solutions. After two years, the verdict was that Joe's business unit had surpassed all projections.

Mike Garnreiter, a partner in a national public-accounting firm, makes his living performing an intangible service. Mike takes pride in his education, the position he holds in the partnership and community, and in his relationships with clients. But when he found out that his KCI result was 5-5-4-7, he felt disappointed. "I wanted to be more of a Quick Start and less of an Implementor," he confided. "I felt out of step with others around me and believed I needed to change to be good at what I was trying to do." It took Mike months of introspection to appreciate the special contribution he could make through his instinctive efforts. He was one of the few accountants who could speak the language of clients in mining, agriculture, and manufacturing industries. When his resistant–Implementor managing partner expressed awe over a cabinet Mike had built, it came home to him that "I'm good at some things he wouldn't even try. I'm not sure he'd be as good working with some of my clients, either. It made me realize I'm fine just the way I am—and so is he, by the way."

It took almost as long for someone with a 3-2-9-4 KCI result to stop trying to become more orderly and systematic in her efforts. Deborah believed she wasn't going to make it in the corporate world unless she shaped up her Follow Thru. She even tried to force herself to keep lists and to act as efficiently as the folks who wrote neatly in their daily planners. "I may not *be* one of them," she said, "but I'll figure out how to *act* like one of them." Of course, she didn't really change, and when she finally realized that trying to do so was futile, she too settled into her natural stride and has been promoted over several others whose MOs she had envied.

TRUSTING OTHERS

DISCOVERING WHAT YOU CAN TRUST OTHERS TO DO REQUIRES UNDERSTANDING WHO they are instinctively and striving cooperatively to identify how they can contribute. A machine-tool operator who led with Implementor worked for half his shift to repair a faulty piece of equipment. When his manager discovered this, the tool operator was admonished for not sticking with the schedule, which didn't match his resistance to Follow Thru. The worker's insistence in Implementor made it predictable that he would get caught up in the repair work. Both he and his manager would have benefited from placing him in a role that utilized his innate abilities. Instead he spent most of his hours on the job functioning in his resistant–Follow Thru mode. Disciplining him didn't change him, nor did threats. The only thing that would have worked would have been to trust him to utilize his talents. This might have allowed him to contribute and kept this situation from escalating into an irresolvable dispute.

Trusting another person's instincts does not mean you will always agree with him. It is possible for people of good will to be at cross-purposes. That's what healthy competition is all about. It can be a confidence builder to go toe-to-toe with a worthy opponent whom you can trust to put forth his best striving capacities. In fact, victories are far more significant when you are up against someone whom is contributing her greatest effort. It is not as satisfying to beat the basketball Chicago Bulls when Michael Jordan is out of the game.

Contracts that require someone to operate in a certain way must reflect the contributor's innate abilities. A resistant–Follow Thru performer cannot be tied to requirements for routine rehearsals. Implicit in the trust you give another person to represent you in matters relating to the use of your talents is the belief that she will accurately reflect your instinctive needs.

SEPARATING WANT FROM WILL

ALL THE HIGH PERFORMERS I HAVE INTERVIEWED HAVE SACRIFICED CERTAIN AC-tivities in order to carry through on the ones they have committed themselves to achieve. By separating the *want*, or desires, from the *Will*—that which people are committed to achieve—they unleash energy for goal-oriented pursuits. When we muster up energy in a resistant mode so that we can help another person or a cause, we are showing true dedication. The constitutionally untidy person who keeps a shared area orderly deserves special thanks. It's a genuine sacrifice to suffer the frustration of intentionally going against his own grain. Just don't expect it to last forever.

A person cannot overcome a lack of commitment with pleasantness, intelligence, or by putting in long hours. The fact that he is not committed to do something will be obvious. The Follow Thru will stop keeping an orderly Rolodex, and the Fact Finder will not dictate file notes. This is where the phrase "Actions speak louder than words" comes into play. Don't believe people when they say they care, unless that caring shows up in a contribution.

When people merely give you their conative leftovers, it is the biggest insult of all. When an insistent Implementor with the skills to repair things says, "I don't have time to fix the fax for you, but I'll call a guy I know you'll like," you know you're low on her list. The resistant Implementor who says, "I'm afraid I'd just make it worse, but I'll find you the number of a guy I really trust to fix it," is a real friend talking.

Another difficult situation occurs when someone is sure he can teach you how to do something. Even though his instinctive strengths may be quite different from yours, he may see your inability to follow his instructions as a rejection of his commitment to transfer talent. If an insistent Implementor puts energy into explaining to you what's under the car hood, you may be afraid you'll have to move so he won't see you aren't changing your own oil. Some Fact Finders insist on cutting out articles from magazines for other people to read. Denying these commitments to share in instinctive methods would be unkind, but responding in kind would be phony. I recommend telling do-gooders how appreciative you are that they would share their talent with you, but how impossible it is for you to take full advantage of it. Those who understand the Kolbe Concept have been known to simply say, "I'm out of Fact Finder; please don't expect me to read it very soon."

MISPLACED TRUST

OVER THE LAST DECADE, THE CORPORATE WORLD HAS CAUGHT ON TO THE IMPORTANCE of trust. Yet it has often missed the mark by not identifying Striving Instincts. Some "trust activities" went down the wilderness path, trying to relate situations of physical survival to office environments. This could have worked had they known, for instance, that the Implementor-insistent people were more adept at handling equipment or building a lean-to. In debriefing sessions they could have pointed out that people insistent in Follow Thru could be trusted to organize the supplies and keep track of what was left. Fact Finder campers are the ones to turn to when it comes to distributing scarce resources wisely. Had the group known to trust the intuition of the Quick Starts, it might have taken the shortcut that would have saved it hours on the trail.

The citified version of this experience has included putting people on the top step of a playground slide and having them fall backward into the intertwined arms of others. Trusting coworkers not to drop them is not the same as trusting them to get the billing out regularly or to provide an in-depth analysis at next week's go/no-go session. The exercise at least gets the word *trust* bandied about, but it doesn't lead to measurable increases in job satisfaction or performance levels. Not by itself. Making the catch didn't require an ongoing commitment to common goals. There were no distinguishable roles within the group that required a true commitment of creative effort along with the physical and affective involvement.

One of the primary causes of lack of commitment is fear of failure. If you're afraid you may not succeed in reaching a particular goal, you can protect yourself by withholding effort. Understanding the equal power of Striving Instincts in every individual assures us that we *can* fulfill commitments based on reason.

CHAPTER FIVE

HOW HIGH PERFORMERS GET MORE DONE

Ighly productive people have the same amount of instinctive energy as everyone else; they just make better use of it. Instead of squandering time working against their instinctive grain, they find outlets for their natural talents. They get tired, but it's usually the well-earned fatigue that follows mental effort. They spend their creative capacities and are then able to unwind and relax—and thoroughly enjoy doing absolutely nothing. This is the reward for operating on pure instinct.

Once front-runners find the methods that work for them, they stick with them, recognizing the power of their instincts. These people usually laugh when I tell them scientists don't believe humans have instinct. The chief financial officer of Eastman Chemical Company, Virgil Stephens, has a 7-8-3-2 KCI result. His advice to others: "Trust your instincts, that small voice within. Sometimes you'll hear another approach, but don't just go with that. Don't give undue weight to another method. Be open, but when it comes down to it, if your own instincts still say you're right, it is right."

Virgil, as an insistent Follow Thru, needs to get his in-box completely clean—and recognizes that he'll feel stress if he isn't able to sort out the top-priority projects, leaving the less important work for later. "It's a natural tendency," he said, one that was not well explained on the aptitude tests he took years ago. He's found a way to use his instincts in corporate finance, where, he said, "My role is not just bringing in the numbers. The president looks to me to share in decision making. Now that I know my instinctive bias, I understand how I help with the interplay. I know when to let things play themselves out and when to push for closure." Virgil recognizes where his ability to structure and his need for completeness will facilitate corporate decisions. He also realizes his resistance to Quick Start may limit his ability to see multiple alternatives, so he needs to look to others on the team for such insights.

Virgil knows his instincts are at work when his life has a sense of order. For Freida Caplan, whose company imports the kiwifruit and other exotic foods into the United States, acting on instinct occurs when she "feels it in my elbow." As she says it, she palms her elbows, naturally drawing herself inward. She knows when she is acting as herself.

Ed Hurd, president of Honeywell, Inc.'s industrial-businesses division, went through a stressful time when he was in a position that required attention to minute specifications. As a highly acclaimed design engineer, he felt personal stress having to check and recheck every part of every plan. It isn't surprising that Ed's KCI result is 3-5-7-6. "I discovered that working with that kind of detail didn't give me personal satisfaction," he said, "nor personal or professional growth. I trusted my instincts too much to do that to myself for very long." He moved on to lead a group that brought out three innovative products selling for over $500 million each. "Many times these products would have been dumped," Ed reflected, "but I kept trying to keep them from being watered down by the wrong kind of consensus. I trusted my intuition."

When Dr. Harry Davis, whose KCI result is 3-2-8-6, was the deputy dean at the University of Chicago Graduate School of Business, his administrative responsibilities inevitably caused him conative stress. He is articulate in describing the frustrations of working contrary to your nature. "I've always known I didn't suit the traditional research-oriented role," he said. "Academic writing, for example, is very painful for me. My KCI result confirmed why I'm not like most of the people around here. It was very freeing. Now it's clear why I've been more energized when I'm developing new programs."

When Harry could innovate rather than hassle with administrative matters, he engaged his Quick Start talents and reduced his stress.

Discovering why this was the case not only freed him of guilt over his often negative response to some required methods, it explained his innate drives. "I'm always energized when I work on something new, innovative, different," he said. "I became more comfortable with my own approach when I learned of my conative needs. I always built prototypes with my Implementor instincts, but not with as much comfort or realization of how much value it had for me to do that."

Sometimes what seems an ideal outlet for your talent satisfies only a narrow band of your total conative capabilities. The way to avoid conative stress is to recognize that you have to satisfy the needs in all four of your Action Modes. For instance, Craig Barrett, executive vice-president and chief operating officer of Intel Corp., left a job as professor of materials science at Stanford University so that he could exercise the full range of his talents. Though his 8-4-4-3 KCI result indicates Craig initiates solutions through the Fact Finder mode, he found pure research too confining. To alleviate the stress he felt in academia, he found a position that freed his accommodating energies and allowed him to pursue "big-picture results." As a business leader, he said he "monitors the heck out of everything," but he also uses his Follow Thru and Quick Start to develop innovative programs and management policies.

Craig achieves on his own terms now. Recently *Business Week* described him as the heir apparent at Intel, a "Mr. Inside" who is "transforming Intel's once weak manufacturing arm into a fortress of respectability." He's found a natural fit in a role that balances his insistent–Fact Finder needs for research with his accommodating–Follow Thru involvement with process and accommodating a Quick Start ability to drive product development. Still, as an insistent Fact Finder, Craig confided, "Every once in a while I long to solve an equation."

PATHS OF LEAST RESISTANCE

IF WE ARE GIVEN COMPLETE FREEDOM OF ACTION, WE WILL NATURALLY GRAVITATE to what works best for us—the path of least resistance. But it sometimes seems as if the world is intent on making us do things the hard way. And sometimes the people who take us out of our own game are the ones who care about us the most.

Gustav Reiner is a highly successful executive in the automotive industry. Yet one Saturday afternoon when his significant other, Valerie, asked him to help her fix windows that wouldn't open, Gustav found the project overwhelmingly frustrating. At one point he pointed his finger at her and yelled, "Every time, it's the same damn thing! You just don't understand; my whole life I haven't been able to do anything like this. People talk me into trying to fix or build things, then when I goof up they want to know what the hell is the matter with me! I won't be humiliated! I won't do it! Leave me alone!"

Not understanding the reason behind his frustration, this highly energetic problem solver stomped off, curled up, and took a long nap.

Had Valerie asked Gustav to help with her taxes, it would have been a different story. He has ample Fact Finder instincts for such calculations. Or had she suggested they play a competitive board game such as Monopoly, he would have joined in without hesitation. That's because he also maneuvers easily in situations requiring Quick Start risks. The problem was that she needed him to use his hands, and he couldn't even visualize what she was trying to do, let alone attempt to help. She was asking him to participate in an activity that relies on an Action Mode he naturally resists. Gustav is talented in a great many ways, but Implementor mechanics are anathema to him.

This had always been a sore spot for Gustav, the son of a carpenter. His father never understood his son's fear that he would look foolish if he tried working with his hands. Gustav always wanted to hear that his dad was proud of him, but managing huge sums of money didn't add up to his father's perception of "real work." So Gustav's outburst—so confusing to Valerie—actually stemmed from a lifetime of having his natural instincts devalued on the homefront. And Valerie's assumption that men were naturally handy didn't help matters.

On the other hand, BYU's Dr. Maren Mouritsen, whose KCI result is 2-2-8-8, would readily put aside her work papers to take a group of students on a hike and would welcome the opportunity to get involved in handcrafting. She often stays up most of the night making home repairs and somehow still finds ample energy for the next day's challenges at work.

In addition to her Implementor talent, Maren is an insistent Quick Start who handles multiple crises as dean of student life at a major university. Whether it's budget slashes, people traumas, or program changes, she cuts right to the bottom line and makes urgently needed decisions. Still, over decades of marveling at her abilities as a therapist, administrator, program developer, missionary, artist, and lecturer, I've rarely seen her follow a schedule. When my kids were young, it was best not to let them anticipate this good friend's on-again, off-again arrivals from out of state. It's just not wise to plan on her for dinner.

"I need the freedom to operate instinctively; to go where my guts tell me I'm most needed, when I'm most needed," Maren told me. "The energy is always there when I can control my own schedule, but I get incredibly bored with the tedium of a set agenda." Showing her resistance to both Fact Finder and Follow Thru, Maren added: "I've gone through periods when I had to sit through all-day meetings and stick to a rigid routine, and I could barely get going those mornings. Yet after a few hours of sleep I'm ready and raring to go when I get my hands on an innovative project."

Maren, Gustav, and the rest of us are able to make our most outstanding contributions only when we are each free to follow our own path of least resistance. Maren gets as frustrated as the next person when that path is full of roadblocks, forcing her to expend more energy taking the long way around.

FOUR PATHS TO ACCOMPLISHMENT

EACH ACTION MODE THAT STEMS FROM AN INSTINCTIVE NECESSITY LEADS US TO perform in a particular way.

Fact Finder

Suppose you are in business with a Fact Finder–insistent partner, Hal, who initiates meetings and comes with an agenda. He needs every *t* crossed and *i* dotted in order to make his best decisions. He always insists on having one more piece of information because thorough backgrounding and in-depth analyses are essential to his success. The two of you may miss some business opportunities because you can't convince him to make a decision until comparisons are exact—but he'll also save you from many potential disasters. Once Hal becomes experienced with something, his expertise amazes others. He has a knack for retaining specifics and historical information, and a need to correct even the slightest error or piece of misinformation. But don't ask Hal to give yes or no answers; he'll have to explain the nuances of each pro and con. If you push for an immediate opinion, he'll back off until he's reviewed priorities. And don't ask Hal what he thought of a movie you haven't seen yet. He has the constitutional need to tell you all the details and possibly ruin it for you.

Follow Thru

What if you and Hal are working with a client who leads with Follow Thru actions? Mr. C needs an overview of your program so he can be sure it's all-inclusive. Give it to him sequentially, without interruptions or distractions. Show him how it plays out, being certain that he sees all the guarantees and assurances that are part of your plan. After all, with him it's a deal breaker if he can't take into account every contingency. Also, if your presentation lacks structure, he may stop you so he can put options into context. You'd do best if you anticipated that need and provided a framework or flowchart. You shouldn't introduce Hal's complex solutions before Mr. C has had a chance to deal with the big picture. Mr. C will benefit from visuals, but not the kind your partner usually uses with facts and figures. Concentrate on graphs and diagrams.

Quick Start

The new marketing director you hired, Suzanne, is as insistent in Quick Start as Hal is insistent in Fact Finder. Suzanne's entire first day is taken up by Hal, who insists on giving her background information on the company. You watch her eyes glaze over. She throws out several ideas, and Hal disregards them because he's convinced she couldn't possibly have sufficient experience. If you're wise you'll take him aside and suggest that the three of you meet, pose some marketing challenges facing your company, and encourage Suzanne to brainstorm possibilities. Then give her a project that's deadline intense and let her jump right in. Ask her to present as many ways of achieving the goals as possible. Don't force her to work in isolation, though, because she'll need to bounce ideas off other people. And try not to confine her to specific hours. She'll work best if she can immerse herself in the project without watching the clock. This may seem inappropriate to Hal, but it's necessary for Suzanne. Above all, encourage her to take chances and be willing to let her play some of her hunches.

Implementor

Let's say your major investor, Hilda, is insistent in the Implementor mode. Hal's book-lined office is probably not the best place to schedule a meeting with her. She needs a true hands-on approach, so offer to walk Hilda through your plant or show her the plans you want her to invest in as they are coming off the computer. Forget sit-down meetings with lots of paperwork; instead use prototypes she can manipulate. Don't let Hal get too wordy, either. Hilda needs more tangible evidence than words—spoken or written—will provide. Quality is a primary issue with her, so point out your first-rate equipment and materials, including the special paper you used for her copy of the business plan. She'll see a lot more significance in what's happening in the shop today than she will either in Hal's historical perspective or Suzanne's vision of the future. Stick with the here and now, and you'll be more likely to satisfy Hilda's needs. It's also a good idea to be prepared for her visits, because she'll size up your operation based on what she observes firsthand. Wasted space will bother her, as will anything that's broken or poorly maintained. Don't be surprised if Hilda stops and adjusts a piece of equipment. That's one of her contributions.

Facilitator, the Means of Mediation

Another essential talent on this team is that of a *Facilitator*, someone with no need to initiate action. For such people, the scores in each of the KCI modes will either be accommodating or resistant. They are able to act as Mediators among people with various insistences. Their reward comes from team play, from being a utility infielder or being cross-trained in many roles. They need to work with initiators who provide opportunities for them to respond. They can be good leaders through their knack for bringing consensus. They need to work in environments that have a lot of instinctive diversity, but without their acting as the glue, everything would surely pull apart.

My research indicates that 20 percent of the general population is insistent and 20 percent resistant in each Action Mode; however, only 10 percent act as Facilitators, with no need to insist on a particular method of problem solving. This makes Facilitators particularly sought after by many organizations, but that doesn't mean they get all the credit they are due. Facilitators have no need to stand out, so they are rarely in starring roles.

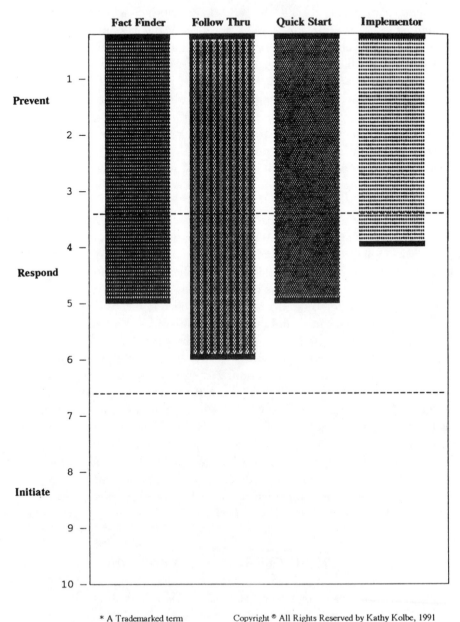

Kolbe Talent Analysis
KOLBE CONATIVE INDEX® Result

I M A Facilitator

THE FRUSTRATION OF TRANSITIONS

UNDERSTANDING HER OWN MAKEUP HELPED MAREN MOURITSEN RELIEVE THE STRESS
that at one time caused her such energy drain that she was in what I term
conative crisis, or a transition period. She described it as similar to trying
to drive an old clunker up steep hills. Even though she floored the gas
pedal, she could only inch along. There just wasn't enough *oomph* to get
her where she wanted to go. All of us have suffered that feeling of
exhaustion at one time or another. This weariness is particularly dis-
couraging when you have nothing to show for your efforts.

People are often puzzled by tiredness that doesn't come from physical
exertion. Gustav's nap wasn't a response to physical fatigue, nor was it
an emotional escape. The draining process of butting up against obstacles and seeking detours—in his case, ways to get out of being a Mr.
Fix-it—can be debilitating.

Once Valerie understood that Gustav's reaction was instinctive, she
supported his need to withdraw from such activities; in fact, he got out
of ever helping her fix anything around the house again. And she encouraged him to rely on her Implementor talents. "There are so many
ways he does make a difference in my life," she said, "that I realized my
inclination to make everything myself didn't need to involve him." Now
she understood how he would take to her do-it-yourself ideas!

Unlike Valerie's window project, most jobs have some flexibility in
how they can be performed—actually, a lot more flexibility than most
managers, friends, and parents allow. Too many bosses insist that a job
be done the way *they* would do it. Instead of encouraging people like
Maren to build prototypes and then let others on her team work out the
details, they force her to function against her instincts. It is both ethical
and sensible to manage people in ways that bring out their instinctive
strengths. Anything short of that will reduce productivity and workers'
job satisfaction. A true total-quality management process can exist only
in organizations built on the premise that *all employees are high-potential
employees if they are free to act on instinct.*

THE POWER TO PREVENT

THE POWER TO *PREVENT*, OR RESIST A FORM OF ACTION, CAN HELP YOU GET MORE
done. High performers count on their resistances to avoid the pitfalls that
would trip them if they initiated or responded in all four modes. They

realize that what they won't do is important, preserving energy for what they need to do. Imagine a seat-of-the-pants emergency-room doctor who didn't understand this. She might save a trauma patient's life and then apologize for the mess created in the process. Or a gardener who grows roses might labor over writing a magazine article about how he does it. Different strokes for different folks. And the truth of that old cliché affects our sense of accomplishment, hiring decisions, customer satisfaction, and leadership responsibilities.

Fact Finder Resistance

Preventing a preoccupation with data and minutiae are hallmarks of a resistant Fact Finder. Maren Mouritsen, for instance, just won't micromanage. Rather than specializing in any particular area, she will always be a generalist. As dean of student life, her programs for students incorporate intellectual, physical, social, and spiritual dimensions. She has the intellectual capability to know a great deal about something, but she will opt to keep adding new dimensions rather than going in more depth in one field. She's proved this by becoming a renowned artist, and then moving on; an Academy Award–winning set designer, and moving on again; and now she is a nationally recognized college administrator. Resistant Fact Finders build on past experiences *intellectually*, but they won't dwell on the past or act on precedent.

Follow Thru Resistance

Sometimes companies run very efficiently but not profitably. This can happen when established procedures create a false sense of security. Organizations that are mired in Follow Thru routines often don't realize the need for more productive alternatives. Such companies could use a resistant Follow Thru to stir up things. This person's natural drive prevents the complacency that often sets in when an organization is overcome by policies and procedures. The resistant Follow Thru's spontaneous nature often generates shortcuts that wouldn't normally be discovered through orderly processes. Acting out of sequence has its place, especially when it allows you to seize unusual opportunities. For instance, if Suzanne the marketing director were resistant to Follow

Thru, she would not be distracted by multiple interruptions and therefore could have several projects—and clients—concurrently.

Quick Start Resistance

Resistant Quick Starts prevent chaos and keep others from taking dangerous plunges. Dr. Frank DeCastro is a psychologist–management consultant whom I have trained to use the Kolbe Concept in his practice. Frank, a 10 in Quick Start, tells a story about himself and fellow military helicopter pilot trainees on a day-off adventure: Climbing rocks near a river, he watched the man ahead of him suddenly dive over the side of a cliff. Frank thought it looked like fun, so he tried it. Ninety feet later he hit the water flat on his back and was knocked unconscious. Due also to his resistance to Fact Finder, Frank didn't investigate the situation or figure out that the other guy was an Olympic-level diver. "I would have been saved a lot of pain had we had a resistant Quick Start calling for caution," Frank reflected. That's the benefit of having such an inclination in any group.

Implementor Resistance

Seeing isn't always believing. Resistant Implementors make decisions without tangible evidence, acting instead on an ability to deal with abstract notions. You don't have to literally demonstrate things for them, because their instincts are more conceptual than mechanical. They prevent situations from becoming overly concrete and don't rely too much on a "show me" approach. Two members of the YPO (Young Presidents' Organization), sitting next to each other in a seminar I was conducting, were delighted to discover they were well suited to their service-oriented, non-Implementor–driven businesses. As these two resistant tactile doers reached up to execute a high-five, they both fanned the air in all three attempts.

HABITS THAT INHIBIT SUCCESS

LEARNED BEHAVIORS AND TRAINED HABITS OFTEN CONFLICT WITH INSTINCTS, BUT inevitably instincts prevail. You may have learned the "right" or traditional way of accomplishing a task, but your Striving Instincts are in control when it comes down to how you are most comfortable doing it. Most managers know how to balance a budget, but some will still go out on a Quick Start limb and make unallocated expenditures that they believe make sense. Entrepreneurs often show up for management-by-objectives–type seminars, but the good ones rarely do exactly what's suggested—at least not for very long. They know how *smart* it is to set specific goals, and they *want* to be objective about decisions. It's just that they find themselves unable to let an unexpected opportunity go by even when their plate is overflowing.

The high performers I've worked with are recognized by others for their noteworthy accomplishments. But they don't do it all. Clearly they don't take charge in every situation, nor do they try to become players in every activity. That is a crucial element of their success. We all have a particular capacity for bringing ideas to fruition, but too many of us misunderstand and misdirect this innate power that lies within us. Our efforts are diminished by:

- unrealistic self-expectations
- unrealistic requirements that others place on us
- conflicting needs between ourselves and others

Gustav's fatigue in the window episode stemmed from the unrealistic expectations his father had placed on him in the past. Experiences like this over the years had led him to feel guilty about not being an Implementor. His friend Valerie's request for help, which wasn't really a very complicated hands-on effort, was not a requirement. She's not the one who needed to make a change; Gustav's self-expectation was the problem. He beamed when I showed him his KCI result, which he felt gave him permission to simply say he preferred not getting involved in do-it-yourself projects. And he could now send out broken equipment to specialists for repairs. He was beginning to realize a resistance is *not* a weakness.

If Valerie, who does initiate in Implementor, had insisted that Gustav participate in such projects, the conflict between them would have compounded his stress. Anytime someone tries to get you to work against your instinctive grain, you will direct your energy against doing so. You may go about the task as diplomatically as possible, but your instincts will fight for their free expression.

Maren's debilitating energy loss resulted from *unrealistic requirements* from a new job situation. She was faced with having to spend her time explaining existing policies to a new Fact Finder–insistent boss who always had one more question. When she was away from those demands, she was full of her usual energy. The moment she understood the cause of her frustrations, she was able to redirect her efforts toward Quick Start and Implementor projects, turning to others to fill in the specifics and provide structure.

PERSONAL FULFILLMENT

YOU DON'T HAVE TO ALTER THE COURSE OF HISTORY IN ORDER TO FIND FULFILL-ment, nor do you have to find the cure for AIDS to have self-esteem. But you do need to make a contribution doing something that matters to you. It needn't be work related. Your greatest efforts may go toward family matters, friendships, community endeavors, or recreational pursuits. When I asked a group of fifty women publicly recognized for professional achievements what had brought them their greatest sense of accomplishment, over 80 percent listed family or relationship triumphs. Many said their ability to balance family and career demands had given them their greatest satisfaction. Often, rearing well-adjusted children topped starting their own businesses, being the first female partners in professional firms, or conquering scientific challenges. Men also frequently mention family as a source of accomplishment. A majority of my male clients note that their community involvement and family activities are essential to their sense of completeness and are among their most rewarding outlets.

No job is without its tiring moments—especially those times when you have to work against your grain—but the fact that over 70 percent of those in the work force report high stress or lack of job satisfaction is unacceptable. Many people's jobs, to them, are simply a way to pay the bills, and their conative abilities are directed toward non-work-related activity. Recreation can, indeed, use your instinctive energy in a rewarding way and even recharge your mental batteries. Yet, if you are getting up every workday regretting what you will be doing, it is time for a change. You don't have to love every minute of what you do, but on balance it needs to provide a positive outlet for who you truly are. You probably expend most of your mental energy doing it, so it's important to seek ways to make the effort worthwhile.

People who find themselves in jobs unsuited to their talents and who don't have the freedom to determine their own methods of completing assignments wind up missing work frequently, changing jobs often, and having very little job satisfaction. They invariably mention feeling tired, listless, or aimless. If your instinctive path is different from the one you are presently taking, you'll probably put in long hours without having much to show for it. A significant amount of your energy is absorbed in overcoming frustrations that inhibit your free flow of effort.

Conative restraints are like large rocks in a river, forcing you into protective maneuvers to keep from damaging your craft. They cost you time and energy. They limit your forward momentum. These obstacles are ever-present in the waters you are trying to navigate.

Every high performer has succeeded not by emulating others but by seeking productive uses for his full range of instinctive energies. They are people who have learned what it means to trust their guts. As you'll see, their effectiveness is even greater when they are in enterprises filled with similarly stress-free producers.

CHAPTER SIX

REDEFINING SUCCESS

AVOIDING STRESS

Often managers demand that employees work in ways that are outside their instinctive strengths, telling them "that's what it takes to succeed around here." Such methods never work. Instead, when employees are given opportunities to work according to their Striving Instincts, the result is a true win-win situation: Employees succeed, and the company benefits from their productivity.

Research on multinational corporations as well as small businesses confirms that conative misalignments between talents and required tasks is a costly problem. Absenteeism and turnover have shown to double among employees with high levels of conative stress. Workers who are working against their Striving Instincts are unproductive and often become disenchanted with their jobs. The problems are avoidable.

Judeth Javorek, the CEO of Holland (Michigan) Community Hospital, has a KCI result of 4-2-8-6. Her Quick Start, which she says "doesn't quit," wasn't being utilized in previous jobs. She told Kolbe consultant Mari Martin, "I never felt that my personal gifts were validated until this CEO appointment. But if someone had told me four years ago I'd be here now, I would have laughed. It wasn't a career track I was on." Like Judeth, employees often stay on career tracks that don't fit but for which they are well trained. In her new role she uses her instinctive knack for improvising, as well as her knowledge and experience. Like many people who turn to others for advice early in their careers, she found "the mentors I had were not helpful in saying 'You can be who you are.' " Judeth suffered stress until she discovered that she could succeed by being herself.

Judeth says her job requires her to call on her Fact Finder talent, "which I can accommodate, but I have no joy in it. The frustration comes when I'm forced to do presentations following logical sequences. Now I understand why, when I have to get ready for a meeting, I leave it until the last minute. I don't anguish over it anymore. I just know that it's going to come together." Judeth started allowing herself to respond to last-minute deadlines, which meant that she was finally listening to her Quick Start needs. Previously, when she was director of pediatrics at a different hospital, "I made more changes than anyone was comfortable with," she reflected. "I thought of advancing my career there, but knew it wasn't going to happen. So as I approached my next opportunity, I didn't make the same mistake." Instead she found her current position at a hospital that is more encouraging of her risk-taking, pioneering spirit. It is a much more productive fit.

Objective proof of on-the-job stress comes by comparing natural talents—*who a person is*—with self-expectations—*how he believes he has to perform.* The problem usually isn't that workers are lazy, stupid, or crazy. Differences between instinctive realities and self-expectations validate that the pain is real, not imagined. One form of stress occurs when we place self-imposed restrictions on our freedom to operate naturally, thereby stifling our instincts. The problem is diagnosed by comparing KCI results with the results of an instrument I call the KCI-B.

Rather than traditional testing, which measures skills, knowledge, or attitudes, the KCI-B focuses on the methods a jobholder perceives are necessary for success. It is a pencil-and-paper questionnaire similar to the KCI. The results are given on the same four-mode grid, making it simple to detect similarities and differences between realities (the KCI) and self-expectations (the KCI-B). This information highlights obstacles that keep workers from functioning through their instinctive strengths.

The KCI-B focuses on functional issues, forcing the person taking it to consider trade-offs in the problem-solving process. Selecting the most and least necessary ways to strive in a role is key to knowing whether it's the right one for you. The following sample KCI-B questions are answered by marking one choice that describes how you have to function in a job *most* often and one choice for the method used *least* in the job.

Select *One* Most and *One* Least:

	Most	Least
1. On this job, presentations require		
documentation	_____	_____
charts and graphs	_____	_____
spontaneity	_____	_____
models	_____	_____
2. On this job, it is essential to		
handcraft	_____	_____
promote	_____	_____
systematize	_____	_____
gather evidence	_____	_____

DIAGNOSING STRESS

DIFFERENCES BETWEEN THE INDIVIDUAL KCI (THE KCI-A) AND KCI-B RESULTS EXplain why you shine in some roles and are pulled in the wrong conative direction by others. For example, the two results show why an otherwise successful journalist was suffering high levels of stress at an early time in his career. His KCI-A result indicated a resistance in Quick Start, which meant he suffered stress during crises.

The KCI-B he filled out showed his job demanded high levels of risk and a strong sense of urgency. When the differences on the two instruments is four or more units in any one Action Mode, the person is suffering a form of stress called *strain*. This problem results from self-imposed expectations. The journalist innately functioned at a level 2 in Quick Start. However, his KCI-B result showed that he believed his job required him to perform as an 8 in that mode: The variance of six units created strain, which made the job unsuitable for him. Sometimes you can redesign a job to fit your needs. In this case, daily deadlines were a fact of the newspaper business, but because the journalist's *interests* involved writing, he sought other outlets that better matched his *instincts*. He began writing for technical journals, which allowed him ample lead time and placed no emphasis on uniqueness of presentation. He'd finally found a good fit.

Kolbe Talent Analysis
KOLBE CONATIVE INDEX® Result

Journalist

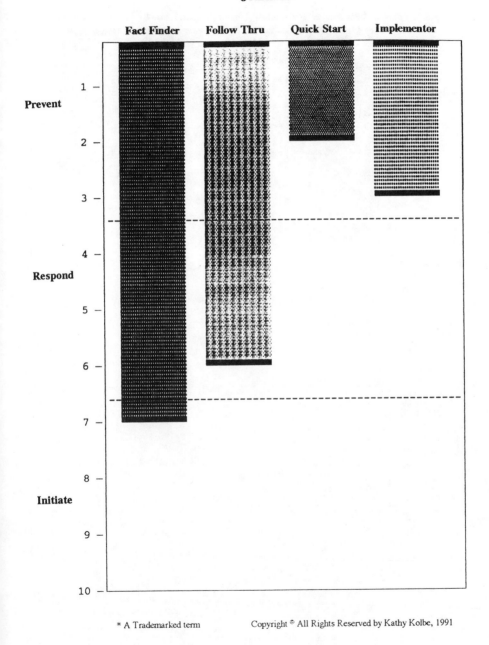

KOLBE CONATIVE INDEX®   "B" : JOB - KCI
Journalist

Strain is the most difficult form of conative stress to allay. It stems from a betrayal of your own instincts and means that you are ignoring internal urges in favor of external rewards. It indicates an attempt to bypass your Striving Instincts and act only according to detrimental motivations. Therefore it interferes with your Creative Process. A person suffering from strain limits her potential for success by not valuing, understanding, or using innate capabilities.

Ignoring any aspect of the Creative Process can lead to particular types of stress. *Cognitive stress*—not understanding the reason something needs to be accomplished, or not having the necessary skills—can be relieved by training and education. *Affective stress*, such as a fear of failure (or success), and social attitudes that interfere with objectives, are motivation-based problems that often can be relieved through counseling. However, you cannot alter your instinctive imperatives; they must be fulfilled if you are to succeed. *You* don't have to change or "improve." The situation causing conative strain has to change.

If Judeth Javorek created high Follow Thru expectations for herself in her hospital CEO role, she would have false expectations for herself because as a resistant Follow Thru she would not meet them, and they would not be true to who she is and how she can best accomplish her job. Burnout, absenteeism, and increased health costs are often attributable to this form of stress. Employees may well put in extraordinary hours at a job without achieving acceptable results. It becomes a downward spiral that can lead to a loss of Will.

STRAIN: A FORM OF SELF-DENIAL

DENYING YOUR TIME-DEFINED NEEDS IS THE SUREST WAY TO CAUSE STRAIN. FOR instance, a resistant Quick Start will be frustrated by the pressure of working against tight deadlines. Other sources of strain include:

- Trying to live up to false self-expectations by

    believing you can change who you are if you try hard
      enough
    confusing hard work with achievement
    undervaluing your ability to take action
    not recognizing a resistance as a strength

attempting to rein in your instinctive impulses until you can rationally think things through

thinking you aren't contributing unless you initiate action

- Trying to live up to other people's expectations by

   trying to do things the way you are told to do them
   trying to be just like someone you admire
   believing others know what is best for you
   promising you will do things differently
   taking criticism of your methods to heart
   knowing it annoys someone when you are just being yourself

- Trying to function within the system by

   trying to conform
   believing you can contribute best by altering your approach
   doubting what you have to offer is needed
   doing what's necessary to satisfy team needs
   containing your inclinations in order to get to the top
   knowing there are already enough people who do what you do best

REDUCING ABSENTEEISM

EMPLOYERS FIND THAT USE OF THE KCI TO MATCH A PERSON'S TALENTS WITH TASKS significantly reduces their rates of absenteeism. When people suffer less stress, they are able to perform at a consistently higher level without as much illness or fatigue.

A recent study focused on sixty employees from a national marketing firm, half of whom had the highest rate of absenteeism in the company and half of whom had the lowest. They were given the KCI-A and KCI-B. The results highlight the causes of job-related stress at this company. In addition to false self-expectations, a boss's misplaced requirements can lead to frustrations. Each employee's supervisor completed a KCI-C, which indicates the conative requirements for success in the job. Stress is indicated when significant differences occur in any mode between the A and B versions, or between the A and C versions.

In this study, 50 percent of the high-absenteeism group were experiencing one of the forms of conative stress, while only 20 percent of the low-absenteeism employees were experiencing similar stress. The Kolbe process had accurately predicted which employees showed a high rate of absenteeism due to being mismatched to their jobs.

Kolbe System as a Predictor of High Absenteeism

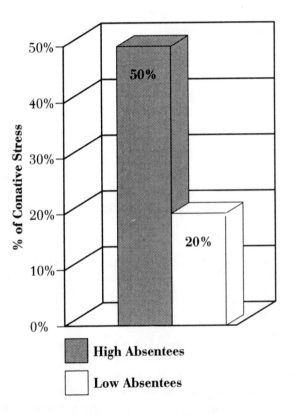

PREDICTING TURNOVER

THE KCI HAS BEEN USED TO SUCCESSFULLY PREDICT BRANCH MANAGER TURNOVER AT a national financial-services company. An initial study identified a conative range that predicted high productivity in the position. The study divided 483 branch-manager trainees into three groups: (1) trainees not given the KCI; (2) trainees given the KCI, whose scores fell outside the recommended range but whose managers were trained by Kolbe-accredited consultants to mitigate the mismatch; and (3) trainees whose scores fell within the recommended range.

At the end of one year, *none* of the conatively matched trainees had left the company for job-related reasons. This was a 100-percent reduction from previous turnover among those predicted to have low stress on the job. Of those whose supervisors were aware of the conative stress and worked to reduce it, there was a 47-percent reduction in turnover. Among those with conative stress for whom nothing was done to reduce frustrations, there was no reduction in turnover. Using the KCI to help select and manage branch managers significantly reduced job-related turnover and the associated recruiting and training costs.

According to Wayne Goodman, personnel administrator of a similar national financial organization, "In the consumer-finance industry, the turnover rate's about fifty percent during the first year for manager trainees. And that's what we set out to use the Kolbe Concept to help us reduce. So all of the information we've received in almost two years of using the Kolbe Concept have really given us some positive results."

RELIEVING STRAIN

FALSE EXPECTATIONS CAUSE STRAIN, SO THE SIMPLE SOLUTION IS TO CHANGE YOUR expectations. This doesn't necessarily require changing job or career. If your success is being limited by self-induced pressure, your first option is to try to redefine what it means to succeed. You can often do that within the context of your present role.

> *If strain at work results from the way you perceive you need to accomplish your job, you can reduce strain by:*
> • Redirecting talent. If you are insistent in Fact Finder, you can use your talent in that mode to target more specific objectives. Follow Thru insistence can help you plan more structure. Quick Start initiation will lead you to add alternatives, and Implementor talent can direct you toward more tangible methods.
>   Be careful you don't try to change the task rather than the method of accomplishing it. The conative bait-and-switch

Use of KCI
Reduction of Turnover

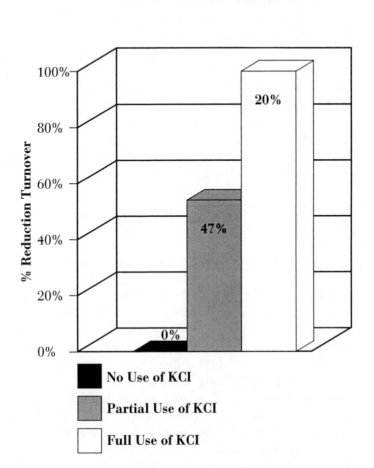

technique where someone agrees to do something in a way that is not instinctively possible, then actually does it in another way, almost always fails. For instance, it doesn't work if an insistent Implementor agrees to manage a construction crew, then spends his time working on the building instead of assigning priorities. In this scenario, the Implementor had accepted a manager's role that was stressful for him, so he attempted to change *what* the job was—by employing his natural talents—as well as *how* it could be accomplished. He could have used his Implementor talent as a manager to demonstrate how machinery works or to evaluate the quality of workmanship needed for the building. But by redefining the job itself, he limited his ability to perform well as a manager. Such tactics usually backfire. Few employers are happy when workers try to redesign jobs. Going beyond a change in methods is unnecessary and inappropriate in most situations. Instead:

• Seek work-related projects that will allow you to use instinctive talents underutilized in your present assignment. Your regular assignments may not show off what you can accomplish, so volunteer for additional assignments that will energize you and highlight your strengths for others to see. Volunteering for the right role is one of the surest ways to be considered for the type of job that suits you best. But be sure the new project isn't just another situation that traps you into further misuse of your talent.

If strain in your job results from how you are responding to others:

• You may be acting on an insistence, when what's needed is your talent for accommodation. Often the most important contribution to an endeavor is a supportive response. For instance, a basketball player who is an accommodating Quick Start may feel strain if he's always trying to initiate a play, which requires taking Quick Start risks. He'd have more success being ready to grab the pass and make something happen. And an accommodating–Follow Thru office worker can effectively monitor the use of policies and procedures to ensure consistent quality. The mildly endowed Implementor may not build the model, but she could be the one to deliver it without damage.

• Avoid unnecessary responses. Three of Intel COO Craig Barrett's Action Modes—Follow Thru, Quick Start, and Implementor—are at the accommodation level. As one of three executives sharing the office of president, he can offer support to the others through those modes by promoting systems development, innovation by other team members, and the need for quality in production of Intel's high-tech materials—but not in data gathering, which Craig needs to initiate. In addition to his Fact Finder strategies, his forte is responding to rapid marketplace shifts, fine-tuning Follow Thru–driven projections, and accommodating Implementor concerns for plant construction and equipment needs.

If strain at work results from your resisting actions needed to accomplish your job, you can prevent problems by:
- Not promising to function through a mode in which you are naturally resistant. It's bad enough when you try to function out of kilter yourself, but when others rely on you to perform contrary to your instincts, their disappointment will add to the problem. A resistant Follow Thru is wise not to guarantee completion of forms according to a prearranged schedule. A risk-averse resistant Quick Start had better not promise to make a quick guesstimate—it could be embarrassing.
- Bartering with someone who has the talent needed for the action. Trade your strengths for others' input. While a resistance is helpful in preventing overindulgence in certain activities, the result of a KCI-B helps diagnose when such avoidance isn't constructive. Since your instincts can't dredge up the energy to provide the needed action, you are better off bartering than wallowing in the problem. Chances are others around you have modes in which they need the assistance you can more easily provide. The arrangement will likely be a two-way street.

EXTERNAL PRESSURE:
THE FORCE BEHIND TENSION

TENSION IS CONATIVE STRESS THAT OCCURS WHEN OBSTACLES, POSED BY PEOPLE OR circumstances, force you to function against your Striving Instincts. There are two victims of tension: the jobholder who does not perform as others require, and the supervisor or other person whose demands will not be met. From the perspective of one business owner, the problem is a constant frustration. "I hire people to do the job the way I think it needs to be done," he said. "Then I pay them while they rebel against the requirements. I can't afford that. I have to figure out how to get people who just naturally do what needs to be done the way it needs to be done."

When conducting seminars, I frequently suggest participants spend a period of time solving a problem through a method contrary to their instincts. For instance, I'll ask the resistant Fact Finders to write a detailed set of priorities or ask Implementors to prepare a speech using no props or body language. The room immediately fills with tension that they later describe as making them feel:

paralyzed	irritated
frustrated	tuned out
set up	defeated, as if spinning their wheels
sweaty palmed	

When I suggest they then reach the same goal through their natural strengths, the atmosphere is immediately charged with renewed energy. They later describe having felt:

confident	trusted
appreciated	valued
engaged	validated
reenergized	reconfirmed
unencumbered	

I designed the KCI-C to diagnose the functional characteristics required in specific roles. As these sample items indicate, it is taken in the same manner as the other two KCIs. It can be completed by a supervisor, peer, or subordinate.

Select *One* Most and *One* Least:

	Most	**Least**
1. This job provides the freedom to be		
innovative	_____	_____
exacting	_____	_____
comprehensive	_____	_____
tangible	_____	_____
2. This job requires a person who is		
strategic	_____	_____
tactile	_____	_____
spontaneous	_____	_____
disciplined	_____	_____

THE ABCS OF CONATION

FOR EASE OF DISCUSSION I USE AN ABC APPROACH IN DISCUSSING THE THREE KOLBE diagnostic tools:

KCI-A = Individual's instinctive talent

KCI-B = Jobholder's self-expectations

KCI-C = Job requirements or functional necessities

Comparing A and B gives you a sense of how much strain you may be under because of the pressure you put on yourself. Comparing A and C indicates whether another person or the organization is limiting your opportunity to achieve, therefore causing tension between you and that person. Comparing B and C can explain differing perceptions of the role.

If a manager's requirements (as indicated on the C results) are causing tension, she needs to know:

- how a team member performs when at his best (as indicated on an A result).
- how much difference exists between that person's talent and the manager's requirements (a *Tension Report* based on A and C results).
- whether the team member has found a way of using his instinctive strengths to do the job (comparison of the A and B).
- what opportunities are available for the team member to make a greater contribution (Cs for other job possibilities that may be better suited to the person's talents).
- who in the organization can contribute the missing elements (other team members' A results).

Armed with this information, employee and manager can work out solutions that not only improve everyone's performance but also avoid placing blame. Although conative tension is counterproductive, it is prevalent in training programs that try to instill methods of operation, management practices that require employees to adhere to problem-solving techniques, and counseling that tries to bring people in line with how others desire them to act.

Circumstances can also produce tension. Your instinctive needs may be blocked by social, economic, and physical conditions over which you have no control. You may have to hold off taking the plunge into Quick Start ventures because of economically hard times. Your outdoor Implementor adventures may be thwarted by months of bad weather. Though you may have the instinctive talent to be a jet pilot, you may lack the eyesight or educational prerequisites. Societal prejudices based on gender, age, race, and physical handicaps act as barriers for many opportunities. Few people enjoy total freedom to express their instinctive selves. Even high performers lament that they are frequently unable to "really go for it." As one said: "If I were ever able to act on pure instinct for a year without interference, I could single-handedly increase the gross national product at least two points."

People react to tension within the context of their conative talents. For instance, Quick Start–insistent people try to go around obstacles, while those who lead with Fact Finder will argue against restrictions with facts and figures. But there also is emotional fallout from tension that differs from the self-inflicted guilt and fatigue caused by strain. It often causes a more outward hostility toward coworkers, bosses, or "the company." Nobody wants to be treated as if her form of contribution is unacceptable. Rather than judging a person as simply uncooperative, consider *actions* that will turn around the situation.

SYMPTOMS OF TENSION

You can identify when you are suffering from tension caused by external pressure to conform by identifying the following distress signals.

- *Acting superficially*. If you are acting in ways that other people want you to act instead of making your best effort, your efforts will be shallow and often accompanied by sarcasm, petulance, or other indications of frustration.
- *Getting by on personality*. If you are attempting to mask lack of productivity with a "nice-guy" attitude, exuding concern or being glib, you may be all show and no go.
- *Giving rationalizations*. You give lots of *reasons*, excuses

and irrelevant justifications that serve only to mask the real issue. Shakespeare had a good phrase for it: "Methinks he doth protest too much."

- *Denying responsibility.* The "not my job" mentality dodges tension by attempting to get out of contributing in *any* way. This is basic "hiding out" behavior.
- *Defying demands.* You respond to job expectations with a confrontational, unnecessarily belligerent take-it-or-leave-it attitude. This is typified by the phrase "If what I have to give isn't okay, I'll show them, by God."
- *Withholding effort.* If you would ordinarily just fix something, but now you refuse to lift a finger, you may be a self-starter. If you are waiting to be forced into action, you are probably experiencing tension.

People caught in these defensive behaviors expend fruitless energy avoiding rather than addressing the problems causing their tension. Such responses further erode the possibility of productive contributions. Tension will not go away by ignoring or avoiding its source; it must be addressed in order to be resolved.

REDUCING TENSION

"IF ONLY I'D KNOWN MY KCI RESULT TWENTY YEARS AGO . . ." I HEAR SOME variation of that statement all too often. Whenever the victims of tension discover the source of their stress, they naturally wish themselves out of the frustrating situation. Whether it's your job, a personal relationship, or a computer you hate to operate, it's never too late to make it work for you. You can reduce tension by redefining success into instinctive terms. For instance, try:

- *negotiating to redefine requirements* to suit your MO. ("This task really doesn't have to be done so meticulously. Will you accept that I've done what needs to be done if I get a general agreement on the conditions by tomorrow night?")
- *removing the need* to satisfy unnecessary standards. ("If you're satisfied with the way I keep house, why does it matter what your mother thinks?")

- *seeking a substitute* who is better equipped conatively for the role. ("Why don't we just call a copier-machine service rep?")
- *declaring a truce.* ("I'll do the best I can if you'll never ask me to do it again.")
- *putting an end in sight.* By seeing light at the end of the tunnel, you can survive almost anything for a short term. ("I'll stick with the security of my job until the economy turns around—or for six more months, whichever comes first.")
- *changing the requirement.* ("Could I provide a written report rather than doing the speech?")

REMODELING THE PROCRUSTES BED

A MYTHOLOGICAL TALE CALLED "THE PROCRUSTES BED" EXEMPLIFIES WHAT TOO many people try to do to one another. A robber named Procrustes welcomed passersby into his home, offering them food and shelter for the night. Many gratefully accepted his hospitality. But if they didn't exactly fit the dimensions of the bed, he would trim their limbs or stretch them out until they conformed to it.

In today's world, we may welcome people into our places of business, our families, and our teams with the best of intentions, then try to stretch them outside their natural form or cut them down to size. This happened to an operations manager who anguished over having asked an Implementor-intense production foreman to prepare an oral presentation for a corporate evaluation team. The foreman literally worried himself sick over how he would speak to this august group. Resistant in Quick Start, he tried desperately to get out of the assignment. Finally the operations manager reshuffled the program so that only those who volunteered had to speak, but he made this announcement too late: The foreman died of a heart attack. "I'll never know," the manager said, "how much that contributed to his untimely death. But I can't help wondering. And I'll never knowingly put another person [under] such preventable stress."

DIAGNOSING PROBLEMS

JOHN BLUMBERG IS A MAJOR PLAYER IN RECRUITING AND TRAINING FOR AN AC-counting firm's worldwide headquarters. When he and I first discussed the A, B, and C KCIs for himself and his role, he was also administrative manager for one statewide office. He was then under considerable stress. Both he and Jack Henry, the state's managing partner, indicated on the KCIs that his job involved primarily Fact Finder–insistent activity. John is a dedicated professional who had tried to do what was necessary. That commitment had caused him to go into conative crisis, the transition period during which he tried to change his natural way of functioning. His KCI result was 5-6-5-4.

Within a few minutes of discussing his result with John, it was clear that his attempts to satisfy both his self-expectations for initiating Fact Finder documentation and Jack's requirements for him to do the same were causing John the predicted high levels of stress. Coupled with his Fact Finder responsibilities to the Chicago operation, he was on the verge of being overwhelmed. "I can honestly tell you that I know I *can* do the job," he said, "but I'm frustrated most of the time because I just don't feel I'm doing it the way it needs to be done."

Adding to the problem was Jack's resistance to Follow Thru and strong inclination to initiate Quick Start, deadline-oriented action. John was trying to respond to Jack's need to have everything done yesterday and also to assure the managing partner that it would be done without any glitches. The first thing we had to do was involve Jack in redefining John's role in the state operation. An in-depth interpretation of John's result led me to believe he was naturally an insistent Quick Start, which proved to be true when he later retook the KCI and the result was 3-5-7-5.

Only when a Facilitator-Mediator retakes the KCI is the result expected to change significantly. Transitions often cause people to restrain their impulses. This false accommodation contributes an added dimension of stress when they have a negative emotional response to change. Staying with instinctive approaches that are your natural strength is the best way to reduce anxieties associated with a new situation.

John was fortunate that his boss worked with him to redesign his role and to lean more heavily on the staff around him in order to relieve his stress. Both men realized that work with the firm's world headquarters, involving a diversity of special projects, was more in line with John's Striving Instincts. So they allocated 50 percent of his time for those

Kolbe Talent Analysis
KOLBE CONATIVE INDEX® Result

Jayne

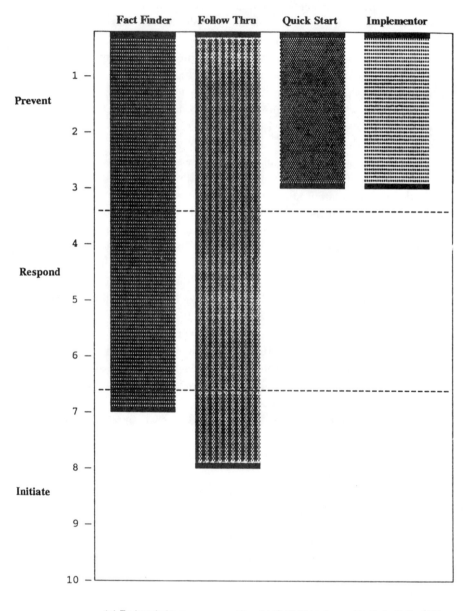

KOLBE CONATIVE INDEX® "B" : JOB - KCI
Jayne, Product Mgr

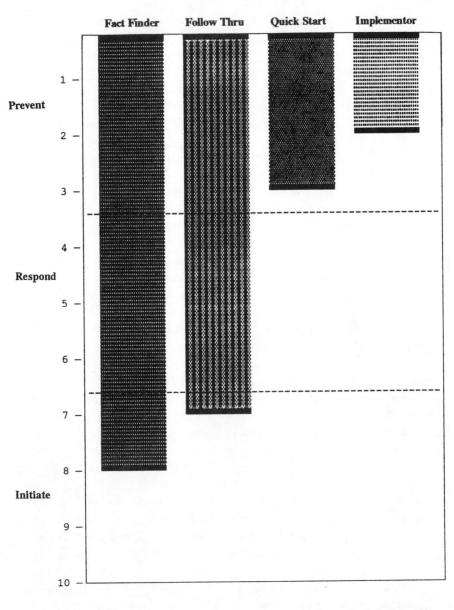

commitments. When both the person undergoing stress and his boss understand the implications of conative stress—and are willing to do what is necessary to relieve it—the benefits of the Kolbe process can move from diagnosing problems toward prescribing solutions. John and Jack took the advice to heart, and John soon became more productive and considerably more energized. "It was an amazing relief," he said. "Knowing my true MO explained so much. It has made a huge difference in my life. At the point I knew something had to change, I didn't care what the change was. You couldn't take something of value away from me, because nothing I was doing was good for me. Now I have unique challenges, and I'm thriving."

In another situation, Jayne, a product manager for a midwestern electrical-appliance manufacturer, told me, "I never do anything half-baked if I can help it." Earlier her boss had complained to me that this employee was not performing satisfactorily. "She's just not a team play-er," he had said. "She has to hold on to everything herself and won't let others help. And she's not getting through it fast enough."

Her boss had already completed a KCI-C, specifying his requirements for her job. The result of this KCI-C was 8-6-4-2. Her individual KCI was 7-8-3-3, which indicated that her instincts did in fact match the job as her boss viewed it.

This was clear from the fact that the instinctive difference between the requirements for the job and the person filling it was no greater than four units in any of the Action Modes. Therefore, conative tension was not the reason Jayne was letting down her boss.

Jayne also was intellectually well equipped to handle the job and had a good attitude. In addition, her KCI-B result, 8-7-3-2, indicated a match between self-expectation and inclinations. After we had elimi-nated both conative strain and tension as causes of her problem, we had to determine whether or not she was allocating her innate talents effec-tively.

Both the company's CEO and Jayne specified what Level of Effort she needed to expend on various activities. Under the heading *Commitments*, there was a list of sixteen obligations; under *Attempts*, only one notation; and under *Intentions*, only two. The obligations included responsibility for managing all the details for a complex business unit's start-up, including obtaining business licenses and legal registration in several states, plus building and training a staff. "It's as if I'm suffering from mental gridlock," she said as she looked at all she had to do. "I guess this is why I just can't seem to move things along in a satisfactory way.

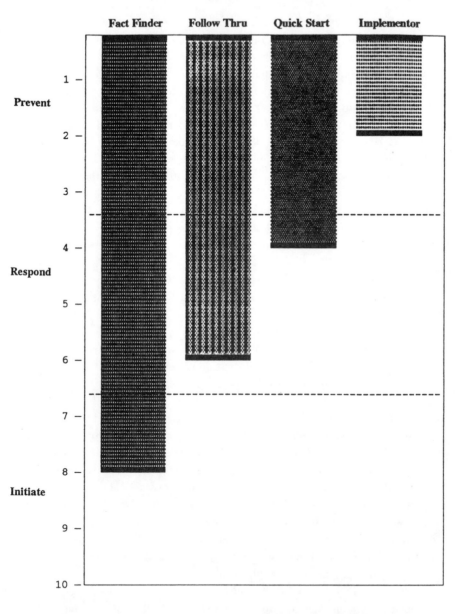

KOLBE CONATIVE INDEX®   "C" : JOB - KCI

Product Mgr   by   Supervisor

Yet, realistically, these items have to be commitments at this point. They're intertwined. If I don't do one, I can't complete the others."

The CEO, whose KCI result is 4-2-9-5, said Jayne needed to make only three commitments. His insistence in Quick Start, along with his mild accommodation to Fact Finder, made these tasks bottom-line generalities that he didn't perceive as separate obligations. Whereas fact-driven Jayne had listed, by state, the eight specific licenses necessary, the CEO had merely given the assignment "to get government approvals." Because the CEO was not specific about what the licensing process entailed, in his mind it didn't require a major commitment of time and energy. His direction to "just do it" didn't take into account the problem Jayne faced in acquiring each state license or the fact that she didn't have a trained staff to whom she could delegate these tasks that the CEO saw as simplistic. The issues were conative. The problem was one of time and energy. Once this surfaced, I urged Jayne's CEO not to fire her. She didn't really have a bad attitude. She was the right person for the job, but she needed management's assistance in freeing up some of her time and energy.

To solve this situation, pressure was taken off Jayne by removing all attempts and intentions from her "to-do" list for the next ninety days. If there was no chance that she could accomplish these tasks, why have them anywhere on her goals list? Taking them off gave her space to turn some of her many commitments into things she would either attempt to do or intend to do. "I've known these things were way down the list," she sighed. "It's a relief to get them off it completely for a while."

Because Jayne was extremely resistant in Quick Start, the next step was for her to rely on her powers of risk prevention. She reframed goals with benchmarks instead of waiting for final completion before checking off progress. This allowed her to measure her movement without having everything dependent on a single, final outcome. For example, she particularly wanted to be sure that new software was installed and completely operational before the salespeople were on board. Since software is always being revised, this goal was unlikely to be achieved. Instead of waiting for perfect software, she set up her list so that the development and testing of each functional part could be ticked off, allowing her to measure her progress toward the goal.

Jayne could use her insistent–Fact Finder instincts to set priorities among her commitments. She couldn't set any of them aside completely, but some could move down to the attempt level. This step was easier when both she and the CEO worked through another conative goal-setting process, assessing her project's main targets. They put her various customers in an order of priority, using an archery target of concentric circles.

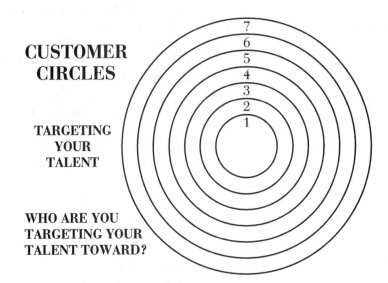

CUSTOMER CIRCLES

TARGETING YOUR TALENT

WHO ARE YOU TARGETING YOUR TALENT TOWARD?

7
6
5
4
3
2
1

It immediately became clear that she was directing too much energy toward secondary customers such as her salespeople rather than primary audiences, including the corporate board of directors. Once an instinctive approach was taken, the situation turned around. For instance, the Quick Start CEO became more involved in promotional efforts, freeing the Fact Finder manager to produce classic marketing analyses for senior management. This cooperative approach increased the unit's performance. Not only is Jayne still gainfully employed with the company, her business group is very profitable—and she's had two raises in the year following this redefinition of goals and commitments.

EFFECTIVENESS CHAIN

THE PROCESS THAT LED TO THIS POSITIVE RESULT BEGAN WITH IDENTIFYING JAYNE'S talents, assessing the degree to which she freely acted on those talents, and how well they fit with the bosses' requirements. Having the three KCI results helped build her confidence and remove many of her bosses' concerns. Trust was reestablished on both counts. Only after dealing with those three pieces of information was it possible to move on to the steps needed to increase her effectiveness. Then she had to decide how much time and energy to give each goal.

Unlike Jayne, people who are very insistent in Quick Start are notorious for overcommitting because of their tendency to jump spontaneously into new projects at a high Level of Effort without downgrading other priorities. This is especially true if they are also resistant in Fact Finder. People who are insistent in Follow Thru need to fit new commitments into their plans, which means they are more likely to integrate new tasks into their ongoing system first and commit later. Fact Finders get particularly frustrated when others try to force them to make an immediate commitment; their instincts tell them to take time to check out the ramifications. Those with Implementor talent are likely to commit only after they've seen tangible evidence that the task needs to be undertaken.

Then there are dual insistences. Consider, for instance, a person whose KCI result is 7-3-7-3; an insistent Fact Finder–Quick Start with resistance in Follow Thru and Implementor. This person sets goals both deliberately and urgently. Such an individual needs to fully but rapidly research the choices he makes. This calls for even greater self-control so that both talents can be put to their best uses. Carefully calculating odds before making commitments involving risk would come naturally to the MO, as would self-editing rapidly changing commitments.

To walk people through the process I used in Jayne's situation, I have developed a seven-step *Effectiveness Chain.* It begins with identifying instinctive realities, self-expectations, and requirements. If instinctive resources are not taken into account in setting goals, the results are immediate and dire: people are placed in stress-filled, unproductive positions.

If you begin the process by quantifying what is doable, you immediately increase the odds of reaching the desired results. You may be forced to recognize some highly desired goals that have to be moved down the list or taken off altogether. But those goals were unlikely to be reached anyway, certainly not without bringing different people into the organization. When you start out by identifying the conative talent available, you will structure your personnel policies to ensure consistent conative strength. For example, you wouldn't make the mistake of offering severance packages based solely on tenure. You may need people with particular instincts to stay on board more than others. The tactic of laying off people may help you save money, when the greater commitment should be *to make a profit.* All too often shortsighted, single-quarter corporate goals drive decision making, at the cost of long-term goal setting that focuses on retention and developing talent.

The following Effectiveness Chain illustrates the steps needed to get to the heart of organizational problems and opportunities.

EFFECTIVENESS CHAIN

EFFORT	*INSTRUMENT*
1. What you have to give.	KCI
2. What you believe is needed.	Job KCI (B)
3. What your boss requires.	Job KCI (C)
4. How much you will give.	Levels of Effort
5. How much does your boss require?	Levels of Effort
6. Which customers do you have to satisfy?	Customer Circles
7. When do you have to satisfy customers?	Time Frames

Redefining success within an organization in terms of allowing workers the freedom to be themselves implies significant change in management practices for most companies. The objectives don't change; people don't change. The big change is that people are given a chance to perform to their potential and become more productive.

CHAPTER SEVEN

CAREER DECISIONS

IT'S NOT *WHAT* YOU DO, BUT *HOW* YOU DO IT

I n 1989, when *The Conative Connection* was published, it included a story about a property manager who had been promoted from a job that required daily supervision of a shopping mall. He had moved into an executive position overseeing all the other property managers at his company and was miserable in the new job, despite it being a promotion. When he saw his KCI result of 3-2-9-3, and his own analysis of his new role, 7-7-1-7, he understood why he dreaded going into the office every day. While it wasn't easy for him to turn away from all the perks of senior management, John James followed his instincts back to his original job, which had allowed him to use the full range of his natural abilities. He has now stepped forward to share the long-term benefits of a move that allowed him to thrive.

"I often think of that day when you told me I was in the wrong job. I felt the weight of the world lifted off my back," says John James, also a former New York Yankee pitcher. "This is much more fulfilling than anything I've ever done. I decided when I got out of the corporate job that I had the opportunity to fall flat on my face, and I was thankful for the opportunity! Now I can do my own thing, and surround myself with people who provide other talents. I can hardly wait to get to work each day." John has helped turn the previously slowpaced Scottsdale Fashion Square into one of the busiest malls in America. It's gone from nothing special to a premier mall. "The comments I get from friends and associates is, 'I thought you were crazy when you changed jobs, but you sure made the right decision.' "

A day rarely passes that I do not receive a letter from someone whose KCI result "freed," "liberated," "encouraged," or "empowered" him to make a career change. I treasure each and every letter because helping people find a sense of accomplishment is the heart of my work, and such letters validate it. Dr. Shirley Bourne (KCI result, 7-6-2-5) of Southern Illinois University wrote: "I did the KCI and was empowered to be me. And out of that came a whole new career. I'm now an assistant professor and director of a military program." A European management consultant who uses the Kolbe Concept in her practice, said, "My clients use words like 'liberating' to describe their reactions to the KCI because it enables them to value their own talents and spend time doing the things they are most productive doing."

If you've ever had difficulty deciding whether to take a particular job or career path, it's probably because various elements within your creative self were leading you in different directions. The risk-taking, adventurous part of me has always yearned to scuba dive, but my practical side holds me back because, as a dyslexic, I'd probably turn dials on my gear in the wrong direction at times. Deep-sea diving might suit my need for excitement, but it would certainly not suit my need for safety. Just as dangerous are situations in which desires are out of kilter with instincts.

Job decisions need to take into account every element in the creative process, including:

Motivation: Interests, values, social style, attitudes.
Instincts: Mental energy, urges, necessities, innate abilities.
Will: Determination, Level of Effort.
Reason: Education, training, job experience, special skills, intelligence.
Conation: Talent for initiating, responding, and acting preventively.

Most career counseling takes only motivation and reason into account. Striving Instincts are typically overlooked, as are the Levels of Effort and the conative match between natural talent and opportunities. Because of this, millions of unfulfilled people have not found outlets for their talents. At an early age, most of us discovered that the kinds of opportunities made available to us were based on how smart we were. The smart kids in class got the prestigious job of helping the teacher grade papers, while the not-so-smart kids only got to clean the chalkboard. Being smarter than others has always had an impact on financial and job opportunities. But the heavy emphasis that has traditionally been placed on intelligence causes instinct and Will to be overlooked. Conative talent is derived from instinct, and so it too is ignored.

Since educators and career counselors have not been aware of the instinctive dimension, they haven't been able to reinforce a person's greatest strength: her natural abilities. It is impossible to receive effective career guidance when neither you nor the advisor understands what compels you to do what you do. Through skills testing, professional counseling services can tell you what you were smart enough to learn, and through personality testing they can tell you what jobs you would like. However, without a test to measure instinct, they have not been able to tell you what you will do best. One career advisor even stated to me, "Regardless of what we say, finding the right career fit is mostly a matter of luck." No, it's not. With an understanding of instinct you can create a fit as perfect as a custom-tailored suit.

When you find a career that matches your instinctive talents, it not only offers you the freedom to be yourself, but pays you for the pleasure. The right job may not pay you the most you could possibly earn, but this is not a chapter on how to make more money. Materialistic desires often throw people off their instinctive courses. A paycheck will provide little compensation for the frustration you'll feel. I often see people in the twilight of their careers who are just discovering what kind of work would have truly fulfilled them. "If only I had known" is a haunting phrase that inspires me to reach out to young people and to others who have a chance to start over, and help them fulfill their potential.

LEVERAGING TALENTS

SEAN'S A DELIGHTFUL YOUNG MAN WHO'S EAGER TO PLEASE. EVERYONE EXPECTED him to excel in whatever career he chose. After receiving his master's degree in economics, he was able to get a job with a management consulting firm. His entry-level position was tailor-made for someone who needed only a general overview of the company's operation in order to write up evaluations of potential consulting projects.

Sean's insistence in Fact Finder was immediately frustrated when he discovered that he wasn't going to get as much background information as his instincts needed to assist one of the partners in making appointments and conducting status reviews of cases. "Even though the decisions I make are at a rather low level," he said, "I still ought not to be making them without more thorough background. What I am doing is too superficial. I am not given sufficient time to consider all the consequences of actions before I have to act as if I know what I am doing."

Management consulting may have been a good choice for Sean had he entered it at a partner level, but working his way up through ill-suited roles was unsatisfying. Had someone who understood his stress been his mentor—especially another insistent Fact Finder, who could have explained how to deal with it productively—Sean could have survived and gone on to excel within the company. But instead he became one of the bright young people who passed through the place without anyone quite understanding why such a high-potential hire had not succeeded there. Later in this chapter I will discuss ways in which some unsuited roles can be tolerated for a short time. We've all had to suffer through transition periods that ultimately led to greater opportunities for using our conative talents.

Instincts are important to consider, whether you're choosing a career or reentering the job market. After Lois spent several years raising a family, she decided not to go back to teaching, although the classroom had given her some very fulfilling years. Education had undergone too many changes, she believed, for her to pick up where she'd left off. Before she knew anything about her instinctive makeup, a career counselor had reviewed the results of her vocational preference test, interviewed her extensively, and suggested she look for a job in a small service-oriented company where she could help with personnel training and office management.

Lois followed the advice and found a job with a new and rapidly growing local bank. While the *type* of work was well suited to her talents—which included an insistence in Follow Thru—the *atmosphere* was not. She found herself in a company that was very resistant to Follow Thru. Lois was asked to deal with sporadic assignments, work irregular hours with frequent interruptions, and operate without sufficient policies or procedures. It was an insistent Follow Thru's nightmare.

Once Lois realized the problem wasn't the type of work she had chosen but rather the situation, she had to decide whether to try improving the situation or to simply move on. Her boss was too busy dealing with how fast the bank was growing to position people appropriately within the organization. Since Lois couldn't get his attention on the issues that mattered most to her, she decided to leave.

Sean and Lois learned that certain types of jobs and work situations were counterproductive for them. And this is true for all of us. People insistent in Quick Start will not be productive in a workplace where they can do only what they are told to do, are forced to follow standard operating practices, and have few opportunities to brainstorm ideas with coworkers. Those insistent in Implementor will be frustrated in roles that require them to work behind a desk in a windowless room, communicate primarily by telephone, and stay in one place all day.

Resistances will cause just as many problems in the workplace when their needs are not met. The resistant Fact Finder rebels when asked to provide detailed explanations, to wear "appropriate" clothing, and to write extensive and documented reports. Resistant Quick Starts need to find career paths that value, even celebrate, their talent for preventing chaos. But instead these folk are often sent through "creativity training" or motivational seminars that try to "bring out" their spontaneity, turn them into public speakers, or teach them how to come up with more alternatives. Such programs not only demean their talents, they encourage acting out of character. If you have to act artificially to win approval, you can carry it off for a while. But to continue this charade would be digging a conative hole for yourself that goes even deeper.

Many senior executives come up through corporate environments that reward their typical strengths in Fact Finder and Quick Start but put them through unrelenting stress if they also have a resistance in Follow Thru. They get caged in midcareer situations that force them to operate within set boundaries, plan activities in advance, keep complete and consistent records, and establish routines. Yet when they reach levels at which they can discard these duties, they too delegate the very same tasks that had distressed them. While this works well for resistant– Follow Thru execs, it will begin to benefit all those involved only when climbing the career ladder does not require following a singular path.

ANALYZING OPPORTUNITIES

ANALYZING CAREER AND JOB OPPORTUNITIES ACCORDING TO CONATIVE ISSUES doesn't exclude any areas of interest. For example, sports may be of

Kolbe Management Report
SYNERGY REPORT

For

DISTRIBUTION OF TALENT
Presidents or CEOs Hired
To Manage Corporations

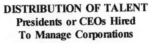

	Fact Finder	Follow Thru	Quick Start	Implementor
1	4%	38%	15%	62%
2				
3				
4	25%	41%	49%	38%
5				
6				
7	71%	21%	36%	0%
8				
9				
10				

particular interest to a nonathletic person. What jobs would be appropriate for each insistence within that broad area of interest?

Fact Finder: statistician, marketer, team manager, diagnostician
Follow Thru: exercise coach, logo designer, scheduler, dietician
Quick Start: promoter, agent, publicist, radio-TV announcer
Implementor: property manager, trainer, clubhouse manager, groundskeeper

Don't make assumptions based on job titles or past experiences in particular positions. Titles can be misleading. For example, if a job as

Kolbe Management Report
SYNERGY REPORT

For

DISTRIBUTION OF TALENT
Entrepreneurs

	Fact Finder	Follow Thru	Quick Start	Implementor
1	16%	34%	8%	55%
2				
3				
4	41%	52%	24%	33%
5				
6				
7	43%	14%	68%	12%
8				
9				
10				

an exercise coach does not involve designing the regimens for each athlete, it doesn't really call on as much Follow Thru talent as that role implies. Being a clubhouse manager may include maintaining all the exercise equipment, making it more of an Implementor task than a Fact Finder job. In order to find the right outlet for your talent, you'll need to ask specific questions related to the job.

Most careers, like most sports, can be mastered from a wide variety of conative strengths. I've found an interesting mix of instincts among professional basketball players and the people in the sports media. Among eighty-one National Basketball Association players who have taken the KCI, the most common insistences seen are in Follow Thru and Fact Finder. One reason these modes prevail in the NBA may be that draftees often come up through college programs run by coaches who reward players who take fewer scoring risks and play within the coach's game plan. Surprisingly, the NBA players have less-than-average Implementor intensity than the general public. But 38 percent of the all-star players who have taken the KCI are insistent in the Implementor mode; that's 90 percent higher than in the general population.

The instincts most often found among media professionals depend greatly upon whether the journalists are with TV, radio, newspapers, or magazines. Of the television anchors and interviewers I KCI'd, I found 80 percent insistent in Quick Start and none insistent in Fact Finder. It appears those insistent Fact Finders with an interest in journalism should consider the print media, since successful newspaper and magazine writers have considerably more insistence in that mode. The famous "thirty-second sound bite," or small amount of air time, frustrates the need to investigate and give more background on a story than TV allows. One former anchorperson lamented, "I've always received high viewer ratings but had low self-esteem because all I could be was superficial, and that's not who I am."

All journalism has an immediacy that adds the need for Quick Start but detracts from it as a career for insistent Follow Thrus, who are underrepresented in the electronic mediums of radio and TV and in daily newspapers (except among those who write regular columns). According to the data from twenty-nine journalists, on-air interviews and bylined stories are most suited to those with Quick Start and Fact Finder talents. Producers also frequently have high insistences in Quick Start, while directors and crew have proved to have the backup necessary in the other modes.

We often use recreation as outlets for instinctive energy we don't get to expend at the workplace. You might play golf to engage the Implementor instincts that you didn't release in the office. Or you might take up hang gliding to unleash Quick Start experimentation held in check during work hours. Singing in a church choir, dancing, playing in a band, as well as hobbies such as gardening and hiking—anything that you do with commitment—allow you to express your creativity. If your job provides you with outlets for most of your instinctive energy, your off-hours will truly be downtime. Then you can watch TV or read the newspaper without having to strive. If your career is an appropriate conduit for your mental energy, your achievements will be mainly job

Kolbe Management Report
SYNERGY REPORT

For

PROFESSIONAL BASKETBALL PLAYERS

	Fact Finder	Follow Thru	Quick Start	Implementor	Group Synergy	Ideal Synergy
PREVENT 1	4%	6%	62%	18%		25%
2						
3						
RESPOND 4	52%	69%	36%	68%		50%
5					56%	
6						
INITIATE 7	44%	25%	2%	14%		25%
8					21%	
9						
10						

This analysis is based on a total of 81 respondents.

Kolbe Management Report
SYNERGY REPORT

For

ALL STARS

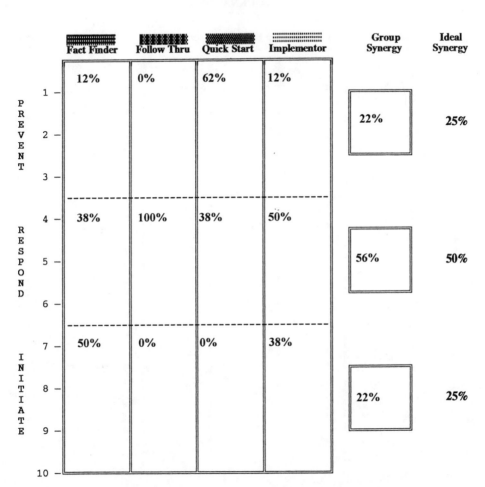

This analysis is based on a total of 8 respondents.

Kolbe Management Report
SYNERGY REPORT

For

JOURNALISTS

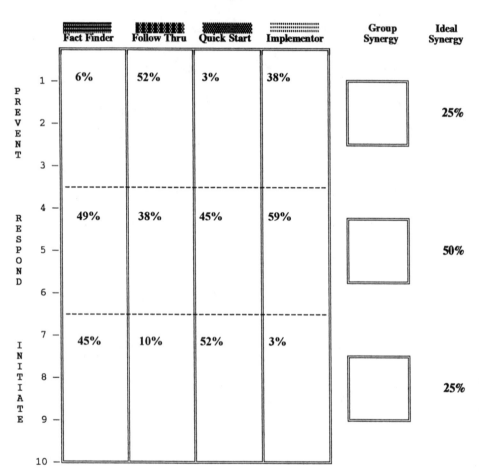

	Fact Finder	Follow Thru	Quick Start	Implementor	Group Synergy	Ideal Synergy
PREVENT (1-3)	6%	52%	3%	38%		25%
RESPOND (4-6)	49%	38%	45%	59%		50%
INITIATE (7-9)	45%	10%	52%	3%		25%

This analysis is based on a total of 29 respondents.

related. People whose minds have been fully engaged are able to relax and enjoy non-striving leisure.

But consider the weekend photographer who spends every spare moment in the darkroom, devoting boundless energy toward perfecting his craft. He sleepwalks through his job and comes alive with enthusiasm and creativity only first thing Saturday morning. He then becomes moody and withdrawn Sunday evening, anticipating another unfulfilling week of merely earning a paycheck.

If you find that you are using more of your instinctive energy on a recreational activity than on your work, that activity could point you in a new direction. Maybe you could get paid for it! Don't we all want to earn a living doing something we enjoy, something that fulfills us instinctively?

Too many people stay in career ruts simply because their résumés reinforce experience in unsuited roles. The weekend photographer, for example, probably stays in his job because his college degree prepared him for it and because he now has twelve years of experience under his belt. He looks no further than his résumé to tell him what to do for a living.

Stanley, a young New England architect, is a rising star in his firm. But his KCI result of 4-3-7-8 shows why he lives for the weekends, when his insistence in Quick Start and Implementor are satisfied out on the boat he and his wife purchased with his year-end bonus. "If he had a choice," a good friend of his observed, "he would be a sailor, a farmer, or maybe a veterinarian." But he was making good money as an architect, and his father—and his father before him—had been architects. So he fidgeted his way through partner meetings, all the while thinking about horses he wanted to buy with his annual bonuses, sheep he could be raising, acres he wanted to plant with nut trees—anything to avoid concentrating on the work of designing buildings. While most architects have an accommodation to Implementor, few have Stanley's insistence in the mode. They also have considerably more Follow Thru, which gives them a greater sense of accomplishment than Stanley has found.

This successful architect is a victim of his own formidable abilities. From as far back as high school, Stanley has been told he should pursue this career. He got terrific grades in the architectural program. His professors praised him constantly. And his career has reinforced the fact that he is *very* good at designing homes. But he has never derived fulfillment from functioning as an architect. Stanley needed to be crafting solutions out in the fresh air, not behind a drawing table.

It's hard to turn your back on something that the world says you ought to be doing. It takes great courage—more than many people ever muster—to stare at a résumé full of honors and promotions and decide to make a 180-degree career change. Conatively suited career recommendations ought to be viewed as roles in which you can succeed *if* you have the interest and intellect for them.

FINDING THE OPPORTUNITY

THE PROCESS OF LOOKING FOR A JOB REQUIRES THE SAME TALENTS THAT YOU HAVE to offer once hired. For example, Roberto is highly insistent in Fact Finder, which means he researches tirelessly to find the companies most likely to make the best use of his talents and to learn of job openings. Before interviewing with a company, he backgrounds himself as much as possible on its financial status, traditions, and historical position in the marketplace. He presents himself best when his Fact Finder needs are satisfied and he can use them to his advantage.

When Roberto does receive an offer, it is important for him to compare it to other job offers, or other *possible* hoped-for opportunities. Though the first job he's offered may seem perfect, Roberto's insistence in Fact Finder will still need to comparison shop before he's confident he's accepting the right position.

Insistent Follow Thrus will rely on a system for their job search. They might try putting job openings they hear about on file cards and checking them off as contacts are made. They should treat job hunting as a job in itself, which will allow them to maintain a sense of order in their lives during the transition period. They should get up at a regular time and work at a desk or designated place for a consistent interval each day. It's a good idea for them to develop a schedule for sending out résumés and making calls. They'll have a greater sense of accomplishment if they stick to it, because regardless of the outcome, they will have done their job.

However, they will be troubled if their job search takes too long. It's best for them to end one approach and then begin a new search by reconsidering their lists and establishing a different system. On the other hand, if they're offered a job before they'd planned on it, they may procrastinate on making a decision, while waiting for other opportunities to play out. They need their career to have an orderly progression, so they'll consider any offers they get in terms of potential advancement, incremental increases in responsibility, as well as issues of financial security. It will bother them if a job takes them backward in any way, even just temporarily.

When they take a job, Follow Thru–insistent people may tie up loose ends, sending thank-you notes to those who either turned them down or are still open considerations. This also allows them to go back to those sources on future job searches, since they keep well-organized records of past contacts.

Insistent Quick Starts seek jobs with an intuitive fit. Their search is hit or miss, and they'll probably take the first opportunity that feels right. They're challenged simply by the possibility of a new job. The bigger the challenge, the better. They need to be in on the action from the get-go; they'll be impatient waiting for a chance to make a big impact. Since Quick Start initiators thrive on open-ended growth, lots of diversity, and the freedom to do their own thing, they should size up possibilities to create their own opportunities within a job environment. Their job searches ought not to end until a role *feels right*.

Donna, a plumber, is insistent in Implementor. She's fairly nonverbal, and writing résumés and answering job-interview questions are particularly stressful for her. She needs to *show* you what she can do. Apprenticeships are the best way for her to showcase her talent. Another way she will get a job is by a former coworker wanting to work with her again.

Donna knows she's short on words, so she may have someone else represent her in labor negotiations. She could benefit from belonging to a trade union, or, like many athletes, let an agent do the talking for her. If she's offered several jobs, she'll make her decision based on location, quality of equipment, freedom of movement, and amount of time away from meetings and desks. Pay and perks are not as important to her as being appreciated for her craftsmanship. In order to feel successful, she needs to be able to stay with a project until she is satisfied with the end product.

RÉSUMÉ REALITIES

THE CURRENT TREND AMONG RÉSUMÉ SERVICES AND CAREER COUNSELORS IS TO advise people to create résumés that obscure their instinctive talents. It is amazing how many people are unable or unwilling to point out what instinctive talents they will contribute to an organization. When every résumé reads alike it wastes everyone's time and energy. Many of my corporate clients ask applicants to take the KCI and are shocked to learn that a candidate whose résumé stresses organization and efficiency is actually resistant in Follow Thru. These clients believed that people knew themselves and would describe their true strengths.

The ideal résumé includes a section on cognitive background, listing education, grades, special skills, and experience. It is accompanied by a cover letter expressing the candidate's goals and aspirations. In addition, it indicates the person's instinctive strengths, including how the applicant naturally initiates activity, how she responds to situations, and what preventive methods will be contributed. With such résumés in hand, applicants poorly suited for a job could be weeded out, which would be in everyone's best interest.

OFFERING THE JOB

BEFORE OFFERING SOMEONE A JOB, DISCUSS WITH HIM HOW WELL SUITED HIS instincts are to the way the job needs to be performed. For instance, if you are hiring Keith, who is insistent in Fact Finder, be specific about job responsibilities, title, and benefits. He needs the details in writing. Give him material to study before his first day, so he has as much information about the company and his role as possible. Encourage him to call with questions. Don't try to force him into a decision before he's reviewed the particulars, or his answer will be no.

Rosa, an insistent Follow Thru, demanded an orderly transition from customer-service representative to office manager. She couldn't make the change immediately and had to "put [her] life in order" before beginning the new assignment. She had to tour the new office and get a lay of the land before making a decision—even though she had been working there for three years. It helped that she already knew many of her future coworkers and that her new boss took time to review unfamiliar policies and procedures. She also benefited from assurances regarding job security.

Clarence is so insistent in Quick Start that he said yes to a job offer even before he knew the salary. Clarence's new boss recognized that he needed to negotiate in some way so that Clarence wouldn't have buyer's remorse and change his mind. So this new boss let Clarence push for something he particularly desired. People who initiate in Quick Start often bargain for commissions, bonuses, or to somehow sweeten the deal.

It was good that Clarence was available to start work immediately; he needs to dive right into a job.

The Implementor in Sally is so insistent that she'll actually go to the new place and watch people use the equipment; maybe ask her future coworkers to let her work the printing press she'll be operating. She'll also need to get a good look at the product she'll be creating so that she can get some ideas on improving quality. Once she's shown you that she can make a contribution in this way, offer her the job.

GETTING YOUR OWN WAY

IN SOME CAREERS YOU FIRST HAVE TO PROVE YOURSELF IN AN ENTRY-LEVEL position that may not fit your instinctive makeup. These are transition jobs that you take in order to get somewhere else. They're stepping stones, and they can be slippery. Even so, if the transition is to a career that will satisfy your needs, you'll want and need to find ways to tolerate—and succeed—at the job. Most entry-level jobs don't offer much opportunity to convert them to fit your particular MO, but you should try to make them work according to your needs. These jobs are never easy, but they are doable.

A resistant–Fact Finder journalist survived proofreading and fact checking to move on to conducting in-person interviews. A marketing boss was once a secretary. A resistant–Quick Start sales manager started out making cold calls. The key to survival is knowing the difference between the goals that you must achieve in order to meet your bosses' expectations and the methods you use to achieve them. Since most supervisors get overly involved in the means instead of the ends, it's a good idea to negotiate so you can tackle your tasks in ways suited to your talents.

Try telling your boss that you'd like to experiment with a new method—one that fits your MO—on a fairly minor, low-profile job. Chances are that when she sees the quality of the work you've done, she'll be more willing to let you use your method for more important projects.

A resistant Follow Thru who balks at daily paperwork and record keeping might convince his manager to let him use his Quick Start and turn it in all at once instead. The manager would still get the data needed, but the Quick Start would be less stressed knowing he could throw it together at the last minute and devote his energy to more satisfying tasks the rest of the time.

Tailoring your methods to your MO will ultimately satisfy everyone. More work will get done, and the quality will be higher. The trick is this: Whenever possible, let your boss see the *results*, but not the process.

"Daphne always has to get her own way!" her boss complained. "That's great," I answered, to his surprise. I knew from his description of her that she was committed to her job. If she insisted on doing things through her instinctive strengths, she was bound to be more productive. I told him I hoped she'd keep it up. "You've got to be kidding," he replied. "It's a problem for us. Her way isn't the normal way. It'd be a mess."

Before speaking with Daphne's boss, I had determined that she was the right instinctive match for the job. She was insistent in Follow Thru, and the position required a lot of Follow Thru talent. Therefore I had no fear that chaos would set in if Daphne was given the chance to work toward meeting her own needs. It was important to let her determine the method she would use to get the job done.

Another example of converting a job to suit a talent is Warren, a school administrator insistent in Quick Start. He figured out how to make a by-the-book role challenging by starting up a variety of new programs. However, once they became part of the system, he asked other people to take over managing them. "But you started the program," a colleague said to him. "How can you let go of it? Don't you have any ego involvement in it?" Sure he did, but the pride he felt didn't overtake his instinctive need for new challenges. "Once I've proved a program's value and showed how it can be done," he explained, "it's a bit boring for me. I take a paternal interest in it after that, but I don't have a need to be directly involved. I have a need to get out from under the repetitiousness of the problems connected with it and have the time to take on other things."

Rather than getting stuck in a dead-end role that doesn't let you prove what you can do, use your creative ability to convert it into a chance for success. Your best means of contributing to an organization is by putting your best conative foot forward. Here are some things to keep in mind while making a job work for you instinctively:

1. Be certain you understand the goals you are expected to meet.

>   Separate the ones you are personally responsible for from those that your team, department, store, or company should accomplish. Establish which aspects of the team goals you have some control over. If you

continue to be confused over who is responsible for what, ask for a memo or a meeting to clarify this.

2. Decide which goals (or parts of them) you can accomplish using your natural inclinations.

> This may require some research, observation, or discussion to find out how things are usually done and how free you are to do things your own way.

3. Find out if you can barter your talents with others, trading what you do well with what they will do for you.

> Be certain that this is permissible; others could view it as dodging work.

4. Isolate the activities that cause you to be less productive than you usually are and find out how essential they are to your job.

5. Seek alternative ways of accomplishing these tasks.

> Try to explain these to your supervisor, providing a plan that shows how your method reaches his goal.

6. Volunteer for additional assignments that are better suited to your instinctive makeup.

One example of how this works: An entry-level customer-service representative made up for his lack of Follow Thru in a job requiring consistency and efficiency by using his Fact Finder talent to assess the primary reasons for customer complaints. In his off-hours he researched the standard problems in the industry, comparing them with his observations of his company's issues. When he asked his supervisor what the specific goals for his job were, he was told they included identifying causes of problems. He asked permission to prepare a report of his observations. The supervisor was so impressed with his initiative, she overlooked his tendency to be late for work and to keep odd hours.

A fishing-fleet owner was taken aback when a crew member at the bottom of the totem pole didn't seem to carry his load when it came to setting and repairing nets, making the best use of storage space, and other Implementor tasks. "He was a klutz, but a nice guy," the owner remarked, "and I knew he had a family to support, so I encouraged him when he came to me with a proposal. Although he wasn't a good boatman or fisherman, the guy had a knack for cutting deals with the local markets. He suggested he could increase profitability by negotiating for the full day's catch rather than haggling individual prices for different types of fish. He had some pretty weird ideas for selling what we caught before we'd caught it and running up a tab with customers. We only tried about half his ideas, enough so we doubled profits over the season. Now he's my director of marketing. And he's still a lousy fisherman."

If you handle entry-level jobs from a smart, instinctive point of view, they can move you *up* rather than *out*. If the transition job is a required springboard, as it is in many companies, at least you know there's light at the end of the tunnel. However, if you can tell that you'll be in an ill-suited job for a long time, it may not be worth it. There's always more than one career in which anyone's talents can shine.

THE SINGLE-CAREER OPTION

VERY OFTEN PEOPLE GO INTO THE JOB MARKET WITH ONLY ONE CAREER IN MIND. I saw an example of this recently when I spoke to a class of gifted high-school students. Over half told me they wanted to go into film. Although colleges have multiplied their film courses to meet the demand, by no means does this reflect an increase in openings in the field. If I could convey one thing to people setting their hearts on a single career choice, it would be that their sense of accomplishment shouldn't rest so heavily on "the breaks." Luck does play a mighty role in some careers. For instance, becoming an opera star often has less to do with your drive or talent than with who you know. Making it into the big leagues in baseball isn't entirely dependent on whether you have the talent, it's also whether the scouts are in the stands the days you play well.

Many young people focus on a particular career early on so that they can more easily answer the question, "What do you want to do when you grow up?" However, being inflexible about your career direction can make it harder to live up to your own self-expectations. It's a shame that kids who say they want to make a difference somehow by contributing their talents may be smiled at and told, "Don't worry, when I was a senior in college, I wasn't sure what I was going to do, either." The truth is, those kids are a lot more purposeful and directed—especially if they've identified their talents—than someone who simply says she wants to go to medical school. Career counseling has been caught up in *naming* specific jobs or career paths instead of identifying personal goals and the methods of achieving them.

There's no need to dissuade a child from wanting to be a fireman just because he's resistant in Implementor. My fear is that doing so would give youngsters a message that limits their views of what they ought to do and what they'd be best to try. The young person's version of the KCI does not give results with numbers but instead lists attributes to build on. And that's how I wish adults would view their results as well. The KCI isn't meant to limit us to particular careers, nor do most careers keep us from using our natural instincts. For instance, the entire crew in a fire station is not made up of people insistent in Implementor. If it were, who would keep the records and write up the reports? It's tough to let go of the dream of becoming something in particular. People who don't get into law school can make marvelous contributions with their talents; they can't go through life thinking they failed. If they do, it's because they viewed success too narrowly; too much according to what they *want* to be or are smart enough to do, and not enough in terms of discovering careers that would give them the freedom to be themselves. Sometimes when people are "sized out" of a job—or just plain fired—it's actually a blessing in disguise; an ideal time to expand their conative horizons and consider new fields.

OUTPLACEMENT OPPORTUNITIES

UNFORTUNATELY, OUTPLACEMENT PROGRAMS USUALLY TRY TO FIND PEOPLE NEW jobs that closely approximate their old jobs. But the obvious question is rarely asked. Were they productive doing it? If a person didn't feel much satisfaction as a secretary, why help that person find another secretarial job?

Outplacement specialists who use the Kolbe Concept, such as Anne Coulter in Chicago, are able to ascertain why a person succeeded or failed in previous jobs. "By comparing someone's KCI result with his KCI-B for the position he is vacating, it is possible to zero in on problems he shouldn't repeat," Coulter said. "Most importantly, the process re-enforces a person's instinct-related capabilities, which may or may not have been well used in the past." Coulter finds a person whose instincts have been validated through outplacement is more likely to wait for the right job.

Outplacement should dwell on the future, using information about the past only as examples of opportunities that were or were not appropriate. It should operate on the assumption that each person has instinctive strengths that should not be thwarted. Job frustration is a sign that the person was trying to succeed; capturing that drive for productive purposes will help the person achieve. Time wasted overexplaining the past, "getting back at" the company that let him go, or searching for a similarly unsuited role could be spent on more constructive goals.

Outplacement firms shouldn't receive compensation based on how many jobs they get for people how quickly, but on how many people are still *thriving* in jobs at least a year later. There's nothing very affirming about losing your job, unless you use it as an opportunity to discover your innate abilities through proper outplacement practices.

HEADHUNTERS

WHEN YOU CONSIDER THAT MOST HEADHUNTERS RECEIVE 20 PERCENT TO 30 percent of the first year's salary for each placement they make, you would think they'd try to find the right fit. Some do, but too many follow the trend of jamming a square peg into a round hole.

This happened to a manufacturing company looking to hire a new plant manager. Company executives preferred someone with experience, of course, but also someone better able to respond in a crisis than the person who had been in the job. They asked a national head-hunting firm to conduct a search, and in a short time were presented with three highly recommended candidates.

But after flying all three in for a full day of interviews, the top management people still couldn't make a decision. The president called me. "I can't tell you exactly what it is, but I just don't feel right about any of these candidates," he said. "They met all the criteria we had listed. They were nice enough. But something's wrong, and we all want to step back and find out what it is. Do you suppose it's that you've taught us so much about our instincts that we're actually trusting them?"

For the first time, applicants for a professional position in this firm were asked to take the KCI. And each executive team member completed a KCI-C. The latter's results revealed they were looking for someone whose instincts fell somewhere between accommodating and insistent in Quick Start. Unfortunately, all the candidates recruited by the head-hunting firm—though qualified in many ways—were resistant in Quick Start.

Another requirement, insistence in Fact Finder, was available with all three candidates. Most of them had more Follow Thru than was necessary, and one had more Implementor than the job called for. These talents would have been useful at the company, but they weren't enough. When the president saw the KCI results, he turned down all the candidates, telling the headhunter that none of them had the right instincts for the job.

This guy came unglued. He couldn't imagine why they were turning down "perfectly qualified" candidates. The president reminded him that all along they'd said they needed someone who was good in a crisis. The headhunter responded: "But all these people are good in a crisis. They prove it day in and day out in the jobs they do. How could they have moved up in corporations if they weren't able to handle a crisis?" It's true that everyone can handle a crisis in his own way. But when a job demands that you take risks and deal with a variety of unknowns in a rapidly changing environment, you're talking about a particular kind of crisis handling.

Had the president been able to explain the assignment accurately to these candidates, it's unlikely they would have wanted it. Recruiters who use the Kolbe Concept can do exactly that. They let the candidates know, usually without revealing the company name, what characteristics are needed to succeed in the job. Not only does this help companies find the right people, but it keeps applicants from ending up in the wrong job for them.

Employing the Kolbe Concept was less than 5 percent of the cost of flying candidates in. The manufacturing company had wasted the other 95 percent of its expenditure as well as lost time. It was also an unnecessary loss of time and energy for the candidates. Laying out *all* the parameters ahead of time and prequalifying candidates according to cognitive, affective, and conative characteristics would have saved everyone's resources.

CHAPTER EIGHT

SELECTING AND PROMOTING PEOPLE WHO WILL SUCCEED

C loe runs an entrepreneurial business in New Mexico with a very small staff jammed into tight quarters. Being true to her instincts (her KCI result is 6-2-8-3), she hires people without giving them much detail about their jobs. Instead she sells them on the terrific variety of what goes on in the office and how their many projects will quickly grow into greater opportunities. Cloe hires people based on her hunches that they'll fit in. After all, her Quick Start intuition serves her pretty well most of the time. And she doesn't think she can afford the cost of giving the KCI to applicants.

Yet she's paid plenty for the problems created by missuited employees. One new hire went to lunch her first day and never came back. Another left after two days, saying, "Variety is one thing; chaos is another!" Another stuck around only long enough to add to the chaos. Cloe's been in business ten years, so she's proved she can succeed, but not everyone fits into the environment she's created or the roles she assigns. Quick Start intuition does not give her the objectivity needed to overcome the personal likes and dislikes that influence her hiring decisions.

Charles, another Southwesterner, chose education as his major in college so he could fulfill his dream of teaching young Native Americans. After graduating with top honors, he sought a classroom assignment on an Indian reservation. He went to a job interview on a reservation with great hope and anticipation. When Charles, a Native American, arrived in the school superintendent's office, the man looked up from his desk and said, "Oh, I'm very sorry. Someone should have told you we have no openings for janitorial positions." Because of the color of his skin, Charles was dismissed without consideration. A decision maker in a publicly funded program approached selection in this manner in 1992. The law doesn't allow what happened to Charles, but our society does.

Cloe, many of her new hires, and Charles have all been victims of misconceptions regarding the selection process. Most people—potential employees and employers—have been victimized by stereotypes of one sort or another. Perhaps you've been turned down for a promotion because you didn't socialize with the right people, or have turned others away yourself because they didn't seem to "fit in." Maybe you've been rejected as an applicant just because you're introverted and don't interview well, or because you couldn't afford the education necessary for the job you knew you could do. Almost everyone has a story about an unreasonable selection situation.

"It's not fair!" has been an all-too-true statement regarding selection and promotion decisions. It's not fair when people aren't given a chance to perform in roles for which they have the right instincts. It's not fair when a worker agrees to do a job and quits without giving it any effort. It's not fair to judge people's abilities or a job's opportunities on a superficial or subjective basis. Yet, until we could measure the Striving Instincts, "Life isn't fair" was about all that could be said. No other method of selection has ever proved to predict how people will perform *and* be unbiased by race, gender, age, or handicap. Now it is possible to offer an objective, job-specific process I call the Kolbe FairSelection System.

I kept the KCI from being used in the selection process for several years after I had developed it, instead focusing on team building and individual counseling applications. I did this because I'd seen what could happen when a testing instrument was misused in hiring or promoting. My father, E. F. Wonderlic, created the first personnel test used widely by American businesses. The Wonderlic Personnel Test was also the instrument that the United States Supreme Court, in a historic civil-rights case, ruled had been used to discriminate against racial minorities in a company's promotion decisions. Because I had been so hurt by seeing how my father's work had been used improperly, I waited to establish the FairSelection program until I had sufficient independently analyzed data proving that the KCI does not discriminate against any group, as well as legal advice supporting that conclusion and ironclad procedures that eliminate misuse of the instrument. Dad had challenged me to find a way to select people without such potential problems, and until I could be certain I had met every one of the federal guidelines for selection, I did not feel I had met that challenge. (See Appendix II for data summary.)

A lawyer, speaking at a recent American Psychological Association conference, believed no one was trying to meet that challenge. According to the head of research for a major personnel-testing company, "He accused industrial psychologists and test developers of not trying to find an unbiased selection method. It isn't that we don't want to be absolutely fair to everyone," the researcher added, "we just don't know how to develop a test that overcomes the way society discriminates. If people are not given equal educational opportunities, they simply won't be able to test equally well."

The KCI overcomes this problem. Because it measures Striving Instincts, which are not influenced by education, experience, age, gender, skin color, or other physical attributes, its results do not discriminate against any group, and it is reliable over time. It predicts how a person will initiate action, respond to situations, and prevent problems. When these relevant issues, rather than personal prejudices, are the basis for selection and promotion, everyone wins. Employers such as Cloe can identify who is most likely to stick around and get the job done. Job candidates can be judged on their potential for success rather than on irrelevant issues.

The Wall Street Journal ran a story recently that quantified the benefits of selecting employees on an equal-opportunity basis. It reported that a Chicago-based firm, Covenant Investment Management, found that from 1988 through 1992, companies rated in the top 20 percent for hiring women and minorities outperformed the stock market by 2.4 percent, whereas the bottom 20 percent with the worst record for hiring women and minorities trailed stock-market performance by 8 percent. "Companies with poor employment records face stricter regulation, lower productivity, and more litigation," said Covenant President Anthony Carfang.

Companies do not become more profitable simply by hiring women, minorities, the elderly, or the handicapped. They become more profitable by hiring people with the highest probability of getting the job done. Selection decisions based on Striving Instincts, which are universal and evenly distributed among all groups of people, give everyone an equal opportunity for success.

If a candidate pool is unbiased, using conative talent as the initial selection criterion also assures a company that it will select an approximately equal percentage from both genders, all races, all age groups, without handicapping anyone, including the company. Helping all people to use their talents productively is certainly a better answer than University of Chicago professor Richard Epstein's solution. In the February 1993 issue of *Forbes*, he stated that "If we want to subsidize a 'protected class,' it can be done more efficiently by just giving grants."

The Kolbe FairSelection process becomes an affirmative-action program that doesn't have to cost an inordinate amount and doesn't lead to accusations of reverse discrimination favoring minority applicants.

Most companies want to do what is right and smart when it comes to fair-selection practices. However, without nondiscriminatory tools to help them, they resort to methods that often reinforce the status quo. According to a 1993 PBS program on women in the workplace, only 8 percent of American executives are women, and they fill only 1 percent of corporate-board positions. Obviously most affirmative-action programs, which attempt to help companies seek out minorities and women for job placements, have been ineffective. Yet in 1993, *Forbes* estimated the *annual* price tag since 1980 for affirmative action in the United States to be $113 billion. It found many companies wouldn't even report costs for such programs, for fear they would seem to be complaining about the price of doing what's right.

Companies of all sizes the world over are making selection decisions today in ways that are not right. The truth is that they have no idea what it's costing them. It's difficult enough to put a price on turnover, but lost opportunities are even more impossible to gauge.

THE HIDDEN COSTS OF SELECTION

PEOPLE ARE EXTREMELY IMPORTANT TO ANY ORGANIZATION, BUT FOR TOO LONG they have been its least quantifiable asset. Renee, a personnel specialist for a Rust Belt manufacturing company, has been trying for years to quantify performance, "but we only keep attendance and payroll records; we don't track contributions." People have to be chosen carefully and their contributions to an organization measured objectively. Based on the many cases I have studied, the true cost of employees working counter to their instincts shows up in absenteeism, turnover, and other measurable losses in productivity. Error rates and sales figures are also objective criteria.

The cost of correcting a placement mistake can be horrendous, both financially and emotionally. Executives report to me that personnel problems cause them more lost sleep than any other issue they face. One executive said, "I broke out in hives when I had to tell a lifelong friend he wasn't cutting it." An office manager reported that she hadn't been able to concentrate or make decisions on other matters the week before she finally fired a hard-working but ill-suited worker.

In most cases employees are selected because someone *likes* them, not because they have the right instincts or capacity to get the job done. But what happens when someone we like doesn't perform well? Studies over the decades have shown that a low-performing employee accomplishes half as much as a high-producing worker. That's why it often takes two people to replace a top-notch performer, and why some companies have found they can reduce their work force and still get as much done. It's possible to get more done with fewer employees if you can figure out which workers will be the highest performers.

Even in tough economic times, when staff cutbacks are justified as cost-saving measures, undesired turnover is detrimental to profitability. Insurance companies put the price of turnover for one sales agent at between fifty thousand and eighty thousand dollars, which includes the outlay for hiring, training, and replacing the person. A national accounting firm estimates the turnover of one clerical-staff employee can cost as much as fifteen thousand dollars. The greatest hidden costs to turnover include lost productivity during the several months it usually takes for a new hire to get up to speed on a job. During that time, coworkers have to carry the burden of both showing the person the ropes and covering those aspects of the job he is not yet able to accomplish.

According to a 1993 article syndicated by Knight-Ridder-Tribune Information Services, employers are becoming more and more reluctant to add full-time workers to their payrolls because of increasing regulations and rising benefits. The article states: "Employers say government regulations have made it more expensive to hire and keep full-time workers and are contributing to what some are calling the 'contingent' work force."

It's tough to build team synergy from part-time, on-and-off workers, yet the article also makes the point: ". . . . Recent civil-rights laws giving more legal rights to women, racial minorities, and the disabled may be deterring companies from hiring full-time workers because of concerns over potential lawsuits.

" 'People are much more cautious,' said Lawrence Lorber, a Washington lawyer who represents business interests.

" 'It increases the liabilities of trying to hire employees. If they can get by on overtime and hiring fewer people, they'll do it, because every time you hire somebody, there's a risk.' "

HOW COMPANIES LIMIT THE PROBABILITY OF FINDING THE RIGHT EMPLOYEE

AS EXPENSIVE AS IT IS TO MAKE A MISTAKE IN SELECTION, MANY COMPANIES eliminate some of the highest-potential employees for reasons that have nothing to do with the ability to produce. They discriminate against certain classes of people. Unfair biases are not only immoral and illegal, they greatly decrease a company's chances of hiring the highest potential performer. Companies that discriminate for non-job-related reasons significantly reduce the talent available to them.

A good-old-boy network that doesn't consider women for significant roles cuts its candidate pool by 50 percent. If racial minorities also are excluded, the applicant field drops, in many cities, by another third. Age discrimination, if it starts with candidates over fifty, may reduce the remaining group by about 20 percent. Any company that follows such unfair practices could eliminate *75 percent* of the job-seeking population from consideration. And that's if it discriminates against only three demographic groups and doesn't have any academic or other standards that must be met.

If an employer used only the KCI in her selection process, she could be assured of a bias-free approach. However, the group available for testing needs to be as broad-based demographically as possible. One firm I work with went through the initial steps of the FairSelection process to establish ranges needed in each Action Mode for a particular job. The program includes ranking job candidates according to their instinctive fit with the job requirements, from Excellent to Poor. Approximately 20 percent of all applicants, regardless of gender, age, or race, are expected to fall in the Excellent or Very Good categories. Those are the people whose KCI results are within or close to a Range of Success in all four modes. Therefore they have the highest probability of success and are the ones to interview. When I heard that this company's final candidates were all white males, I knew the candidate pool was biased even before testing had begun.

Indeed, it turned out the company had sought applicants only at a local private college and through ads in a professional journal. Such sources artificially skewed the candidate group. Checking further, I found that none of the senior managers already employed at the company was either female or a minority. The firm's policy of promoting from within further reduced diversity in its ranks. Not only did this company need help establishing a reliable and unbiased approach to testing, it needed assistance in its recruiting practices. Sometimes this problem stems from recruiting in ways that draw out conative clones and has nothing to do with other forms of discrimination. As you'll see, academic requirements frequently narrow the conative field.

When recruiting problems result in discrimination against protected groups, the answer is not for the company to lower its standards so that women and minorities will fall within the acceptable conative ranges. If enough minorities are in the pool, they will have an equal opportunity to qualify on the KCI. Setting separate standards for women, minorities, or handicapped people leads to reverse discrimination against males, whites, and the nonhandicapped. Congress decided in 1991 that separate norms for classes of applicants are unacceptable.

This company needed to broaden its search for potential employees and recruit in nontraditional ways. I advised its employment officers to advertise jobs in community newsletters that reached minority populations and to use bulletin boards in places where the missing segments of the population would likely shop. Neighborhood associations and women's groups also proved helpful in communicating job openings. Broadening recruiting practices can increase the diversity of talents along with a diversity of other characteristics. This process resulted in finding 19 percent of applicants in the required conative ranges for the job, with women and minorities more equally represented.

THE NEED TO BE FAIR

AS AN EMPLOYER, I DON'T WANT A GOVERNMENT AGENCY TELLING ME WHO I CAN and can't hire. I don't want to be regulated to a degree that I can't make the best decision for my company. No bureaucrat knows my company's needs as well as I do. I must be able to make my own decisions without being overburdened by paperwork and without playing nonproductive quota games. Personally, I have never been willing to be the token woman and have never wanted to place another person in that type of situation. I have three sons, and I don't want them excluded from job opportunities because they are white males and don't fit a racial or gender "need." I know I have a problem when a client doesn't want to work with a young person, a female, or a black employee; the marketplace isn't always fair. But giving people the opportunity to perform in roles for which they have the right conative makeup is our best chance of eliminating many of the wrongs that affect people's opportunities to succeed. It's a cost-effective way of taking affirmative action without giving preferential treatment to any one group of people. (A 1993 poll conducted by *The New York Times* and CBS News found Americans divided on the issue of whether preferential treatment should be given to blacks in hiring and promotion as a means of correcting past job discrimination. Fifty-eight percent of whites opposed such preferences—which would discriminate against them. Even twenty-four percent of blacks opposed such a method of righting a wrong.)

Trying to operate within both the letter and the spirit of nondiscrimination laws has made hiring such a hassle that many employers are worn down to a mentality of taking the first people in the door. "We don't even try to figure out who we ought to hire anymore," explained a personnel officer for a national telemarketing company. "We'll just have to fire those who don't produce." More than one executive has admitted to me that employee layoffs are not always tied directly to downsizing the organization but to correct poor hiring practices. Is it any wonder the economy has been slow to recover?

Too many of the methods we've used to assess human productivity have not been predictive and have been discriminatory. It's time to put an end to these problems. We're making progress, but still have a long way to go. For instance, I recently found myself in an awkward situation when discussing strategic issues with a CEO whose management approach I generally respect. His company was undergoing a significant reorganization that led to a redefinition of roles within his senior-management team. When I suggested the only woman in the group had the right instincts for a very tough assignment, he said, "Yeah, but I'd be concerned putting her in that spot. Women are so indecisive." He'd probably never sat through such a long silence as the one that followed. "What I mean," he finally added, "is that I don't want to put her in a bad position where people will take advantage of her—or, I mean, where she won't get the respect she deserves. You know what I mean." I did.

Then we compared the candidates' instinctive fit for the role. He referred to my earlier suggestion and said, "I guess I'd better rethink that idea. Her KCI result is right on the money. Maybe I ought to give her a chance." He didn't make the final decision that day, but within a few weeks she had the job. It has allowed her to excel.

This woman was promoted because she was the right person for the job, according to objective criteria. Had she not had the necessary instincts but been promoted to fill a quota or to prove the boss was unbiased, it could have hurt her career and slowed progress for other women in the company. Without the talent for the role, giving her the opportunity would have been unfair to everyone. She would have been set up for failure and furthered the stereotype that "women don't have what it takes."

The FairSelection System alone is not going to make up for all past discrimination. For instance, since only 5 percent of degreed engineers are black, I cannot assure my engineering clients that this system will give them a racially balanced talent pool. But now we have a greater chance for nonbiased hiring among available qualified candidates.

STEPS FOR IDENTIFYING
THOSE WHO WILL SUCCEED

THERE ARE TWO TYPES OF FAIRSELECTION PROCESSES: ONE FOR A JOB TO BE FILLED by many different people (sales, data entry, customer service), and the other for a unique position with unreplicated needs. They allow anyone who hires (from small-business owners to employment offices in large organizations) a powerful way to improve prediction of job success and a way to cut the high cost of turnover.

Even hiring dozens of people for a replicated role involves low start-up commitment, low risk, and high accuracy. The process includes identifying the instinctive differences between high and low performers among incumbents. With such comparisons, it is possible to pinpoint essential characteristics and to isolate detrimental methods that will detract from a candidate's probability of success *on this particular job*.

A Range of Success in each Action Mode is determined rather than seeking one ideal MO. These are the conative boundaries within which a job can best be performed. Most jobs allow considerable latitude in one or more modes. However, there is often one method that is essential, such as a prevention of Quick Start chaos, or an initiation of in-depth Fact Finder action.

Many of my clients explain that today's economy doesn't allow them to keep low performers on the payroll very long in hopes things will improve. The shorter time frame employees have to demonstrate their instincts for doing a job well, the greater the importance of hiring the right person in the first place. Otherwise the revolving door of employees ties up resources required to recruit, select, train, manage, and outplace the workers who later proved wrong for the job.

Whether or not a job is filled by multiple people, management's job requirements, as seen on the KCI-C, are an important consideration. Working against the methods your boss considers imperative certainly influences your stress and your ability to succeed. "It's not unusual to find that a boss believes a job needs to be done one way," said Bill Lee, a consultant specializing in the lumber and hardware industry. "But successful performers prove otherwise."

For this reason, the high performers' KCI results are the best predictor of candidates' potential, and the supervisor's requirements are treated by Bill and other Kolbe Selection Specialists as an important influence on potential job satisfaction. Additionally, the system involves a job analysis, which validates the information obtained on the KCIs. By determining in conative terms the nature of the actual work that is to be done, it's possible to reconfirm the ranges within each mode that will predict success.

In one study we found top real-estate agents had a wide range (2–8) in Fact Finder. A job analysis clarified that those agents with insistence in Fact Finder were selling more expensive properties than were those resistant in Fact Finder. The job title was the same, but the target markets were considerably different. The firm for which we were doing this study used the information to add the right balance of each type of salesperson. It knew which applicants would be more inclined to do comprehensive Fact Finder work on real-estate comparables and complex financing, and which would go for a greater number of small sales that could be closed without requiring such detailed studies.

Where one person is sought to fill a unique role, consideration is given to the instincts already available among other team members. The process also involves reviewing KCI-C requirements from all those in a position to evaluate the work of the new hire. If you're selecting a personal secretary and have never had one previously, we would con-

sider your MO and your C results. Those are the two factors most likely
to affect your secretary's ability to stay in the job and not suffer too much
stress. One entrepreneur continually hired the wrong secretary because
he was concerned only with typing speed and telephone skills. Eight
secretaries later, he tried finding the right conative fit. She's been with
him four years now.

EMPLOYING THE CREATIVE PROCESS

INSTINCTS AND THEIR RESULTING CONATIVE BEHAVIORS ARE NOT THE ONLY FACTORS
that determine whether a person ought to be placed in a particular job.
Other elements of the Creative Process, such as motivation and reasoning abilities, also need to be considered. A good interviewer concen-
trates on issues such as Level of Effort. Other hiring processes should
identify intellect or previously demonstrated skills. The problem, however, has been that identifying hard workers willing to give their all does
not ensure their talents are those most needed in a specific job. Or that
cognitive criteria won't discriminate against people who have not had
equal opportunities previously.

"I'll do anything I'm asked to do" sounds great. The question the
interviewer has to have answered in advance is, "Does this person have
the right instincts to do the job the way it needs to be done?" Highly
motivated people are likely to tell you they will gladly do a job just the
way a boss wants it done. On that basis, a highly insistent Follow Thru
(5-9-1-5) was given a job collecting money at an airport parking garage.
He worked as fast as he could, but he just *had* to take the time to sort
dollar bills so Washington's face was always showing—turned in the
same direction—and with the wrinkles smoothed out. He was conscien-
tious. But motorists regularly grew exasperated at waiting in line at his
booth. He was in the wrong job. The expense of trying to train him to act
with a little more Quick Start urgency and a little less Follow Thru
structure proved useless. Everyone's time was wasted trying to change
his method of operation. He gave up stacking bills in a particular way.
For a while. Then another equally time-consuming system emerged.

The results of a personality test indicated this individual *preferred* to
act by taking risks. That was how he wanted to be perceived and how he
wished to contribute. But such social-style instruments did not predict
his performance. The way he acted may seem unreasonable, yet results
of an intelligence test showed he was smart enough for the job. The

reasoning aspect of his Creative Process was not what hindered his productivity. He had the skills to use the computer at his station and the knowledge necessary to make change quickly. Testing whether he could operate at the level of thinking required on the job did not forecast the instinct-based needs that frustrated both him and the delayed motorists.

While all aspects of the Creative Process need to be taken into account in the selection process, until research was completed on the KCI, the only testing methods available measured either social style (motivation) or learned behaviors (reason). They did not predict *how* a person would perform. And they dealt with aspects of human ability influenced by lack of equal opportunities among people.

Laws regarding selection practices in this country attempt to level the playing field for all job applicants. Selection is an area where traditional practices, such as asking employees to bring in their friends for interviews, may not only result in unproductive employees, but may cause legal problems because of biased selection practices. There's too much at stake not to do it right.

The Civil Rights Act of 1991 and the Americans with Disabilities Act both reconfirmed this country's commitment to fair hiring practices. These laws, and similar laws dating back to the Civil War, have tried to ensure that people's race, color, religion, national origin, age, gender, or disability will not limit their opportunity to be considered for a job for which they are qualified. These laws place the burden for fair employment squarely on the employer.

The following is a summary of the current legal requirements for selection and promotion or classification of employees:

To comply with government guidelines, an employer must be able to show that its selection and classification system either:

Has no adverse impact (defined as selecting one group less than 80 percent as frequently as another),

OR,

1. accurately predicts employee performance on necessary job-related criteria, and,

2. is the least-discriminatory means available for identifying productive employees, and

3. is reliable and does not test skills acquired on the job.

My passion is to prove that all people have equal potential for productivity and to remove obstacles that keep anyone from fully using his or her talents. Some employers still use the excuse that they can't find a "qualified" woman or person of color to fill a particular role. Since conative talents are equally distributed in all segments of the population, that's a hollow argument. What's missing are enough people from these groups who have not been subjected to prior discrimination. They are underrepresented in boardrooms, management councils, and professional partnerships because of our historic inability to assign roles on an appropriate basis.

The United States Supreme Court, in one of its most important decisions on selection law, *Griggs v. Duke Power Co.* (*1971*), described unfair experience and educational requirements and biased testing practices as "hidden headwinds." These headwinds, which exist in many companies' hiring practices, limit individuals' opportunities to use instinctive abilities in ways that could substantially benefit them and potential employers.

MEETING LEGAL REQUIREMENTS

THE KCI HAS BEEN THE SUBJECT OF SEVERAL UNIVERSITY AND BUSINESS STUDIES, which determined that it more than satisfies the requirements of the federal Equal Employment Office (EEO). For instance, Dr. Robert T. Keim, director of the division of information, management and systems technology at Arizona State University, conducted a study with a sample of 4,030 KCI scores. He analyzed them for biases when grouped into seventeen conative patterns that simulate job-selection ranges. He concluded that "the KCI is not biased by gender, age, or race" and that it more than met the government guideline "at the .05 level." The KCI did not discriminate against any group by selecting it less than 80 percent as frequently as the most frequently selected group. (See Appendix II for details.)

In a recent study conducted by Dr. Clyde Stutts of Macy's department stores, the bias-free nature of the KCI was also put to the test. Over 150 employees at two different retail stores were given the KCI, and the data were studied by independent university researchers, as well as by Stutts. It indicated there were no significant differences in KCI results on the basis of race, gender, or age. Stutts, a PhD in industrial psychology, was amazed. "I had felt that the KCI was an attractive alternative for selecting employees," he said, "but I never believed that it could be as bias free as it claimed. It has proven its character to me."

Stutts also stated, "Affirmative-action programs, in the past, have not had good methods of selecting minorities who would perform well. With

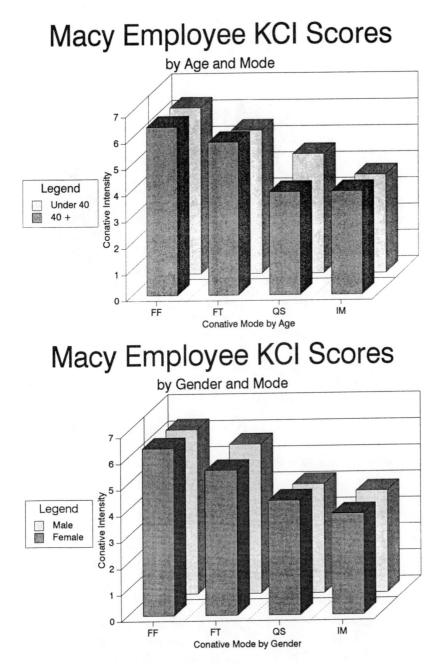

Macy Employee KCI Scores
by Race and Mode

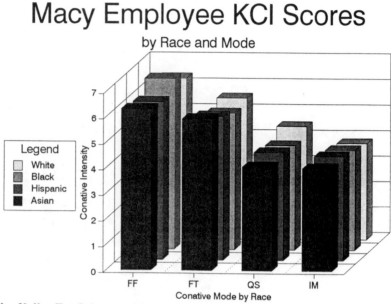

Conative Mode by Race

the Kolbe FairSelection System, you can pick people of different races, ages, and genders who have the highest probability of success." A former head of the EEOC (Equal Employment Opportunity Commission) didn't think it was possible for racial minorities to play on a level field with the use of *any* test of which he was aware in 1982:

> There is not any way in which black people tomorrow as a group are going to, no matter what kind of test you give them, score the same way that white people score . . . . And I think test validation gives them an A-1 out, because if you validate your tests you don't have to worry about exclusion of minorities and women any longer. *

TRADITIONAL SELECTION PRACTICES

Interviews

Some employers believe that if they simply avoid using selection tests altogether, they won't be subject to problems with the law. They argue

---

* Quoted in "Personnel Testing and the Law," by J. C. Sharf, in *Personnel Management*, edited by K. M. Rowland and G. R. Ferris, published by Allyn and Bacon, Boston, 1982.

that the best thing to do is not to test anyone, but to select only on the basis of an interview. "We can't be accused of doing something wrong," one executive said, "if we do nothing." The interview, however, has *proved* to be one of the least reliable and most bias-prone methods of selection. The school superintendent who thought a Native American was fit only to be a custodian probably did not think of himself as using a selection test. Yet he put Charles through the worst possible scrutiny and judged him on the color of his skin. By law, the selection process must either be free from bias, or it must be proved predictive, nondiscriminatory, and reliable. Interviews don't meet that test.

An interview is clearly subject to the bias of the interviewer. Even if there is no intent to discriminate, stereotypical characteristics may limit opportunities for the handicapped, females, minorities, and older applicants. For instance, one study identified significant stereotypes between interviewers' perceptions of "ideal" male and female candidates for the same job. Men needed to be "persuasive," "highly motivated," and "aggressive." Women applicants for the same job were highly rated if they had "a pleasant voice," "good clerical skills," and "immaculate dress and appearance." Such hidden headwinds unfairly discriminate against people with such non-job-related criteria.

Like the weighted application, interviews have proved ineffective in predicting job performance. Studies of the relationship between interviews and supervisors' subsequent ratings found that interviews were predictive of success only one out of every ten times.

Although interviews are as subject to the law as any other selection device, the vast majority of companies never validate their interviewing process to determine whether it has any bearing on job performance. Worse yet is a selection process that requires a spousal interview, which, shockingly, still takes place in the 1990s. In fact, a manager in a Fortune 100 company recently touted spousal interviews as "the best way ever" for selecting salespeople. That this approach was condoned by several other managers in the company indicates the high level of misinformation about selection standards that exists in corporate America. One well-known business-book author even boasts that he never hires employees without first going to their homes and meeting their families. How could the way your spouse keeps house, or dresses, or handles conversation possibly be proved to relate to your success on the job? I doubt many executives could prove their ability to manage people by how well their kids behave in front of company!

The interview is one of the most costly methods, both because of the time it requires, usually of several people, and because of the potential liability it creates.

Educational Considerations

There may be certain roles that require specific education or training. However, such criteria are not always predictive of success. Historically, they have also discriminated against minorities and may hide some conative biases as well. According to the U.S. Department of Commerce, Bureau of the Census, *Current Population Report*, high school dropout rates vary greatly by race. It compares the percent of 1980 high school dropout rates as follows:

White: 10.2
Black: 18.6
Hispanic: 35.2

This factor may, therefore, lead to bias when a company believes a salesman with a college degree is more effective than one without. Since this discriminates against minorities, a company should go to great lengths to prove this belief holds up statistically. Employers often use education as a screening device simply because they don't have another method of identifying the true requirements for a position. I have rarely seen a company using such a prerequisite base it on having hired people without the educational requirement and then tracking results.

Recently, a multistate communications company asked me for help in selecting technical-support personnel. They were anxious to know whether additional educational requirements or other selection criteria would predict job success. After analyzing how much physical and mechanical ability the job required, I thought it likely that someone with an insistence in Implementor would be more suited to the assignments than someone with the Fact Finder talent usually necessary to achieve in an academic setting. Research confirmed that 73 percent of high performers in the roles were accommodating or insistent Implementors. Fact Finder insistence proved to be irrelevant to success. Additional educational requirements for such jobs would have constituted a hidden headwind that would have excluded the very employees who would be most likely to succeed.

Most cognitively based tests are more accurate than interviews, but they still correlate with job success fewer than four in ten times, or, .40. The same .40 range has proved to correlate job success with social-style instruments such as the Myers-Briggs Type Indicator (MBTI), most of which are not recommended for use in selection by their developers. The Myers-Briggs instrument focuses on how a person *prefers* to act or be viewed by others. While preferences are important to understanding motivation, they often do not tie to actual performance. The National Research Council notes in *In the Mind's Eye: Enhancing Human Performance* (1991) that a study by McCarley and Carskadon (1983) concluded that only 47 percent of respondents retained their initial types over a period of five weeks. "Changes in the type designations of these magnitudes suggest caution in classifying people in these ways and then making decisions that would influence their careers or personal lives." In other words, the methods of mental measurement previously available have had a low probability of predicting on-the-job performance. (For interviews, the correlation with job success is only .11)

KCI results, on the other hand, have proved in independent university studies and in corporate environments to correlate with success eight times out of ten, with a correlation of .80. That means it is twice as predictive of job success as other instruments and eight times as effective as an interview.

Admissions Exams

Because education is used so often as a prequalification for jobs, it is especially important to consider the basis on which candidates are selected or rejected for educational opportunities. To be admitted to most colleges or universities, students must achieve acceptable scores on college-admission exams. Many firms interview only potential hirees from certain universities, so the test cutoff scores used by particular academic institutions have great importance for future job candidates. A primary source of such tests is the Educational Testing Service (ETS), which developed the Scholastic Aptitude Test or SAT (recently renamed the Scholastic *Assessment* Test), as well as a multitude of other exams for graduate and specialized educational placement.

In order to do well on the SAT, the test taker needs to have had prior educational opportunities, since it assesses knowledge and skill. Not only does this tend to discriminate against minorities, it primarily measures the potential for success in another academic situation, not on jobs. Such instruments, which are a major factor in determining future job opportunities, need to be considered in terms of their ability to predict on-the-job performance. They are heavily dependent on linguistic skill and therefore biased in favor of insistent Fact Finders. They are biased against Implementors and Follow Thrus. So they are inappropriate tools to select or reject people for jobs that are not dependent upon book learning for results. They reward Fact Finders through their emphasis on word definitions, analogies, and reading comprehension, as well as mathematical computations. They don't reward the Implementor talent for constructing manual solutions, since they're strictly paper-and-pencil exams. The SAT, for instance, penalizes guessing and encourages skipping questions. Therefore it can lower scores for an insistent Follow Thru who needs to answer in an orderly way. As a recent Follow Thru initiator said after taking the SAT, "I had to finish one page before I could go on to the next, even though I knew I was being penalized for it."

Weighted Applications and Recommendations

A weighted application often assigns relative values to particular addresses, certain schools, familial traits, or desired levels of income and can be a hidden headwind, limiting equal opportunity for employment. Such weightings may be strongly biased on ethnic, racial, or other cultural criteria. One researcher found, for example, that having an urban Detroit address versus a suburban address distinguished prospective employees who were likely to steal from their employers from those less likely to do so. Such criteria, according to a study in *Personnel Psychology* magazine, discriminate against nonwhite applicants.

Not only are weighted applications potentially discriminatory, they are relatively ineffective as predictors of job success. One of the most often-used is the Aptitude Index Battery (AIB), which is particularly prevalent in selection in the life-insurance industry. Despite the fact that it has been rewritten and rescored a dozen times, it still identifies successful salespeople less than 40 percent of the time, according to *Psychological Bulletin*.

Another hidden headwind is recommendations from other employees or supervisors, who are often used as a source of job applicants. The courts have censured such practices because they tend to perpetuate any existing discrimination, and have found that more open recruiting and selection is necessary to "break the chain of discrimination."

Recommendations from former employers are notoriously unreliable.

We can laugh at obvious double entendres in letters of recommendation such as "I cannot recommend this applicant too highly" or "I cannot calculate the contribution of this employee to our company," but many statements from former employers are impossible to evaluate fairly. Companies that use recommendations for selection do so for the same reason they use educational requirements: They are seen as "better than nothing." In a legal environment that requires the least discriminatory methods, employers would be better off with nothing at all.

Skills Testing

Skills are essential in many jobs and cannot be ignored, even though they may cause an employer to select fewer people from one demographic group than another. Since few minorities and women have gained the skills necessary to qualify as astronauts, most United States astronauts have been white males. NASA can't right the cultural wrong by sending people into space who lack the experience and training necessary for a successful flight.

There is no question that some jobs have skills-related prerequisites. But the entrepreneur who believed his secretary had to type over eighty words per minute turned out to be wrong. It would have been terrific if he could have found a secretary with the right instincts for the job, *and* who typed over eighty, but the level of skill proved to be a desire, not a necessity. Since he's a 9 in Quick Start, he had to stop choosing people with a resistance in the mode. There are minimal requirements for a secretary (Can she type?), substitute requirements (Does she word process?), and training requirements (If she has the right instincts and wants the job, we'll train her on our system). If the candidate can word process on a computer, old standards that may have seemed necessary, such as minimum typing speed and accuracy, may no longer be applicable.

Hiring biases cannot be solved simply by lower minimal-skill requirements. No matter how slow a typing speed you accept, it is often difficult to find any men who will apply for secretarial jobs. Our culture has stereotyped the role as a female career path. When companies advertise for the same skills using titles such as marketing or editorial assistant, men with the needed skills apply. And they generally have more Quick Start than the females who apply for secretarial positions. People with predominately Fact Finder–Follow Thru insistences seek jobs that fit more traditional roles. Those with high accommodation or insistence in Quick Start will venture into situations that are considered more daring.

Many skills can be learned on the job and therefore are mistakenly used as prerequisites. They unnecessarily eliminate conative *A* hires. The secretary finally hired by the entrepreneur had to be trained to use a computer for more than simple word processing. Before long she was doing graphics and some desktop publishing, which added considerably to her value as an employee. Had this level of skill been required of her at the time of selection, she would have been eliminated from the candidate pool, even though she turned out to be the best secretary he has ever had.

THE KCI AS A SELECTION TOOL

THE FAIRSELECTION PROCESS INVOLVES A SEQUENCE OF CAREFULLY MONITORED steps:

- identifying an objective measure of employee success or effectiveness. Companies have to find ways to quantify levels of performance, which is often a major challenge. Reliable measures are difficult to develop, but essential.
- comparing the range in each Action Mode for high performers, low performers, and supervisors' KCI-Cs; then establishing recommended ranges in each mode by specific job title.
- conducting a job analysis to confirm the recommended ranges.
- testing on the Selection KCI all job applicants who meet minimum cognitive prerequisites (skills and experience). Answer sheets can be faxed to central computers, so results can be available within minutes. No demographic information is included, as an additional protection against any perceptions of bias.
- Selection KCI results are given to qualified people within a company in the form of letter grades.
- An applicant whose talents fall within the recommended range in all four modes is an *A*, or Excellent match. A person who is outside the range a small degree in two modes would be a *B*, or Very Good hire. Anyone who falls

below a $C+$ is unlikely to fulfill the requirements of the job
without high levels of stress. The chart that follows is typical of the report generated by the computer for a replicable
job title.

SELECTION KCI SCORING RESULTS
================================

COMPANY:	DATE SCORED: 04/28/93
CONTACT:	I.D. NUMBER: 660000
TELEPHONE:	FAX NUMBER: 17142223513

==

HYPOTHETICAL PROFILE FOR A STUDENT

PROGRAM OF STUDY:1234	MATCH:	APPLICANT CODE:	GROUP:	MO:
RATING: EXCELLENT				
	A	400054		6743
	A	400057		7861
	A	400076		6772
	A-	400035		7572
	A-	400063		8671
	A-	400074		8771
RATING: GOOD				
	B+	400038		7581
	B+	400075		6582
RATING: FAIR				
	B-	400068		9661
	B-	400070		7591
	B-	400079		8623
	C+	400077		9532
	C+	400078		8381
RATING: POOR				
	C	400081		7391
	C-	400073		4294
	D	400072		32102
	F	400061		2297

- The company interviews only those applicants whose talents match the job characteristics. It determines whether
  that cutoff is at a $B+$ or other level.
- Those not interviewed are told that their conative talents
  are equal to all other candidates, but that the role would not
  provide them with opportunities to use their full capacity to
  perform. They can be encouraged to apply for other types of
  positions and can be assured the selection process was
  unbiased and fair to all applicants.

Dr. Clyde Stutts of Macy's explained why the selection process should involve the KCI prior to interviews: "If you know when you interview people that they have the right conative talent, you might think twice before eliminating them because they don't talk like you, look like you, or act like you. Instead of the typical search for negative information in an interview, the person conducting an interview with the benefit of a KCI rating will be looking for 'Why not?' Going into the interview with an objective assessment, knowing that the person has the right talent, forces the interviewer to avoid interjecting anything that might be a personal bias."

APPLICATIONS FOR FAIRSELECTION

AMERICAN EXPRESS IN MEXICO WAS CONCERNED ABOUT THE SELECTION OF customer-service representatives who served on the "front line" when it came to responding to consumer and retailer needs. The clientele is affluent and demanding. Jim Radulski, head of human resources, knew that these employees had to be able to respond flexibly to customer requests, but they could not compromise the company's financial commitments. The goal was to increase productivity, reduce turnover, and satisfy customers. After conducting a validation study and identifying appropriate conative ranges for the jobs to be filled, American Express used the KCI to select new employees. After just a few months, employees selected with use of the KCI proved to have higher productivity than that of other employees with the same job title, and their turnover as compared to that of other employees was down over 20 percent. Radulski said, "Our accuracy in hiring has improved dramatically now that we're identifying the instincts that are drop-dead issues. People we hire have a much higher probability of working out well."

Another company, a national food-processing firm, was concerned about employee absenteeism, which had decreased productivity and increased health-benefits costs. Its managers wanted to know how to select new employees to reduce that costly problem. After determining the conative requirements for jobs at issue, the company found that over 60 percent of those employees in the medium- or high-absenteeism group were suffering from conative tension or strain— *three times* the level of conative stress among those with low absenteeism. The FairSelection System identified employees who were least likely to suffer job-related stress and therefore miss less work.

This factor alone saved the company significant lost revenues and improved job satisfaction.

In a manufacturing group, we found that the people who caused accidents were five times more likely to have a resistance to Follow Thru than those with perfect performance records. In another case, we found data-entry clerks insistent in Quick Start were four times more likely to be in the lowest-rated group of employees than were those resistant in the mode.

The Kolbe FairSelection System is not perfect. It vastly improves on previously available tests and interviewers' abilities to predict performance, but it cannot distinguish between a person who is in conative transition and one who is trying to come out differently on the instrument than is true. About 5 percent of the time a person's results will require an in-depth interview to determine the reason for unusual circumstances. It does not replace consideration of the other factors in the Creative Process. A conatively suited person is a lousy hire if he ends up stealing, sleeping on the job, or making stupid decisions. It's important to use the FairSelection System to predict performance and reduce discrimination, but it's also important to use it as a *part* of an objective hiring program.

CHAPTER NINE

TEAM BUILDING

GETTING THE RIGHT MIX

An organization's greatest competitive advantage lies in building employee teams that have a synergistic mix of Striving Instincts. Teams composed of the right combination of MOs will unleash an energy that goes beyond that of a mere collection of individuals.

Conative diversity provides the multiplier effect that converts the otherwise limited creative energy of independent contributors into vastly magnified productivity. Any one person, no matter how intelligent and committed to an effort, can contribute only through one zone in each Action Mode. No one can do it all. Some methods of problem solving will go untried unless a project is undertaken by a group of people with a variety of MOs. *Synergy* is a productive balance of instincts within a team. It is derived from a mixture of complementary, conative talents.

In 1991 the University of Chicago MBA program placed students in project teams, then assessed the conative makeup of each group. The teams were part of a new-product lab, in which corporations paid the university to have each student team develop marketing plans for a commercial product. According to Associate Dean Dan Tepke, those teams with the greatest variety among participants' KCI results were the most successful. One group, with a preponderance of cloned instinctive approaches, proved the most difficult to manage.

Dr. Christine Johnston of Rowan College of New Jersey conducted a twelve-month field study on the effectiveness of using KCI results to increase a team's performance and improve team members' appreciation of their own and other participants' conative talents. The team's progress was carefully documented on twenty hours of video and in extensive journals kept by team members. As the group first began to work together, Johnston noted, "Even at the first convening . . . when its task was not yet clear, the influence of the conative proclivities of each member appeared. . . ." Later, Johnston said, "The team's awareness of its members' conation assisted it in working interdependently when seeking to develop plans and make decisions." She found she could predict a work group's level of productivity by knowing the mixture of instincts within it. If too many people were similarly inclined in their natural methods of problem solving, the group would get bogged down. But when there was a conative balance among them, team members were able to "plan, analyze, implement, and reflect upon the team's productivity, as well as its ability to work collegially."

One of the cornerstones of conative teamwork is collaboration. The team fails if those on it don't succeed, and they won't succeed unless they can trade off of one another's instinctive abilities. For a team to be effective, the members must recognize the importance of interdependence and understand the nature of one another's instinctive needs and contributions. As participants in the Johnston study wrote in their journals after learning to work on a team with diverse conative talents:

- "Felt a natural high after the . . . session. [When I] viewed the video of the session, I was fascinated with the validation of the conations demonstrated visually and verbally. I thought I was aware of and tried to accommodate each team member's conative and cognitive strengths with the project while meeting my own need for Follow Thru as I facilitated the activity."
- "These training sessions have been very interesting to me because they demonstrate even in a silly problem-solving situation how our conative styles can't hide. This made me aware of my conative 'needs' and those of others."
- "Everyone blended so nicely—each meeting his or her own needs; each participant aware of each other's conation. When finished, I felt very good. This feeling is quite vivid."
- "This exercise showed me that if we consider *all* the factors that each individual needs, a far superior product could be

made. Thinking only in terms of my own conation is not
enough to succeed."
- "The training has given a label to my method of operation
and has helped me understand myself and [my] methods in
a more scientific and organized way. I find myself far more
tolerant of others . . . [and] delegate more effectively and
feel more comfortable with my work. . . . I know more
precisely whom to call on for suggestion and input. . . .
The training provided me with an excellent opportunity to
learn about my team in a rather quick fashion."

Project teams designed with maximum conative synergy have proved
as much as 225 percent more productive by company-established criteria than have strictly skills-based work groups. Textron Corporation
Inc.'s Hank Van Kampen, an organizational-development specialist,
credits the KCI with enabling the company to be much more proactive in
structuring teams. He said, "Before we set up any groups, now we're
using the KCI to take a look at the makeup of that group."

Textron's fuel-systems division has utilized the Kolbe method for
predicting how synergistic, and therefore productive, a team will be if it
is managed in ways that encourage contribution of available talents. In
one example, Van Kampen says a team that was stymied in reaching its
goals was found to have sixty-six percent of its instinctive effort falling
in the accommodation zone. Fifty percent is the ideal distribution; a
team starts losing energy with a five-percent variation from that standard.
So the fuel-systems group put in a person with two resistances and two
insistences. Just one person—as identified by the KCI—changed the
balance of the team and infused sufficient initiation and prevention to
change the dynamics.

According to Van Kampen, "The group is now doing much better in
terms of staying on schedule and making things happen. We've seen a
real change. We can see an increase in the trust between people, especially on teams, and that is allowing us to shorten the lead times
dramatically. It's a real competitive edge."

Building teams without taking into consideration the range of instinctive energy needed for the task—and how well particular people will
work together—is a sure way for any system or strategy to fail. Too often,
companies spend months making presentations and bidding on a project,
then they throw together a group of available people to perform the
service. This hit-or-miss approach never takes into account who is best

equipped to produce the required result. People in the group might be experts, but if the mix of instincts is off, the team won't deliver.

Whenever I compare organizations that have met goals with those that have not, I find that the differences are primarily conative in origin. As Charles Darwin might have put it, the groups that make it in tough economic times survive because they are instinctively the fittest. Groups with the right instinctive balance have the highest probability of overcoming obstacles. As we've seen in earlier chapters, instincts override all other factors that affect productivity. All the management theories in the world won't make an organization effective if it's not made up of instinctively synergistic groups. One major corporation had a team that I predicted would have significant problems if it did not take corrective action. The leader, a senior person in the company, chose to ignore the advice and shut off the discussion among his team members as to changes they were eager to make. Within ten months the leader had been fired and all but one member of the fourteen-person team had left the company either voluntarily or involuntarily.

Ideal synergy involves not only the right mix of instincts to initiate solutions, but the same amount of energy working to avoid problems as well. In every case where I have found a team successful in meeting its goals, the distribution of its members' instinctive energy has been evenly divided (25 percent each) among insistences and resistances. The pull between conative will and won't must also be moderated, as Textron discovered, by 50 percent of energy in the accommodating zone. This natural distribution, or bell-shaped curve, has surfaced in often-replicated findings in corporations, universities, and government groups. Teams deviating from Ideal Synergy by more than 5 percent, plus or minus, have a serious problem. Those off by more than 10 percent have proved unable to produce acceptable results.

A CASE FOR BUILDING TEAM SYNERGY

THE RESEARCH-AND-DEVELOPMENT TEAM FOR A MAJOR ENGINEERING FIRM WAS faced with a serious problem of conative imbalance. Even though all the team members were highly intelligent, the group was extremely unproductive and had been blamed for excessive costs and minimal results.

Its *Synergy Report* revealed the cause of the team's failure was excessive accommodation. This report pinpoints problems by indicating the zone in which a team varies from Ideal Synergy, and the breakdown of these zones by Action Mode. In this case, the report showed that the group lacked the necessary insistence for Ideal Synergy, particularly in the Follow Thru mode. So many people's instincts were at the accommodation level that they worked *against* taking strong stands or definitive actions. And the few people who were instinctively insistent gained reputations as troublemakers, even though the group should have prized their contributions. It was no wonder the competition had been eating away at its market share.

Too much accommodation stymied this group, but too little has a different, though still disastrous, dynamic. When a team doesn't have sufficient energy to mediate the conative power struggle between people's insistent and resistant energy, it can become paralyzed by disputes.

Group synergy also suffers when there is too much energy at the throttle and not enough on the brake. A large marketing firm was like a runaway train driven by people who were insistent in various Action Modes. It was scary. It was going full steam ahead with proposals but was about to jump the track because it couldn't produce promised results.

The only way to avert disaster was to add some resistant weight in the right places to slow down the team. As a consultant to the group, I didn't want to destroy its momentum, but I could see it taking on more projects than it could possibly complete. The team needed to bid only on those marketing projects for which it could guarantee performance. When a group's synergy is askew, as this one's was, you must bring on new members and perhaps let some off. I try to switch people onto separate tracks by creating project teams instead of adding to the larger load that must be attached to the group as it travels down the track. The trick is to load each smaller unit with a synergistic distribution of talents. The collective effect of several project teams will allow the total group to reach its desired destination.

INERTIA, THE CLONING OF CAPABILITIES

PEOPLE ON SELF-SELECTED TEAMS, WHO GET TO CHOOSE THEIR COWORKERS, TEND to select their instinctive clones—people with very similar MOs—unless they understand the implications of the Kolbe Concept. When people's capabilities are redundant in a group, inertia sets in, and the team becomes passive. Even the loftiest goals won't stimulate such a sluggish group.

This inertia becomes apparent when a team with uniform talents tries

Kolbe Management Report
SYNERGY REPORT

For

XYZ COMPANY
R & D TEAM

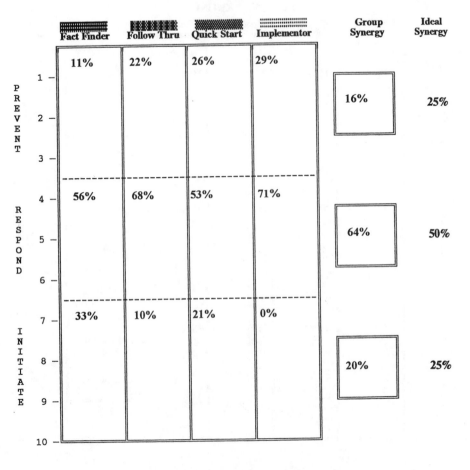

This analysis is based on a total of 43 respondents.

Kolbe Management Report
SYNERGY REPORT

For

QRS COMPANY
MARKETING

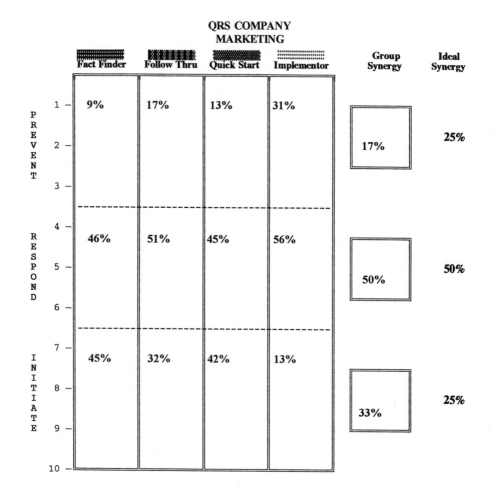

This analysis is based on a total of 139 respondents.

the Glop Shop exercise. For instance, a trio of Quick Start initiators, all also resistant in Follow Thru, work in a helter-skelter fashion, trying to build something without developing a plan. They talk all at once, interjecting one possibility on top of another, without completing any of their attempts. None of them watches the clock, so they are shocked when I tell them they have only one minute left. Since each has been off on a different tangent, the final presentation is disjointed.

A group composed exclusively of Fact Finders resistant in Implementor will agonize over the rules. Their need for defining objectives precisely is so overriding that they spend almost all their time and energy clarifying exactly what to do. They never build anything and are encumbered with materials they won't touch and an assignment they think is irrelevant. Their cloned energy leads them to procrastinate rather than perform. Before time is up, they have given up.

It doesn't matter which MOs are replicated, because cloning strengths on a team will always lead to procrastination and a waste of precious talents. Every participant suffers as the group trudges on. The next time you receive lousy service, look around. Is the place populated with robots going through their paces? Inertia may be the cause. Or does it look like a Keystone Kops comedy, with everyone running around but going nowhere? Same problem, different mode.

MOVING AWAY FROM INERTIA

IN MOST CASES, THE LETHARGY THAT RESULTS FROM INERTIA KEEPS THE TEAMS FROM doing anything about it. Groups of instinctive clones tend to band together to protect their approach to problem solving, even while doing so limits their effectiveness. Whenever I raised the subject of instinctively cloned teams at a consumer-products company I had worked with for a couple of years, its manager became defensive. He would rationalize the need for each participant, protecting the team's makeup and denying any need for change. His defensiveness was put in perspective for me when I realized that, in putting his team together, *he had cloned himself.* Luckily, his CEO recognized the need for improving the group.

We formed smaller subgroups within the larger team and brought in new members who would add missing instinctive elements. We drew these from other employees who were internal customers, staff members who had previously been kept at bay, and external consultants already on retainer. The subgroups didn't become synergistic overnight, but as the victims of cloning began to recognize the benefits of parlaying different methods of striving, a wider variety of methods became acceptable to team members. Also, as team members realized their talents were wasted here—and would be needed and valued elsewhere—transferring within the company was seen in a more positive light and less like a demotion.

ADDING SPARKS WITHOUT IGNITING CONFLICT

ONE DANGER IN ADDING VASTLY DIFFERENT TALENTS TO A TEAM SUFFERING FROM inertia is the possibility of creating conative conflict. This clash of Wills results when people with significant (four or more units) differences in instinctive needs work interactively. It is difficult to meet someone half-way when she is taking a totally different path. Still, as frustrating as such conflicts can be, they are far preferable to inertia. Conflict is the most manageable yet complex form of instinct-related stress. It is a shared problem between two or more people who interfere with each other's progress because of each person's need to act in contrary ways.

Conflicts arise only in situations where there is *interdependence*. When you are first learning the ropes on a job, you may be dependent upon a supervisor and will not try to institute your own ideas for getting work done. However, once you are a fully productive member of the team, you may incorporate some of your own processes into the program—causing conflict. Ideally, by this time you and your supervisor should have reached an understanding, and either you are able to work independently, passing the baton back and forth, or you have found someone to intercede on your behalf, acting as an intermediary.

Virgil Stephens, the chief financial officer of Eastman Chemical, and a 7-8-3-2, talks about "coming to peace" with the instinctive differences between himself and family members, as well as business associates. He and fellow Eastman executive Jack Spurgeon, whose KCI result is 6-5-9-1, conflict in two modes. They've managed to turn the differences into a strength. Jack's Quick Start often drives the organization toward innovation. He heads up the company's information-systems efforts, which means he is responsible for discovering solutions to problems before they happen, and for anticipating the organization's global-communication and data-processing needs well into the future.

Virgil said of Jack's conative bent: "In times when I want something to move, I can go to Jack, knowing it'll be instinctive for him to get it going. I *want* to push, but I know he's the one to actually do it. If at first I get irritated with his approach, I know to let it play out. We never close the door on one another." How well these contrasting talents can work together became clear during an all-day management meeting. Discussions had dragged on until Jack's mind was saturated with seemingly endless reiterations of operational tactics.

Finally, he stood up and politely said he needed to check on some things and would return later. After he left, Virgil explained to the group that Jack needed to remove himself from a situation that wasn't using his talents well. "I knew he understood what was going on," Jack said, "and that he wouldn't take it personally. We play off each other well. It helps that we understand each other conatively, because we can relax and just contribute our energy naturally."

People can work side by side with their conative opposite without it causing frustration, so long as neither person gets involved in the other's way of operating. As soon as they are asked to do a joint proposal, however, both their efforts will be slowed. When there is a conflict of Wills, energies are used counterproductively. Isabel Cobian, the office manager of Genesis, a consulting firm in Madrid, Spain, wanted to be certain her less Follow Thru–inclined coworkers did not disrupt her system of organizing shared reading materials. A translation of the sign she tacked on the library door reads, Prohibited Entry to All Those Who Would Alter the Order of the Library.

The most straightforward solution to conative conflicts is to withdraw from the interplay or keep others out. Discord will be reduced when the people involved work as separately as possible. The supervisor of two coworkers who sat facing each other in a cramped office was mystified that they couldn't cooperate with each other. They had similar training and experience, and were intelligent and outgoing. Their responsibilities were identical, so the boss assumed they would work interactively—until she asked them to take the KCI. She discovered that they had variances of six units in three Action Modes. She then knew why her attempts to get them to exchange efforts had only made matters worse. When the boss stopped asking them to work as a team, they independently became higher performers. Though pairing their two roles synergistically would have accomplished more, this alternative was the best available.

Dr. Richard Deems, of Deems & Associates in Iowa, is an author and outplacement specialist whose own business team had suffered numerous conflicts. "Once we began to understand and appreciate our MOs," he recalled, "the frustrations we had with each other began to dissipate.

We know the differences we have allow us to bring various strengths to the negotiating table. And now we know we need each other as a team. It's what enabled us to triple business in less than two years."

Some people misdirect their talents because they mistakenly fear dependency on the other talents in a synergistic team. A Follow Thru rancher was concerned about becoming dependent upon his Implementor foreman. He spoke of someday having to run the place without the aging outdoorsman in charge of roundup. The rancher set aside his elaborate designs for a new irrigation system and committed his efforts instead to learning the ropes, literally. Mostly he embarrassed himself among the ranch hands, who ridiculed his clumsy attempts. His strain was obvious; and so was the contrast between his strengths and those of his foreman. Within a season he was back at his drawing board, accepting the foreman's talents for as long as they were available—and making plans to train one of the ranch hands to take over the foreman's role when necessary. The rancher had initially thought he could do it all; not only the tasks his instincts suited him for, but those someone else had mastered as well. He eventually realized that the synergy of his team was an advantage, not a weakness or dependency.

BUILDING BRIDGES

SOMETIMES PEOPLE IN CONFLICT IN ONE MODE FIND WAYS OF GETTING ALONG BY connecting through another mode in which they can operate cooperatively. I call this *bridging*, because differences are overcome by turning to a mode with a common Operating Zone. A shared insistence in Implementor can help a couple bridge their Follow Thru conflicts over keeping the house tidy. They escape the ongoing issue by going camping instead. Bridging differences in methodology doesn't make problems go away, but it temporarily makes the situation more tolerable. You'll be foreclosing your creativity's full expression, as well as that of the other person, and eventually you'll have to return home, where the conflict still awaits you.

A more effective bridge can be found in another person or people whose middle ground in a mode acts as a neutralizing force. A bridge person falls between others in a mode and is not in conflict with either. An office manager averted a war of Wills moderating a file-cabinet-filling Follow Thru and a toss-it-if-you-aren't-using-it paper hater. She was accommodating in Follow Thru and came up with a plan that worked for both extremes. In this case, nobody "lost" the battle, and everyone got on with other tasks. Had the office manager been instinctively in line with either side of the process—either insistent or resistant in Follow Thru—the fight would still be raging. Without the mediation that bridge people provide, a fight over record keeping between two people at opposite ends of a mode could be given more attention than clients' needs.

It is important for bridge people to have the same goals as those whose conflicts they are moderating. The role they play is different from the formal judge or arbitrator who makes a cognitive decision as to right and wrong. A conative bridge does not offer opinions, but keeps a process moving. Instead of having all three parties labor over an ongoing dispute, this moderating influence has a multiplier effect on productivity.

Bridge people do not have to act overtly or formally to facilitate the process. They span differences quite naturally, acting as conative go-betweens. It is also not essential for them to be full participants in the existing organization, nor do they have to have skills or political stature equal to those in conflict. Outside executives have served as conative bridges, and secretaries often become the bridges between managers. I frequently recommend creating a spot for a conatively appropriate administrative assistant or deputy director. The increased effectiveness justifies the expense within a few weeks, and sometimes even within a few days.

My conflict with a researcher is a case in point. With resistance in Fact Finder, I keep a team from getting mired in too much detail, but I can also prevent a specialist from moving forward when I don't provide enough specific information. Dr. Robert Keim, of Arizona State University, has been involved in analyzing my case studies. His high insistence in Fact Finder is often confounded by my intense resistance in the mode. We don't have any problems when he analyzes data I provide, but when he needs me to give him the history behind certain figures, or to clarify the source of particular research, a conflict arises. My overview isn't enough for him, and his degree of specification is too much for me.

To form a bridge, Bob and I bring in others who give him the fact checking he needs and don't hassle me for anything but final sign-offs on the accuracy of their assessments. Every time we're together, he tries to sneak in two or three complex questions, and, using my insistence in Quick Start, I take it on as a challenge to tell him more than even he wants to know.

POLARIZED FORCES

POLARIZATION IN AN ORGANIZATION IS LIKE CONFLICT BETWEEN INDIVIDUALS. IT occurs when people in a group are strongly insistent and resistant in a mode, without enough accommodation to balance them. Productivity is blocked when energy gets sidetracked in internal tugs-of-war. The wills and won'ts get so tangled up that management often resorts to feel-good seminars to try to get everyone working together. But sessions that make polarized groups feel better about each other don't have lasting benefits because the cause of the problem isn't resolved. Attitude adjustment is not the solution when a group is divided down the middle by conative needs. The solution can be found in project teams that bring in people who bridge differences in each Action Mode.

One financial-services firm dealt with a polarization of instincts by breaking down into functional teams of sales- and service-minded people. It gave an insistent Follow Thru in sales the responsibility of organizing its database. The general agent who had been trying to manage the team was too resistant in Fact Finder to be setting everyone's priorities. He went back to doing what his insistence in Quick Start had always made him best at: selling. The company went on to hold the national record for greatest increased sales three years in a row.

In another case, the head of a large financial institution exacerbated the polarization within his management team by declaring that his successor would be the one among them to win a contest for which there were no rules. He wanted them to kill one another off. Such an approach fosters conflicts rather than bridging them: Alliances form along instinct-based lines, creating divisions. Sure enough, by-the-book insistent Fact Finders lined up against resistant Fact Finders anxious to avoid getting stymied by traditional methods. And those who were insistent in Quick Start sought one another out after hours and formed a splinter group that promoted one of its members as the best choice. These natural "reformers" sought control so that their innovations would be possible, yet none of them had the instinctive talents to regulate the day-to-day operations. A Tammany Hall–era politician, George Washington Plunkett, was right when he said "reformers are like morning glories." In this case, they didn't have their day in the sun; within two years the board of directors had fired the Quick Start reformer president and all the executives who had reported to him.

Hierarchical structures tend to cause polarization. As discussed in Chapter Seven, the striving mechanisms necessary to thrive in entry-level roles are different from those you use as you go up the corporate ladder. For example, a professional-services firm bases early promotions on the ability to effectively process a great deal of information. In other words, it rewards people who are insistent in Follow Thru and Fact Finder. At the next level, emphasis is placed on research and written analyses, where Fact Finders thrive. Follow Thru talent is needed less as one moves up in the company, and success is defined by the amount of Fact Finder talent you have to contribute.

Then something startling happens: Partnerships are offered only to those gung-ho salespeople who bring in a steady flow of new business and who tend to be long on Quick Start talents. Suddenly an insistence in Quick Start is a prerequisite for advancement in this firm. (In just as many other cases, the traits required at the top are Fact Finder or Follow Thru, and all the Quick Starts go down in flames.) When this occurs, polarization can take hold, with a clash of insistences and resistances running from the top to the bottom of organizations.

One solution to the problems of polarization by career ladder are dual career paths. An individual should be offered a choice of routes up the ladder so that no single conative trait is a prerequisite for advancement. If I can talk companies into even considering dual career paths, I think of it as a victory. For example, when you consider the instinctive talents needed to supervise a construction site, it doesn't really make sense that in order to get that job a person has to prove himself as a superior carpenter. Computer programming isn't the only appropriate road to becoming an information-systems manager. The overall project suffers when instinctive differences are not treated as constructive alternatives.

TEARING DOWN CONATIVE WALLS

FOR ANY SYSTEM TO THRIVE, POLARIZATION MUST BE ELIMINATED. THE KEY TO doing this lies in tearing down conative walls dividing the polarized levels, areas of expertise, union and management.

The restructuring can lead to very interesting changes, both functional and even physical. The layout of a workplace can change dramatically. Conative clones no longer end up in insulated clusters: the Follow Thrus in their cubicles, the Quick Starts with their projects piling up in the middle of the room, the Fact Finders near the on-line databases, and the Implementors out of the office getting fresh air. Instead, synergistic teams are gathered into interactive settings. Energy pulsates throughout the environment as people exchange methods and are mentally stimulated by being a part of a dynamic process.

It's possible to diagnose polarization by having team members do the Glop Shop exercise. When a family-owned company was undergoing the exercise, it was evident that its Fact Finder owners were polarized with the Follow Thru–Implementor workers. Their options were simple. They could continue turning their energy inward, vying with one another, or they could become a team. If they chose to work toward becoming a team, they would have to reorganize into project groups, which meant throwing the owners together with employees, college grads with tradespeople. They'd have to put a halt to culturally based suspicions, even the deeply held dislikes. They had to want to make it work.

The answer came within three days. A foreman in their manufacturing unit called to tell me the owner's son, an insistent Follow Thru, had arrived in the disheveled plant loaded down with organizing materials. "I wouldn't have believed it if I had not seen it with my own eyes," the foreman said. "This usually pompous kid rolled up his sleeves and spent the day straightening out the place, without lecturing me or anything. He just sat there and decided what needed to be kept and what didn't. I'll tell you, it was a blessing to have it done. And a real shocker that he was willing to do it." This company risked tearing down the walls, and when it did, it uncovered a perfect, long-overdue task for an insistent Follow Thru who wouldn't normally contribute talent within the plant.

Sydney Johnson, director of human resources for Oberto Sausage Company in Seattle, said, "The nice thing about building a team this way is that it's positive information. You can tell people why you need them in particular positions."

MAINTAINING TEAM ENERGY

No management goal is more fundamental than finding ways of encouraging workers to contribute their instinctive talents. Bottled-up energy doesn't produce results, and workers struggling to cope with out-of-kilter assignments are unable to help one another. In situations like this, the team becomes fragmented, and its members have to fend for themselves. The negative effect this has on the group's problem-solving potential very often leads to missed business opportunities.

The probability of team fatigue causing collective strain is gauged by a *Depletion Rate*, which is determined by the percentage of participants suffering from false self-expectations in any one mode. It's derived by comparing the KCI-A to the B version. It shows the rate at which energy is lost through misapplication or dissipation of talent.

Imagine a Depletion Rate of 20 percent on a baseball team. Assuming there's a designated hitter, the ten-member group has two players acting out of sync with their natural talents. They aren't trusting their instincts for when to take a pitch or to sense where the ball will bounce off the grass. They are out of their usual rhythm, a step off their natural pace. You can see that something is wrong. They don't get their customary hits and they make errors. It's obviously not any one individual's problem; everyone on a team is affected when a member is suffering strain.

If steps aren't taken to reduce high levels of depletion (30 percent maximum), you can bet the team will limp along with more and more players failing to fulfill their potential. Shooting for 0 percent is always the goal; around 10 percent to 15 percent is realistic. That may be because management is trying to get people to adjust to methodologies instead of adjusting operations to meet needs of employees. The continual restructuring that seems to be a preoccupation of many American corporations is usually an attempt to make people conform to organization charts, rather than building on the instinctive strengths of those involved. The resultant strain is contagious. Once a couple of players drop the ball, it hurts everyone's game. You will have to work even harder to compensate for others' lack of productivity and to pick up the slowed pace.

Picking up a group's pace must start with identifying joint purposes and allocating conative energy in a way that will move the group toward those goals. Any group of people working cooperatively to reach common goals forms a conative system. It can be a project team, family, company, or group of friends. Setting goals together provides the direction that keeps you functioning cooperatively.

Let's say you and some cohorts decided to go out together for the evening. Making plans to do something together involved several of you committing energy. Imagine if someone insistent in Quick Start and resistant in Follow Thru was asked to arrange for tickets to an event but waited until the last minute when the concert was sold out. You suggest stopping by some other places instead, but a couple of plan-ahead Follow Thrus get upset because they had counted on going to the concert. Rather than risk an evening of winging it, their resistance to Quick Start makes them decide to forget the whole thing. The group disintegrates into an aimless, incohesive bunch, regrouping into twosomes and

Kolbe Management Report of Organizational Strain

HIGH TECH COMPANY

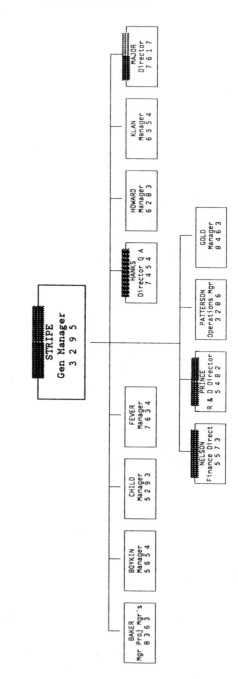

Kolbe Management Report
for
High Tech Company
5/6/93

DEPLETION RATE

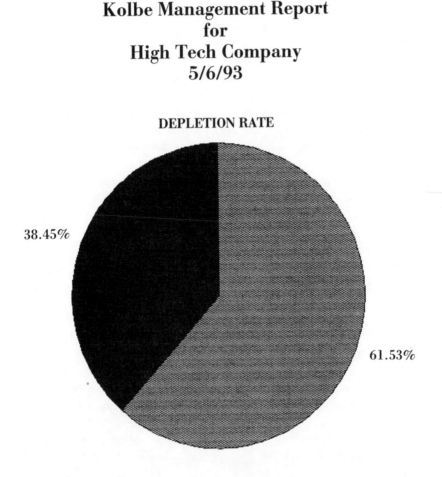

38.45%

61.53%

Plot includes 13 individuals who have completed B-KCI's, from a total of 13.

threesomes and drifting off in different directions. This is the result of unresolved tension limiting individuals from giving the group their best. In this case, some vague goals were set for the group, but individuals' conative strengths were put to all the wrong uses. What's the point of putting a resistant Follow Thru in charge of planning ahead?

If you could rewind the events leading up to the evening, a simple reallocation of energy would have solved the problem. The goal would remain the same—to attend a concert with friends—but it would be more attainable if the organized Follow Thrus ordered the tickets, and the Quick Start people agreed to surprise everyone with postconcert activities. The same energy that caused the group to self-destruct would have then been used to have a good time.

MELTDOWN: THE ULTIMATE CONATIVE DISASTER

MELTDOWN OCCURS WHEN TOO MANY PARTICIPANTS—AT LEAST 15 PERCENT—ARE experiencing tension from being asked to deny their instinctive methods of operation. It results in high levels of frustration and a natural tendency toward self-protection. Team members often lash out when they perceive a threat to their productivity, and a chain reaction occurs. For instance, if a person resists doing requested advance planning, this affects his coworker, who may then refuse to review last-minute documentation. Creative energy becomes a destructive force as people change their goals from a common commitment to their individual survival.

Meltdown can result from misguided peer pressure, bosses' requirements, or subordinates' needs. If coworkers take someone out of his instinctive game, *they* also suffer the consequences, usually without realizing it. Telling a resistant Quick Start, "Come on, just take a chance; what've you got to lose?" is counterproductive. The person will probably lose confidence and withdraw even her usual level of contribution. And the team will then suffer a setback in achieving its goals. Badgering a worker to withhold talent is also fruitless. Imagine telling a detail-driven Fact Finder, "If you keep trying to prove the point beyond a doubt, we'll never meet our deadline." The Fact Finder will be hurt and angry that her valuable talents are being dismissed, and will most likely withhold the data she's so good at generating the next time it's needed.

Jockeying for control over how goals are being reached can halt productivity. In one case, a group of senior managers in a high-tech company brought their decision making to a standstill while each tried to get his way adopted for a project. The result was a 40 percent Meltdown rate, which resulted in decreased productivity.

Meltdown situations also lead to high rates of turnover and absenteeism. Stress-related illnesses have doubled in nine recent years, according to research conducted by Northwestern National Life Insurance Company. In three separate studies, instinctive strain and tension forecasted a doubling of turnover. The studies were conducted with corporations that had analyzed instincts, self-expectations, and requirements. In each situation the KCI-A and KCI-B results were given to employees

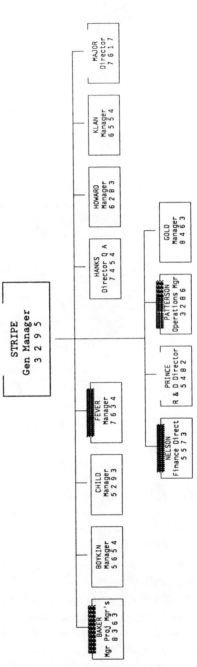

Kolbe Management Report of Organizational Tension
Copyright® All Rights Reserved by Kathy Kolbe, 1991

HIGH TECH COMPANY

Kolbe Management Report
for
High Tech Company
5/6/93

MELTDOWN RATE

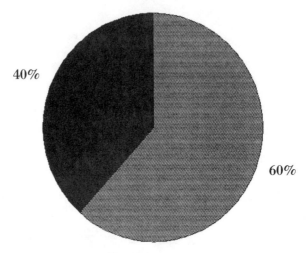

40%

60%

**Plot includes 10 individuals for whom a C-KCI was
completed, from a total of 13.**

but not placed in their personnel files. While senior management had the collective data relating to Depletion and Meltdown, the studies were done prior to most supervisors using the information. In all three companies, which were just beginning to study the benefits of using this approach, turnover within one year was at least 50 percent higher for employees suffering strain or tension than it was for other employees.

Given a choice, people don't stay in situations where they are asked to work against their instincts. They may like the people they work with and the company itself; they may even have the expertise to do the job. But given any choices they will not stay in roles that continually make them look bad and feel ill. They know they won't become front-runners unless they have the option of utilizing their Striving Instincts.

In a corporate setting, Meltdown can be catastrophic. If leadership tries to push a group best suited to consistency and efficiency toward diversification, the demands for change will be overwhelming. A group of quality-oriented Implementors will be satisfied by a low return rate on manufactured goods, but it will be impossible for them to follow a supervisor's orders to produce the goods at a faster pace.

The problems of a conatively dysfunctional group may very likely lead to affective problems such as personality clashes. By definition it is a system gone amuck. Members of this sort of system don't support one another's free will and don't function in conatively appropriate roles. Don Lawhorne, president of the Texas Minority Enterprise Small Business Investment Council, uses the Kolbe Concept to identify strengths in management teams of minority-owned businesses. He observed that when such a system is removed: "You have an understanding of the different conative dynamics needed for different functions in a company. The Kolbe process allows you not only to put the right person in the right slot, it helps teammates understand why one is more prone to risk, while another resists risk. Management has to understand and use the information so requirements don't set up impossible situations."

CAUSES AND EFFECTS OF DEPLETION

DEPLETION IS PAIN THAT MEMBERS OF A GROUP SUBJECT THEMSELVES TO BY EXpecting the wrong sort of performance from themselves. Muddled self-perceptions and counterproductive personal motivations cause resistant Quick Starts to expect spontaneous behavior from themselves. Or insistent Fact Finders may expect themselves to skip over preliminary detail work in order to save time. Some people overinstigate or try initiating action using modes of insistence they simply don't have. Instead of using their full range of talent, overinstigators expect themselves to initiate through every Action Mode.

Eliminating misplaced praise for this sort of counterproductive initiation will help remove such posturing and reenergize performance based on Striving Instincts. Those who have tried to initiate in every mode can refocus on the benefits of contributing their true talents to team effort. Depletion Rates caused by overinstigating can be reduced by providing incentives for group achievements rather than individual contributions.

Another problem stems from participants behaving as if the only contribution they can make is preventing problems. They may think the group needs more resistance than is natural because:

- They have been praised for saving the group from disaster, or view that as their role. ("If you hadn't stopped us, we might have sent out that press release with the chairman's name spelled wrong.")
- They work in an environment where their natural inclination in a particular process is considered uncooperative. ("The standards have already been established. Don't reinvent the wheel.")
- Others on the team are so dominant in a mode or modes that they encourage offsetting resistance. ("We have enough people worrying about the probabilities of error. We need you to tell us when to stop weighing the pros and cons and get on with it.")
- The contrast between them and more highly insistent contributors gives a mistaken impression that they are avoiding actions they actually accommodate. ("Everyone else around here offers to experiment with the new technology. How come you wait until it's on-line before you use it?")

A third source of depleted energy grows out of people not only withholding their instinctive contributions but allowing their artificial preventions to block others' efforts. Insistent Quick Starts who won't reveal their seemingly off-the-wall solutions also refuse to go along with others who they say are "too impulsive." Follow Thrus who disown their neatnik traits also refuse to support others who conform to established standards. A solution to this problem is to use the KCI-B to identify and reduce the stagnating influence of such withholding behavior. The contrast between actual conative strengths and job expectations pinpoints the modes in which someone is withdrawing. Becoming aware of the misalignment is the single most effective way to reduce the problem. Giving credit for initiation is vital, even when efforts don't lead to fruition.

Peter Nichols, World Bank's chief of human resources for Europe, Central Asia, Middle East, and North Africa, helped a team of people redefine their roles to better suit their conative needs. "They had to mix themselves up," as he put it, "and the turnaround was dramatic. It saved one person his job, and the staff was a lot happier."

Another way people restrain their natural talents is by denying their strong insistences so they are more like everyone else. They do this because they've been made to feel guilty about their own inclinations and therefore retreat into other, less committal behaviors. For instance, someone extremely insistent in Quick Start tried to keep his fifth business start-up from becoming yet another flash-in-the-pan venture. He got off to the right start by bringing on board a dynamic group of people with a mix of instincts. He was on his way to attaining team synergy, but before that happened he began to rein in the very instinctive urges his organization needed in order to succeed. "We know how to handle his loose-cannon routine," one coworker confided. "But he won't give us a chance. He's lost confidence in his ability to make it work."

When someone is denying his natural instincts, humor is often an antidote. Another is found in bridge people who can act as conative interpreters and help facilitate the productive use of his efforts. It's important to reinforce the benefits of exceptional insistence in a mode. Do so without stereotyping people as instinctively one-dimensional. While they have an obvious trump suit, it is not the only card they have to play.

DOING IT RIGHT

A GOOD MANAGER WILL KEEP GOAL SETTING SEPARATE FROM THE PROCESSES TO achieve goals. Honeywell President Ed Hurd summarized management's role in avoiding Meltdown: "I trust the people I have; so they can contribute to the fullest extent." Eastman Kodak's Kathy Hudson manages people with a conscious effort to avoid misdirecting conative energy. "I'm going to be my best when my team members are at their best," she reflected. "I don't need control over them. I need to give them the power to be their best. An important thing about working with teams is recognizing there's no single way of getting there. You can easily approach a problem from one hundred and one directions." Besides, she added, having more than one method makes the work more fun and interesting. "Who wants to work in an environment where you are told exactly what to do?"

We all need to express ourselves through the energy of our Striving Instincts. True democracies thrive when everyone's abilities are nurtured, and the same is true for organizations and businesses. Whether it's citizens expressing their choices at the ballot box, customers making their preferences known through purchases, or employees giving their instinctive efforts, each act is one of self-determination. It reflects the individual's power to decide from whom, from what, and where he will derive the greatest assistance in achieving his destiny.

CHAPTER TEN

TRAINING

THE ART OF CULTIVATING SUCCESS

T raining requires applying everything we know about Striving Instincts in order to maximize workers' productive use of them. It is as important to an organization's success as is hiring the right people, placing them in appropriate jobs, and putting them on synergistic teams. For training to be effective it has to be integrated into a company's commitment to building on the instinctive strengths of each employee. Results-oriented training incorporates as many different problem-solving processes as possible rather than attempting to instill a particular process. Too often, however, training focuses on one "right way" of accomplishing a task. In such cases it does not take the diversity of instinctive needs into account and helps only those who naturally use the one accepted method.

For instance, resistant Follow Thrus frequently tell me they have attended time-management seminars because they, or a boss, wanted them to become more efficient. Such programs usually train people on a system that includes a daily planner, goal-setting sheets, and other time-tracking tools. The resistant Follow Thrus may show commitment by attending the seminar and will probably understand the process. But usually their actions change only briefly.

The use of time is ingrained; it's instinctive. Therefore, as with other processes, training people to change is a waste of time. Those time-management programs that recognize this and at least accommodate the needs of resistant Follow Thrus—and every other mode—will have the highest success rate.

An educator transfers knowledge. A trainer enables people to apply knowledge in specific situations. Much of education is passive (though it ought not to be), with information conveyed either through books or lectures. Training cannot afford to be so inactive. Numerous studies indicate people retain information significantly longer if they have been actively involved in the learning process. Therefore training needs to engage the instinctive energy of participants, as well as gain their committed effort.

WHAT TRAINING CAN AND CANNOT ACCOMPLISH

TRAINING PROGRAMS NEED TO SET CLEAR OBJECTIVES FOR EACH PARTICIPANT. BUT they also have to define their own mission. What they can and cannot be expected to accomplish is fundamental to evaluating their success.

- Training programs can assist people in putting their knowledge to work.
- They cannot be burdened with educating employees. If a person does not have basic knowledge, such as a reading level necessary for a job, he needs further education and may not be ready for job training.
- They can establish performance criteria and help each participant achieve at measurable levels of accomplishment.
- They cannot have vague purposes or unmeasurable standards of performance for accomplishing the skills they are demonstrating.
- They can model acceptable methods of performing tasks.
- They cannot demand conformity to a method of operation that is unsuited to participants.
- They can help participants understand their own instinctive needs and the different needs of people with whom they will interact.
- They cannot take leadership responsibility for influencing

work-group cooperation, establishment of goals, or assignment of roles.

- They can help participants find alternate paths for accomplishing tasks.
- They cannot absolve participants of responsibility.
- They can increase participants' self-confidence in trusting
their instincts and can encourage commitment to tasks.
- They cannot change the way participants naturally perform
or make them productive in jobs for which they are conatively unsuited.

Successful trainers trust their own instincts, so, while they have to
cover the same material as anyone conducting a similar program, they
give themselves the same latitude to use their natural talents as they do
their participants. Training programs do not have to follow a canned
format; they *do* have to maximize the productivity of each and every
participant—and of trainers.

CAN HABITS BE TRAINED?

PEOPLE CAN BE TRAINED TO USE HABITS ONLY IF THOSE HABITS CONFORM TO THEIR
natural way of performing. Even if an organization could train all its
employees to adopt "good" Follow Thru time-management habits, productivity would not increase for everyone. Only those who already had
the inclinations for scheduling and planning would benefit. Those resistant in Follow Thru would rob energy from productive efforts to either try
to "do it right" or to avoid following the system. Habits are beneficial
when they improve use of existing talents. When training tries to impose
actions that bypass instinct, it won't take. And it will interfere with a
trainee's ability to live up to a commitment.

When people act on habit rather than instinct, they go on automatic
pilot and ignore natural signals. This is similar to what happens when a
person with chronic pain learns to dull the message of physical discom-
fort that is sent to the brain. Habitual masking of pain can create
problems when it interferes with other signals the body sends the mind.
It can cause a person to react too slowly to heat or other danger. Similarly, habits can mask needs and override natural abilities with artificial
routines. This drowning out of instinct can lull people into conforming to
unsuited behaviors.

Numbing even one of the Striving Instincts interferes with the entire Creative Process. Brenda is an insistent Implementor who has been trained to work on an assembly line. "I have to ignore my instinct to do it better," she explained. She had to disengage the innate energy that would naturally handcraft each item. "I do it the way I've been trained," Brenda added, "but that's *all* I do." Since she can't contribute her natural talent, she's not motivated to do more than the minimum that is required. "And you can bet," she said, "I'll be out of here the moment I find something that pays even close to what I'm getting now." Her only commitment is to getting a paycheck. Brenda was a good student in high school and excelled in a technical program she took after graduation. But at work, her supervisor complains that she makes "stupid errors." Of course she does. Since she disengaged her instinct, her mind has not been on the job.

HOW INSTINCT-BASED TRAINING IMPROVES PERFORMANCE

INSTINCT IS THE MISSING LINK THAT JOINS KNOWLEDGE OR UNDERSTANDING OF information with the motivation to use it. It adds the energy force that leads to action. Without it, training can bring participants to the brink of success—they can be fully informed and ready to go—but they won't *do* what needs to be done. By showing people ways they can perform a task most effectively, the knowledge and desire are put to productive use. People can accomplish what they set out to achieve. This entails helping trainees understand their own instinctive character and when and how to use it for specific tasks.

Let's say you are training a group of data-entry people on how to improve their speed and reduce errors. First, training objectives must be clearly stated and well understood. How will speed be measured, and what rate is standard? How many errors are acceptable? What's typical? Quick Start trainees in particular will want to know the fastest rate anyone has achieved, and they ought to be cautioned that speed without accuracy is not desirable. Ambiguity in establishing goals makes it impossible to evaluate results or to target instinctive energy appropriately.

Then trainees need to know their KCI results, as does the trainer. Every trainer and teacher knows some classes just seem to click. Those are the ones with a balance of MOs, or conative synergy. If an entire training class is conatively cloned, a trainer will have to bring in speakers or outside experts to add diversity; anything to break up the inertia. On the plus side, there would be fewer methods to model, other than to increase sensitivity to the possibility that their coworkers will not always conform to their methods.

With KCI results interpreted for the group, the trainer is ready to focus on tasks involved in entering data accurately and quickly. Rather than trying to demonstrate every possible conative approach to achieving this goal, it's important that the trainer provide examples of what works for some people and then encourage trainees to explore their own best approach. In some cases, there are ways that will not work. Bum Soo Baek of Asiana Airlines has analyzed the nature of airline-pilot trainees and found an insistence in Quick Start "has to be overcome." Since people don't change, the training program has to guide students away from the use of risk taking when in the cockpit. Conative energy can be targeted toward specific tasks, so a pilot could find other outlets for Quick Start, bypassing that form of talent on the job. However, the danger can be great if training has not pinpointed the problem and helped the pilot trainee deal constructively with the issue. In most cases, training a person to withhold talent is so time consuming and frustrating for everyone involved that it is more logical to counsel people to seek other career opportunities.

Rod Strand is a human-resources specialist and trainer for the United States Department of Energy's Bonneville Power Administration. He says that one of the most important goals of training in that predominately engineering-based culture is improved communication. He and another trainer, Ellie Montgomery, use the KCIs A, B, and C at retreats with teams from various Bonneville branches. "We take them through a series of steps," Rod said, "to help them discover ways to understand and communicate their similarities and differences." The first step is to communicate the MOs of team members. "Then we ask them to discuss their favorite and worst jobs," he said, "which inevitably tie back to roles that allowed them to use insistences and resistances. Then we ask them to describe their ideal work environment and the kinds of things that help and hinder their efforts. After this type of communication with each other they go back to work with extremely different ways of looking at their own and others' contributions. It's a much richer level of understanding."

Even though Bonneville is facing belt-tightening budgets, Rod said the Kolbe training "is not a luxury. It has roots in the organization because people have more than intellectualized the information. Ninety-five percent of the people find it an 'awesome' experience and want to keep it as a communication tool." In fact, Rod says, many employees have requested that management post requirements for a new job listing by including the KCI-C results. "Once people are trained on this system, they find it a helpful shorthand for explaining what's needed and what's going on."

WHO SHOULD TRAIN

THE TRAINER, ABOVE ALL, IS AN ENABLER. SO WHEN TRAINING, IT IS IMPORTANT to step back and let the trainee use different methods to solve a problem. It would be ideal if training were done in teams, with people of differing conative abilities showcasing how a job could be accomplished through their strengths. However, a complete conative mix is rarely possible. Nancy Hall, an expert trainer with the North Carolina Department of Human Resources, has conducted a study on the use of conation in training for social-services workers. By administering the KCI to twelve training teams, she says she learned which training partner was more:

apt to leave the prepared script

likely to follow procedures and stay focused

prone to use charts and diagrams

willing to set up the audiovisual equipment

likely to get bogged down answering questions

in need of detailed orientation and background information

"This type of information is priceless," she observed. "It allows team members to understand and use each other's talents without wondering what they can expect." Nancy found knowing trainers' MOs helped her predict the relationship between them and particular groups of trainees. It also pinpointed the types of curriculum that would be most appropriate for each trainer. One of the myths in training, she said, is that a good trainer can train on anything. Imagine a resistant Implementor having to show trainees how to repair complex machinery!

Another area of the research project was the relationship among trainers who have to work cooperatively. Do conative differences enhance or detract from their efforts? To assess training teams' interactions, the trainers were given their KCI results, along with suggestions on how they could work together. Training tasks for a risk-assessment curriculum were then analyzed and separated by the Action Modes necessary for accomplishment. Then training teams were encouraged to use information on their KCI results to decide on a division of labor.

Among the early results of this ongoing study, Nancy found "response [from trainers] has been positive." For example:

- from a Quick Start who trains with another Quick Start—insistent person: "This sure explains why when we train together we are always competing and changing things in the middle of the training."
- from an insistent Follow Thru: "Until I took the KCI, I just thought I was obsessive-compulsive."
- from a resistant Follow Thru: "Sure explains why I was so miserable in [a previous training program that was a] structured job."

The purpose of the North Carolina project is to enhance the effectiveness of training through the trainers' understanding of what they bring to the process. The information is also intended to help form training teams, fit trainers with specific curriculums, and make trainers aware of the instinctive needs of those they are training. Nancy said, "Training is not just putting on courses, it is preventing and solving problems." That takes a full understanding of conative talents.

WHEN INSTINCT NEEDS TO ENTER THE TRAINING PROCESS

TOO OFTEN THE KCI IS GIVEN TO TRAINEES AFTER THEY ARE ALREADY IN A TRAINING program. Only then is it apparent the program is wrong for them. This happens in corporate-sponsored programs, as well as job-training programs for the unemployed. Once an insistent Quick Start is enrolled in pilot training, it is costly both emotionally and financially to remove her from the program. Just as the KCI is used to select people prior to an employment interview, it is important to consider KCI results *before* a person enters a training program. Because every person receives an extensive written report regarding his individual talents, the information can be helpful in making a decision concerning possible training opportunities. When training is required for a job, the selection process itself helps match applicants with the type of program that focuses on the tasks that will be performed.

By identifying the ranges in each Action Mode of trainees who have and haven't benefited from particular training, it is possible to determine the conative nature of those best suited for the courses. This process also provides important information for trainers, who can adjust the methods they use for the needs of trainees who do not fit the norm. Private national job-training programs use the Kolbe process to analyze the conative nature of high-performing students by individual course, so they can better recommend suitable programs to trainees. This also helps them reduce the dropout rate among trainees, which has been an especially costly factor for taxpayers who foot the bill for many job-training programs.

Trainers benefit when participants' KCI results are available before classes begin. Knowing the conative makeup of the group allows them to plan their curriculum accordingly. Bill, who trains first-line supervisors for an environmental-products company, faced a difficult decision when he discovered that in one training class he would be the only person not insistent in Follow Thru or Implementor. "My first reaction," he said, "was to bail out." But then he realized how much the group could teach him. "It was one of the most effective training classes I ever ran, because I wasn't the know-it-all. I showed the group upfront a chart of their KCI results compared to mine. After everyone stopped laughing, we went to work figuring out how they were going to show *me* how they need to do their job. It was a wonderful adventure for all of us. I set the agenda for what had to be accomplished, and they demonstrated systems for making it happen."

WHERE SHOULD INSTINCT-BASED
TRAINING TAKE PLACE?

CLASSROOMS ARE STRANGE PLACES TO CONDUCT TRAINING PROGRAMS OF ANY KIND— except, perhaps, teacher training. They take people out of the workplace, without improving much, if any, on the environment. My first choice for training is the work site. I'd rather train office managers while sitting in the corner of a busy office where we can observe the setting and discuss it in realistic terms. Of course, that's often disruptive to others.

So training gets removed to an off-site location, or a portable trailer at the back of the building, or the lunch room during off-hours. If it can't be close to the action, I prefer it be as far away as possible. Especially among Quick Starts, training near their workplace is an open invitation for frequent interruptions. It's best to take them to an undisclosed place with no telephones.

The training site has to be equipped with everything necessary to demonstrate the skills being trained. That may seem obvious, but years ago I went to a training program entitled "Computers for the Computer-Illiterate Executive." There was not a computer in the room! We were educated in the uses of a computer, but there was no way we were going to be trained on how to use one. People who I assume were insistent Follow Thrus kept asking for pictures to help them understand the coursework. Insistent Implementors would have just walked out, as a few people did.

The physical setting in which training takes place is of special importance to those insistent or accommodating in Implementor. The higher the range in the mode within a group, the more windows you need in the room. Don't cram them into tight spaces or try to contain their energy behind closed doors. Two corporate human-resources executives, Peter Nichols of World Bank, and Honeywell's Paul Brinkmann, have been through several training programs on the Kolbe Concept, enduring long days despite their mutual insistences in both Implementor and Quick Start. How did they survive? By everyone in the room understanding their frequent need to get up and walk around. By sitting near a door and being able to look out a window. And by having activities that allowed them to tinker with materials while they were being trained. Of course their Quick Start needs required opportunities to take off on tangents and switch topics often.

Since training is most effective when it is interactive, *participant* is a more appropriate term for trainees than *student*. In order to participate, the room needs to be arranged so that trainees have space to move about and can have eye contact with one another. A sure way to lower the probability of success is to arrange participants in rows, one behind the other. Then, even if the group has Ideal Synergy, trainees tend to act as independent learners. Instinctive energy is withheld for lack of opportunity to be truly participatory.

HOW TO HANDLE CONFLICTING NEEDS

WHAT DO YOU DO WHEN ONE PERSON'S CONATIVE NEEDS CONFLICT WITH ANOTHER'S in the class? What about the person who is distracted by Peter and Paul wandering around the room? First, the needs tied to each Striving Instinct can be explained. Then the trainees can share their MOs. With the understanding that everyone has equal but differing needs, the participants become more empathetic with one another's idiosyncracies. Peter, for instance, may become frustrated when someone like Al Giles (KCI result, 7-6-7-2), the retired head of human resources for The Bank of Nova Scotia, asks copious questions. Al will find forward-looking ways to incorporate facts into his efforts, but not until he's thoroughly digested the historical underpinnings of a program.

You have to answer Al's questions, but not all at once, and not everyone has to listen. Part of any training program is the underlying responsibility to help people figure out how to work with one another. A lot of it has to do with consideration. So, making Al aware that Peter's getting antsy, and Peter conscious that Al's disoriented until he's grounded in data, is a significant part of any training exercise. It's not good enough to tell people what will happen if they block another's innate path. There has to be time and opportunity for trainees to discover both the truth and power behind instinctive energy.

SCHEDULING TIME FOR MAKING MISTAKES

TRIAL-AND-ERROR APPROACHES WORK WONDERFULLY WITH QUICK START—INSISTENT folk. They'll jump right in the minute you tell them a problem is impossible to solve. So Ben, a 9 in the mode, made sure he had lots of opportunities for people in his training classes to experiment on their own. He'd make up fascinating challenges that defied anyone to solve them using traditional methods. That was great, so long as he was training a bunch of fellow Quick Starts. The problem was that he trained bank-loan officers on risk-assessment procedures. Few of them shared his proclivity for seeking unusual solutions. Nor would financial institutions turn to him for training if the results were that loan officers tried to take uncalled-for risks. So he modified his program. He scheduled time for people to take calculated risks, using their Fact Finder strategies and Follow Thru charts. Then he helped them discover the mistakes they'd made. The resistant Quick Starts learned they couldn't cut corners without causing costly errors. One woman who went through this self-discovery process exclaimed, "I've always wanted to see what would happen if I just cut loose and went with a loan proposal that didn't really add up on the numbers side. Now I know. I'd better stick with what works for me. I blew it and would have lost my boss's trust forever. But it was fun to see how it feels to just wing it."

Resistant Follow Thrus are the most difficult to train. They won't stay with the plan. They lose focus and often take the group with them. They interrupt. Imagine what their parents heard in grade-school teachers' conferences! These are the people who get a bad rap in the deportment department. They're criticized by teachers and trainers for straying from the outline and not turning in homework on time (or neatly enough). Recently David, my law-student son, spent over an hour shelling piñon nuts for a pasta dish he was making. Everyone else in the kitchen was amazed at how this resistant Follow Thru stuck with the task until it was completed. But the real David reappeared when he finally finished, grabbed the cookbook to check on the amount of olive oil, and discovered piñon nuts weren't part of the recipe. It took him extra time to work against his conative grain, and he ended up without piñon nuts in the pasta to show for it. I didn't train him to cook—he's obviously self-taught—but if I had, I would benefit from knowing that's just the way he is.

DIFFERENT "LEARNING" STYLES

MUCH RESEARCH HAS BEEN DONE ON DIFFERING LEARNING STYLES, ALL OF WHICH support the notion that people of equal intelligence and motivation internalize information differently. Whether in training or educational programs, conative characteristics can help explain why some people (Fact Finder–insistent folks) are compelled to write it down and others (Quick Start initiators) excel in oral presentations. The topic in which you are training isn't the decisive factor; it's the person's MO. A case in point is John Chiatalas, an attorney with Sandoz Corp. While his wife, Nancy, was at home struggling with a serious illness and the special needs of their three physically and mentally challenged children, he was working full-time and going to law school at night. He was able to maintain his energy by trusting and using his instincts, having a determined purpose and the support of his family. John (whose KCI result is 7-2-9-3) was literally off and running to meet economic needs and to reach the professional goals he and Nancy agreed were important for him.

"I used a time-compression system," John explained, "simply because my Quick Start needed to have some sense of urgency. I am a shortcut person; I circumvent obstacles." Then, describing how his resistance to Follow Thru caused him stress when outlining and studying in the recommended way, he said, "My other responsibilities kept me too busy to spend all that time getting organized." He then mentioned some waffle-soled shoes and a tape recorder with a power booster. John had created a Quick Start technique for doing two things at once: exercise and study. During lunch hour at the corporate job he'd don his cushioned shoes—which magnified his stride—and a headset that played back his taped notes 40 percent faster than normal speed. Now he could jog farther and review material faster. And he made it to the courthouse to deliver his last-minute filings (remember the 2 in Follow Thru) just on time.

Reggie Behl has taught Quick Start "Sketching for the Traveler" at the Smithsonian Institution in Washington, DC, the Museum of Natural History in Los Angeles, and the Museum of Natural History at the University of New Mexico. She, like sculptress Helen Blair Crosbie, finds there is an artist in everyone, but that equal creative gifts are nurtured through different methods. "Anyone can learn to draw," Reggie said. "You just have to use your inclinations."

Teaching business people, engineers, and others has allowed her to see the diversity of natural talents among them. "Some students can't draw a vertical line, so I tell them to let that be their style. 'Don't fight it, use it.' Some people aren't complex Fact Finders—that's their charm."

Reggie is a trainer who enables people to learn by unmasking their own best efforts. "Some people fight their instincts," she said. "and need to loosen up. I bombard them with seeing, selecting, and making choices—relying on guts—with no time to think. Then they just have to react. They get very excited when they see the results. Within a group you can see twenty different responses to the same thing. It's hard to get rid of habits in my two-day workshop, but they learn a lot about themselves they can put to use afterward. Once they tap into their natural way of expressing themselves, their talent for doing whatever they want to do develops very rapidly."

People often associate learning styles with gender and race stereotypes. But the lack of bias in KCI results indicates that differences in how people react to training or education is not because of innate differences by gender, age, and race. For instance, since there are as many female Fact Finders as males, both genders can be trained equally well to use natural abilities for defining strategies.

Barbara Barrett (KCI result, 7-3-6-4), an attorney who was at the top echelon of the Civil Aeronautics Board and who was the number-two person at the Federal Aviation Administration, noted, "Cross-cultural community courses are in some cases teaching that women and minorities learn in different ways. This information is presented as truth rather than explaining that environment builds different expectations." She stated that even in these times when college students promote "politically correct" notions of equality, "I was quite surprised to hear students repeat the stereotype that women just think about things differently. We're training women to believe they have to go into human resources, public relations, accounting, and law, and not manufacturing and engineering."

Barbara is amused that aircraft engineers don't expect she'll know the technology of F-18 planes, when, in fact, she's an expert. "But then," she acknowledged, "I'm often viewed as a novelty." In the corporate setting there's a notion that women must be trained as the nurturers because, she pointed out, people like Clarence Darrow have promoted the idea that "women don't have the nature of litigators."

"By exercising a little more gumption, I got in," Barbara said of her ability to overcome stereotypes and be trained as a jet pilot, litigator, and political strategist.

EVALUATING TRAINING PROGRAMS

I WOULDN'T WANT MY PARENTAL TRAINING SKILLS EVALUATED BY MY SON'S ABILITY to make a tasty pasta, although I would come out looking pretty good if that were the criterion. Results are what counts, but *which* results are to be counted? In parenting, results have more to do with passing along values than with specific behaviors. Attitudes also count in job training. An employee with a bad attitude can be a bigger problem than one who does nothing. Job satisfaction has proved essential to productivity. A training program should be evaluated both in terms of trainees' approval of it and bottom-line productivity increases. With the high cost of training, it is not sufficient to have employees simply enjoy the training or remain good contributors after having completed it. Performance must *improve.*

Measuring performance on most jobs is so difficult that it is not cost effective to gather all the necessary information. So companies guess at the results of training. If profits are up, they figure the training must have been a part of the reason. In fact, training is most important when profits are down. During periods of expansion, market readjustments, and downsizing, companies tend to ask more of people in the organization. And they ask for something different than was needed in the past. Job requirements are changing, and training should help employees deal with those changes. An effective program will do this by reenforcing the positive qualities of each contributor's conative capabilities. That in itself will help increase performance. If a way to monitor creative output existed, there is no doubt in my mind that the long-range benefits of validating a person's talents would outperform any other aspect of training.

REWARDS: THE KEY TO HARVESTING RESULTS

THE GREATEST REWARD A PERSON RECEIVES FROM EFFECTIVE TRAINING PROGRAMS is the joy that comes with higher levels of accomplishment. Along the way, trainers and managers can increase motivation and commitment to use trained skills by providing conatively appropriate rewards. Training helps a worker understand and use productive methods, but trainers still need to ensure that energy is targeted toward the organization's goals. Offering the wrong rewards, such as a last-minute trip to Hawaii for a resistant Follow Thru, can be worse than no reward at all.

Training that includes the conative dimension helps managers and employees recognize the need to reward the *process* and not just the result. A Quick Start may have come up with a proposal that, in the end, doesn't work. But the contribution was vital to the process. If that Quick Start is rewarded only when his contribution leads to profit, discouragement will set in all too soon.

Jerome, a service manager for an electronics firm, pushed his people to perform at consistently high standards. Occasional customer complaints were treated as serious lapses in an otherwise outstanding record of consistent performance. Though he was proud of his group's record of low complaints, he didn't feel it was necessary to reward people for doing what they'd been hired to do, but he was wrong. In a management-training program, he discovered his mistake. Rewards were necessary to encourage the long-term success of employee-training objectives.

Rewarding employee accomplishments appropriately is an important part of the process of transferring training onto the job site. Jerome should have appreciated and acknowledged the people around him for their accomplishments, *especially* because they were doing what they were paid to do. Yet some managers, like Jerome, think that giving rewards kills a person's initiative. Understanding the indelible nature of instincts ought to clear up that matter. People with an insistence in an Action Mode will use it to take initiative—somewhere. They won't stop initiating because you didn't give them a reward, but they may focus initiating efforts *away* from organizational goals.

For instance, Harold (KCI result, 7-3-4-7) is a midlevel manager with a soft-drink bottling company. He was well trained and conatively suited to his role of coordinating part of the plant operations. But when two and a half years went by with no reward other than a standard raise, Harold grew disgusted with the situation. "I do everything I'm supposed to do, and I do it well," he said. "If they want me to do something more, fine, they can show me what it is and how to do it, and I'll give it my best. But ignoring my contribution isn't helping." Harold's solution was to apply his talents recreationally. He became very involved in Boy Scouts, using his Fact Finder to identify conatively similar mentors for kids, and his Implementor to set up campsites for overnite hikes. Unlike his work for the bottling company, Harold's scouting efforts were praised, he saw personal results, and he became reenergized.

Instinctive energy exists without any inducement, but individuals react to incentives when deciding where to channel that energy. The energy has to be replenished, and the right kind of reward helps do that. If a manager wants to continue harvesting the benefits of a team member's conative talent, then some form of appreciation needs to be provided. Without positive reinforcement, the skills learned in training might soon go unused. However, one person's reinforcement is another person's punishment. When selecting appropriate rewards, it is important for managers to understand the MOs that drive their employees.

Incentives for Insistent Fact Finders

For this group, incentives need to be traditional, practical, and appear fair. A title means a lot to them, as do perks, since appropriate status is essential. Credentials are of sufficient concern to an insistent Fact Finder that tuition for educational programs and work-related seminars would be important. Tie a Fact Finder's raises and other rewards to specific accomplishments, such as meeting a training program's objectives, or the rewards won't mean as much to him.

Incentives for Insistent Follow Thrus

Follow Thrus need their incentives spelled out in advance. Their rewards need to fit the balance sheet in their minds. Steady, accountable raises are better than bonuses or occasional big jumps. Anything that provides security is highly desirable. So consider alternatives such as setting up a scholarship fund for their children or helping them with regular payments.

Incentives for Insistent Quick Starts

Quick Starts react positively when incentives are tied to deadlines, growth, or some other challenge. Bonuses and commissions work well because they give risk takers a chance to make it big. Unusual benefits—including contest prizes—stimulate their continued energy, as does allowing them to purchase stock or take part in a buy-in that could help them entrepreneurially.

Incentives for Insistent Implementors

These need to be tangible and usable. They may select new equipment over other rewards. Getting out of having to attend meetings is a big treat, as is having sufficient time to build a sturdy model. If they're stuck in an office environment, time off will be the most appreciated reward of all for Implementors.

CREATING PERSONAL INCENTIVES

A MANAGEMENT TRAINER ONCE CHALLENGED A GROUP OF MANAGERS WITH THE question, "Do you think you praise your subordinates enough?" A show of hands indicated that a strong majority felt they did. The second question, "Do you feel your boss praises you enough?" brought a much smaller group of hands. The final question, "How would your subordinates answer the second question if they were here tonight?" brought sheepish looks and thoughtful murmurs. Unfortunately, managers do not recognize, praise, and reward as often or as effectively as they should to get maximum performance from their employees. As an employee, the positive reaction to this is to challenge, recognize, praise, and reward *yourself*.

Training people to provide self-approval is even more important than helping a manager develop an external reward structure. Other people may not fully understand what a challenge it was to reach a goal or the trials you experienced in getting there. While others will be more likely to praise visible achievements, the person struggling to reach goals has to self-congratulate when contributing to the process. The personal sense of accomplishment can come from making commitments and acting on instinct, even when it doesn't work out as hoped.

Trainers can help workers understand that using a resistance to prevent a problem usually goes unheralded by others, but it is deserving of self-approval. When someone who was quite resistant in Quick Start put a halt to his company's change in health-insurance plans, he had good reason to feel proud. He saw through the salesperson's flimsy pitch and recognized that the promised savings would not have materialized. Of course, others in the human-resources department were disappointed about the information he presented and had to scurry around to find another alternative health plan, so he didn't receive much appreciation. Still, he knew he'd exercised instinctive effort for the good of the group, and he rewarded himself with tickets to a favorite sporting event.

INTEGRATING TRAINING INTO THE ORGANIZATIONAL DYNAMIC

THIS BOOK ILLUSTRATES THE VALUE OF DIFFERING CONATIVE APPROACHES IN MANY organizational areas. Yet it is not a how-to manual. Clearly, there are specific methods that are useful when working with different combinations of talents, both with individuals and training groups. The samples given here are but the tip of the iceberg. Understanding that people have instinctive needs is a major first step. Meeting those needs itself requires training, time to experience failure, and rewards for making the effort.

CHAPTER ELEVEN

QUALITY

CULTURES THAT
ENCOURAGE PRODUCTIVITY

In the early 1980s, many American companies sought ways to achieve "excellence." More recently, a number have installed "Total Quality Management" (TQM) and "Continuous Process Improvement" (CPI) systems, which they hoped would increase attention on the customer, create a participatory management structure, and monitor industrial processes to reduce or eliminate errors.

To recognize this new commitment to "quality," and to try to bolster perceptions of American industrial viability, Congress instituted the annual Malcolm Baldrige National Quality Award, which is similar to Japan's Deming Prize. It is given to companies that reflect the ideals of involvement, commitment to improving quality, and other laudable corporate goals. Unfortunately, many of the companies that changed their structures in hopes of securing a Baldrige Award or emulating what was perceived to be the great Japanese industrial success story not only haven't improved performance, they have suffered severe economic losses since then.

There are two basic reasons why this "quality movement" has not significantly improved productivity. First, too many companies call for continuous improvement of products and services but don't translate the desire into action. Improving performance quality requires committing appropriate instinctive energy and bringing together the right mix of conative talents.

Secondly, the process necessary to win the award puts too much emphasis on customer service, monitoring of processes, and error reduction, which *all* require a commitment of Follow Thru–insistent energy. So the very process necessary to win the award calls for a conative imbalance. Everything from the copious forms that have to be completed to compete for the award to proving that systems are in place push competing companies toward conative inertia. A company that emphasizes Follow Thru actions to win such awards may be doing so at the cost of other contributions. It's difficult for any award to encourage the instinctive diversity necessary for productivity, because the process requires Follow Thru record keeping and Fact Finder justifications. Few Implementor or Quick Start initiators put their energy into satisfying pencil-and-paper proofs of success. The only place I know of that takes into account the full range of instinctive talents necessary for success is the marketplace.

When Florida Power & Light Co. (FPL) won the Deming Prize in 1989, it was the first non-Japanese organization to do so. It had worked for nearly a decade to reshape its systems in the image of successful Japanese utilities. It instituted "quality circles," required everyone's involvement, and developed "feedback loops" and other customer-focused mechanisms that were supposed to ensure its success. Though it did receive international acclaim for its efforts, that acclaim did not translate into an improved bottom line, more satisfied customers, or more productive employees. Shortly after receiving the award, FPL began a dramatic retrenchment of these processes, dismantling many of the TQM approaches in favor of more broadly applicable employee programs. As its chairman, James L. Broadhead, said, "I was most troubled, however, by the frequently stated opinion that preoccupation of process had resulted in us losing sight of one of the major tenets of quality improvement; namely, respect for employees."

Most companies in a 1992 survey by Rath & Strong, Inc., of Lexington, Massachusetts, gave Total Quality Management *D*s and *F*s for its ability to improve market share, rein in costs, and make customers happy. Arthur D. Little, Inc.'s survey found that a slim 36 percent of five hundred companies said the process had a "significant impact" on their competitiveness. *Newsweek* commented in September of '92 that "U.S. companies have soured on TQM because it provides little protection against hard times." It can play a role in improving Follow Thru operational programs and some Fact Finder identification of priorities, but TQM is not the total answer.

The recent tough times for high-technology "quality-oriented" companies such as IBM and Compaq Computer Corporation have caused the layoffs of so many workers that job security is no longer a reality for most "survivors." This is especially difficult for the security-conscious insistent Follow Thrus, who are likely to have given the TQM approach their greatest efforts. They are often the most devastated when it fails to live up to its unrealistic promises. When businesses have to retrench for economic reasons, the first people to be laid off are often midlevel managers and operational supervisors—the predominantly Follow Thru–insistent rank, among whom are many of those that had been assigned to design and monitor TQM systems.

RECOGNIZING THE CONTRIBUTION PEOPLE MAKE TO THE ORGANIZATION

THE CURRENT RECOGNITION THAT QUALITY CONCEPTS DON'T IMPROVE THE BOTTOM line has led to a raft of new management theories. Yet all you have to do is listen to the buzzwords of many replacement programs to recognize that, once again, systems, not a diversity of instinctive approaches, are the primary focus of these efforts. The variety of people's potential contributions seems to be lost in words and phrases such as "reengineering," "organizational architecture," "core competencies," and "the new molecular organization." There has been a continuing bias toward the mechanics of organizational structures and a denigration of differing creative efforts as the basic resource needed for the successful implementation of any idea.

Ever since Fredrick W. Taylor introduced the concept of scientific management in 1913, which led to the development of efficient assembly-line operations, many management consultants have treated the human factor in organizations as if it were another piece of machinery, one that could be retooled at the Will of the company. This approach has led to one management concept after another failing to achieve promised successes. Employees are not interchangeable resources that can replace one another at Will. They are not identical cogs in some system. They do not accept change at the same pace, or work in the same sequences, or respond in the same way to every edict or opportunity.

Systems and technology are vital to an organization, but no more so than the synergy of its people. Several of my clients are high-tech companies. I often watch them put together highly productive teams that design innovative programs to meet the specialized needs of a customer, only to have the project fail. It didn't fail because the program wasn't workable. The technology was advanced and well integrated into the customer's systems. But the people at the other end, the users, failed to operate it efficiently. In the past, my customers have thought the answer was to provide more training for the customer's employees so that the program would be put to its best use. Now they know training will work only when the right people are in place.

One solution has been to consider user groups as part of the development team and to include their instinctive needs in the original design. Those designing the cockpit of a jet fighter (usually Fact Finder–dominant engineers, with a resistance to Implementor) need to involve jet pilots early in the process. Most pilots, my research shows, are insistent in Follow Thru and accommodating in Implementor. They bring a synergistic talent to the design team, and as end users they bring needs that must be met in order for the project to be of the highest quality.

Where successful use of a product or service relies heavily on the conative makeup of the user, product designers should include conative warning labels on their materials. For instance, some complex programs require that a user thoroughly study the specifics of how they need to be used. While we can't assume every buyer knows that means an insistent Fact Finder needs to be on the case, the user's manual can point out the kind of initiative necessary.

Often the act of defining the instincts necessary for the use of a product or service adds to the recognition that people's creative abilities play a crucial part in determining the success of any effort. It also helps those developing the technology or product to realize ways in which they may need to broaden its usability. Traditional VCRs, for instance, have required a combination of Fact Finder and Implementor insistences in order to be used to their fullest capacity. That's a design flaw that affects customer satisfaction in most households.

OPERATING IN CULTURES THAT DEMAND CHANGE

ONE OF THE MOST DANGEROUS FACTORS IN ANY CHANGE PROCESS IS THE RISK OF major conative shake-ups within well-functioning teams. People who are

Kolbe Management Report
SYNERGY REPORT

For

PILOTS

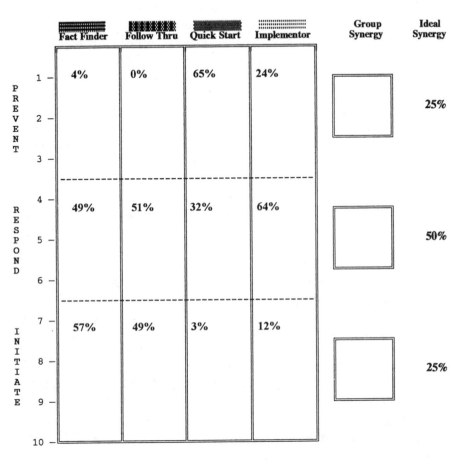

	Fact Finder	Follow Thru	Quick Start	Implementor	Group Synergy	Ideal Synergy
PREVENT (1–3)	4%	0%	65%	24%		25%
RESPOND (4–6)	49%	51%	32%	64%		50%
INITIATE (7–10)	57%	49%	3%	12%		25%

This analysis is based on a total of 205 respondents.

productive operating in manners well suited to their instinctive makeups may suddenly find themselves forced into new roles requiring processes that conflict with their instincts. No amount of training, no analysis of the change process, no new systems, will compensate for the shift.

Imagine what would happen if an insistent Follow Thru who is also resistant in Quick Start tried to supervise a billing department. Over the years, she has devised and honed a system for handling the billing cycle. She succeeds in using it and is proud of her efforts. Suddenly, with the development of a company initiative to focus on time-based competition, she is told to head up a task force designed to reduce cycle time for billings. In addition to the motivation problems created by being told her system isn't good enough—without anyone even looking at it—she is ordered to break apart her system and spearhead change. The required set of actions goes against her nature.

Companies have to look past functional areas and skill sets to engineer change. With the right mix of Striving Instincts, a team effort could have met the goal of improving the accounting system. The supervisor could have been given the assignment of making sure any changes would not compromise the process's fundamental objectives. Others, whose conative roles she understood and accepted, could have added the elements of Quick Start experimentation and Fact Finder comparative analysis.

Any change process needs to be introduced to employees with an understanding of how they will respond to it and why. Fact Finder–insistent people need to have sufficient background on the reasons for change and be able to go through their own processes of assessing various options. Telling such people that the chosen method has proved the most effective makes the false assumption that they don't need to prove it to themselves. Giving them sufficient information to draw their own conclusions will help gain the commitment of Fact Finder energy.

For insistent Follow Thrus to adjust to change, it is important that it be introduced in incremental steps. They need to see how change integrates with what is already being done. Change is a problem for people who need consistency when they are unable to assimilate it in an orderly way. Don't just hit them with the notion and then expect them to sing its praises.

Quick Start–insistent people adapt to change much more easily. The difficulty from them arises when change is forced upon them. It's the old problem of "not invented here." They must be challenged to make their own adjustments to any changes that affect their work. It adds insult to injury if someone tries to solve their "problem" by integrating something new into their work. Just give them the bottom line and let them find their own ways of reaching it.

Change frustrates insistent Implementors if it requires them to use materials or equipment they have not personally tested for quality.

"They're always shoving something new down our throats," an insistent-Implementor technician complained to me. "If only they would let me check materials out before they go and order truckloads of the stuff, I'd save the company a fortune."

QUALITY AS A BELIEF RATHER THAN A REALITY

THE CONCEPTS OF EXCELLENCE AND QUALITY CAN MAKE IMPORTANT CONTRIBUTIONS to corporate success. Yet when these positive ideas become entrenched as a management belief system ("evangelical crusades," as one business-school professor put it), it further limits their effectiveness. When such management beliefs are so deeply held, simplistic approaches can be seen as panaceas. Business executives are often characterized on TV, in movies, and in literature as lacking this concern with quality. On TV's · *The Simpsons*, Homer Simpson's boss is portrayed as your basic evil industrialist, a nuclear power plant owner who bribes people not to disclose safety violations. However, most business people are motivated to fill the needs of their customers. And they desire to fulfill their own creative potential. So the idea of excellence and quality are attractive to them. The fact that the quality movement has been more an attitude than a reality should not diminish the importance of finding better ways to reach the goal. TQM and other quality-improvement programs can provide the motivation that stimulates a culture to move toward creative solutions. As beliefs, they provide the stimulus that can trigger people to engage their Striving Instincts.

Once motivated, the culture has to encourage the contribution of every form of talent. No single Action Mode provides the effort necessary to produce quality within an organization. A Quick Start–oriented management theory that calls for constant change and ever-increasing risk will fail just as surely as a quality program based on Follow Thru initiatives.

Author Robert Pirsig identified the problem in *Zen and the Art of Motorcycle Maintenance*. The real question is, "What is quality? What the hell is it?" He answered, "If you want to build a factory, or fix a motorcycle, or set a nation right without getting stuck, then classical, structured dualistic subject-object knowledge, although necessary, isn't enough. You have to have some feeling for the quality of the work. You have to have a sense of what's good."

Pirsig is right. Most management theories leave out the Striving Instincts, a natural sense of what's good, of what will work. By leaving out all but the motivation in most people's Creative Process, they fail to use employee teams effectively.

Demands for zero product defects cannot be met by a manufacturing group whose innate actions go against the goal. You give me a bunch of Quick Start daredevils, and I'll show you a shop with rapidly produced defective work. Give me an Implementor work force, and I'll show you craftsmanship of the highest quality (even if it's behind schedule). Benchmarks for measuring progress will reach objectives only if they are tied to the availability of the right forms of mental energy. Resistant Follow Thrus, for example, won't continuously improve service; they'll do it sporadically. Resistant Implementors won't produce quality products; they'll discuss the theoretical reasons why it isn't happening.

Instinct-based behavior cannot be changed, and nothing good comes from such attempts. Companies' performances will reflect the instincts of their employees and their suitability to their jobs. Organizations will rise or fall to their conative watermarks, the natural levels of attainment of the people within them. That level depends upon the fit between requirements and realities.

Slogans calling for quality don't change behaviors. The senior vice-president of a large East Coast firm called in a consultant to "build a quality program" into the organization. "Yesterday," he told a visitor, "our president held a rally for all the employees, unveiled a huge court-yard banner, and gave an inspiring speech. He called for a new era in the company, a new commitment to quality. He promised dramatic changes and substantial improvements in productivity, which would lead to greater rewards for employees and more satisfied customers. The problem is, we don't have any plans in place. All we really have now is that banner." He pointed out the window to a mammoth sign that read: Commitment to Customers, Commitment to Employees, and Commitment to Quality. The sign gave no clue as to how the company was going to fulfill these commitments. It was nothing more than another slogan without a solution.

On occasion, slogans or new approaches may achieve short-term improvement. The Hawthorne effect proves that people placed in management's spotlight will tap dance faster—until they run out of energy and collapse. But they don't become better tap dancers. Instead they feel foolish for having tried. After the momentary spotlight has faded, it becomes evident that their efforts didn't change the nature of the performers.

What seemed like a good idea for a short time ends up creating even greater frustration. Without permanent benefits, taking people off their usual tasks to work toward "quality improvement" wastes energy, and the exercise becomes a negative experience. The fact is, such approaches often create the need for another new program to achieve another short-term effect. As *Newsweek* said, "Management plans often have the shelf life of cottage cheese."

QUALITY CIRCLES

QUALITY CIRCLES ARE ONE OF THE MAINSTAYS OF TQM. THEY INVOLVE TEAMS OF employees meeting regularly to evaluate their efforts and recommend improvements. Some of these groups are effective, but most fail to increase productivity. At best, there is a short-term increase in job satisfaction because group members feel "empowered" to make changes.

"I served on a quality circle for over a year," a corporate employee said, "and it was disappointing. We shared our hopes and aspirations, believing that for once somebody was going to listen to what we had to say. It wasn't all that hard to get agreement on what we all hoped would happen. But nothing came of it. Perhaps it was supposed to appease us for the lack of raises that year. In any event, it was very patronizing, and I wouldn't waste my time doing it again."

Quality circles in many large organizations become like high-school homerooms, providing a sense of belonging. But job satisfaction is tied to a sense of accomplishment. An employee who participated in one of the most extensive TQM programs in an American company said, "Mostly it became a place to vent our frustrations, which didn't make any of us feel we were getting anywhere." In this case, the group wasn't getting anywhere because it became mired in attitude adjustment and in wish lists. Because it was not empowered to deal with conative methods for getting jobs done, its members' good intentions were fruitless and therefore demoralizing.

If members of a group are not aware of one another's conative strengths, they will be far less successful in developing the desired synergy. Poorly constituted groups will be ineffective using TQM or any other program. Ask ten insistent Fact Finders to evaluate how you can cut the cost for producing an item, and they'll meet once a week for six months and give you a 110-page report analyzing why it's impossible to be completely accurate in assessing specific costs. Ask ten insistent Quick Starts to do the same thing, and they'll meet a couple of times and give you thirty-five new items that might cost less to produce, without answering your original question.

There's no use talking about what others must accomplish, or talking about what you have to do, if the conative cards are stacked against you. The point is to form project teams with a productive balance and to empower participants to use their instincts to meet shared goals.

PILLARS OF MANAGEMENT

RATHER THAN TRYING TO OVERCOME THE WALLS BUILT BY COMPARTMENTALIZATION or the status problems caused by hierarchical structures with artificial and nonproductive circles or teams, many companies have sought ways to "flatten" the organization. This happens most frequently in organizations beset by economic problems and forced into considerable layoffs. After substantial trimming of middle managers from the firm, they often refer to the process as "pancaking." They point out that hierarchical levels no longer shape their organization chart into a pyramid because they have compressed it into fewer layers.

The organizational-development specialist for one large corporation explained that a plethora of middle managers had made the company slow in responding to customer needs and to adjust marketing strategies. If middle management were only a way station to upper management, such juniors would not be missed when removed. But if the roles being eliminated are career program planners and administrative positions, losing those with the talents for these tasks will devastate the organization and its "survivors."

As a result, many senior executives have found themselves doing Follow Thru planning, when their forte is in setting Fact Finder strategies. They need to leave the tactical maneuvers to others, but they no longer have people with those instincts available. When operational tasks previously done by a cadre of Follow Thru professionals land at the doors of those conatively ill-equipped for them, it costs the individuals involved and the company misspent energy.

A more solid foundation that allows room for a diversity of conative talents at all levels within the organization resembles a set of pillars.

Four vertical columns represent the ever-rising level of responsibility given to those with each form of conative insistence. The Fact Finder column is for those who will progress up the ladder by providing marketing and product research, financial assessments, and organizational

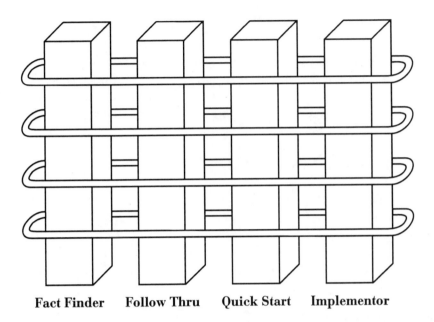

Fact Finder   Follow Thru   Quick Start   Implementor

strategies. The Follow Thru column houses those needed at all levels to provide operational programs, customer service, and systems design. Quick Start is necessary for sales, public relations, and innovations from entry level to top positions in the company. The fourth column is for manufacturing and production, which may not be necessary in a service-oriented company. People with dual insistences may operate within a couple of pillars, but most employees will work up to higher levels of responsibility within one of the columns. This structure allows everyone to use natural talents instead of fruitlessly trying to change conative stripes in order to climb a career ladder.

The benefits of the pillar concept are:

1. Employees with different conative strengths populate each distinctly different pillar, providing synergy for work groups that cut across pillars at all levels.

2. Compensation can be more equitable among differing forms of talents because this system rewards people by their level on a pillar, not by particular pillars. People do not have to move from technical jobs into supervisory roles in order to receive pay increases.

3. Consideration for top management positions can be given to senior people from each conative pillar, allowing non-

traditional paths to lead to the highest levels. Employees don't have to endure the stress of working outside their conative ranges in order to be considered for promotions.

4. If it becomes necessary to cut the payroll, it can be done across pillars without decimating a particular career path or inadvertently eliminating a needed set of talents.

COMBINING QUALITY AND CREATIVITY

WHEN QUALITY IS SOUGHT THROUGH THE CONTRIBUTIONS OF PEOPLE'S STRIVING Instincts, the results are most likely to increase productivity, along with job satisfaction. This is accomplished by adhering to a few basic principles. People need to be selected for roles that allow them to function according to their instincts. They deserve to be placed on teams with synergistic talents.

The two deans at the University of Chicago Graduate School of Business, Dr. Harry Davis and Dan Tepke, have been part of a team that has helped that school retain its prominence as one of the premier business schools in the world. Both are well suited to their roles, and have some complementary strengths. However, because of their mutual Quick Start instincts, their early efforts at improving their academic program were fraught with conative difficulties.

Dan, the associate dean, has a KCI result of 3-3-10-3 (yes, that's a 10 in Quick Start and resistance in every other mode). In describing his management style, Dan volunteered: "I operate on instinct. I'm energized when I go ahead instinctively and don't try to justify ideas I've generated. . . . I find myself selling without the data. Sometimes I get too far out in front of the facts. You have to be careful when you have this Quick Start ability; it's like being a magician. As a manager I am always being asked how I create new programs. All I can tell people is that it takes a little 'pixie dust,' like the sorcerer's apprentice."

Harry, the deputy dean, has a KCI result of 3-2-8-6. He adds an accommodation in Implementor, which brings a tangible quality to his Quick Start drive toward unique solutions. As he says: "It's natural for me to say, 'Let's build it.' While I always used objects to teach concepts, until the Kolbe seminars I didn't have as much comfort doing it or realize it had as much value for me. It's amazing how I can get others to buy in. . . . I have a real energy for going out and selling new products, my prototypes. I've sold several millions of dollars in corporate sponsorships just by talking about new programs—when I could view them as products. Of course I was also improvising the plan for getting there as I was talking."

These two insistent Quick Starts assembled a team of capable and dedicated professionals. For some of those people, Harry's and Dan's Quick Start initiatives provided readily accepted opportunities to contribute toward dynamic change. But for those with a differing conative point of view these "groundbreaking" programs required efforts that seemed to pull the rug out from under them. We used the KCI to identify the instinctive strengths of the entire MBA staff, and compared those strengths to self-expectations and job requirements. The group had a diversity of conative talents that hadn't been fully recognised. As Harry said, "I became more sensitive to the need for balance. Sharing information about our instincts made others more comfortable. From an organization point of view we had a basis for discussing differing approaches." The two Quick Starts were as innovative as ever, but their creative energy was better understood by their staff.

They tell a wonderful story about an international flight during which they brainstormed the curriculum for a new semester-long course—for which they already had financial support and full enrollment—and which was to begin three days later. "Of course we waited until the last minute," Dan said to me, "which certainly shouldn't surprise you. And it turned out to be a better program because it got our riveted attention." Their staff, rather than being distraught because it had not received the curriculum in advance, trusted these two to prepare the class in time and in their own best way.

As Intel makes plans to open a $1 billion factory to manufacture a future generation of computer chips, it selected a conatively synergistic core team to oversee the start-up phase. Plant manager Dave Marsing says of this process, "It forces you to hire and staff in a manner that goes beyond what you've done traditionally. You look at the combinations of instinctive talent that best fit your changing needs. Good teams can be great in particular situations, but thrown into another part of the cycle they can fall apart. We need combinations of talent that survive the transitions from when we first set equipment in place to when we're in full production. We have to do a quality job at every stage."

Marsing and his core team completed KCI-Cs to identify the instincts necessary for various roles in the ongoing operation. Now work groups with required skills can be formed into project teams with the right instincts for different stages in the development of the factory. "I now have a completely different perspective on the way people perform," Marsing said. "It's not just a matter of skills and motivation."

When efforts to achieve quality include building and managing project teams according to instinctive strengths, the process changes from trying to make people work harder for the company to making the company work better for people. Then quality is no longer a belief, it is a reality.

CHAPTER TWELVE

THE INNOVATION PROCESS

Innovation has always been an essential part of the culture and legends of American business, and lately it has become a magic word. Joel Barker has introduced business people to the scientific concept of a *paradigm shift*, and they have embraced it. Books such as *Thriving on Chaos* and *Dancing with Elephants* focus on the importance of innovation. On top of that, the recent focus is on speed. Organizations are told they have to remake themselves on a regular basis to stay ahead of the competition.

At the same time, seminars are taught on the dangerous tendency of humans to resist change, and this has spawned a new breed of consultants who teach organizations to develop "change masters" and build innovation teams. In spite of this emphasis on innovation and the time and money put into the concept, many organizations are having little success incorporating it. New-product developers come in too late with ideas that cost too much. Research-and-development departments have stagnated, only to be replaced with innovation teams that disintegrate into conflicts and turf battles.

This chapter explains why commitments to innovate often miss the mark and how to increase the odds of creating changes that will improve the bottom line over the long haul. It isn't as simple as gathering all the insistent Quick Starts in a room and telling them to come up with something new. If you want innovation to work, you've got to involve all three zones in Quick Start as well as initiatives in other modes. Each person has a perspective on change that can help in developing new products and services.

A new-product development specialist who trains corporate employees on innovation asked me how I had originated the Kolbe Concept. I explained that I had initially developed it through an intuitive process, trusting my instincts. He was surprised when I didn't respond to his suggestion that my example could be used to help teach people to become "true" innovators. People he trains all have the instinct to innovate, even if they often don't know it and don't have the freedom to use it. Innovation doesn't need to be instilled, it is a potential that cries out to be engaged.

The instinct to innovate is universal. It results in change, diversification, newness, and variation, as well as prevents too many distracting differences. People contribute to that process by initiating risk, accommodating change, and preventing chaos. Our perspectives, or ways of reacting to change, vary according to our zone in the Quick Start mode. Every point on the Quick Start scale offers an important point of view on innovation. The generalization "People just don't respond well to change" is true only for 20 percent of the population. Those individuals, who are resistant to Quick Start, will resist change until they find a way to incorporate it into their actions through other modes. They enhance the innovation process by seeking its irrevocable benefits. But for 20 percent of the population—the insistent Quick Starts—change, risk, and diversity are a driving force.

A CONATIVE APPROACH TO INNOVATION

I RECENTLY SAT IN ON A MEETING OF THE BOARD OF DIRECTORS OF A PUBLICLY traded company, listening to one report after another filled with the gloom and doom of the early nineties. Three decisions were made by the end of the marathon session: (1) lay off 10 percent of the workforce; (2) cut back on expenditures, including salaries, inventories, and capital expenditures; (3) appoint an Innovation Team of the highest-qualified people to develop new products and programs that would position the company for growth. My job was to help the board put together this team, based on the instinctive strengths of the remaining employees, who were suffering through the worst financial setback in the corporation's history. They had tried traditional research and development without success. This time they wanted to ensure innovation would take place.

The board had considered several creative problem-solving approaches for resolving its financial dilemmas. Innovation is not always the best solution to a problem. For example, a retail outlet with faltering sales might find customer surveys, traffic analysis, and pricing strategies are better approaches than diving into the development of a new-product/ merchandising mix. However, Fact Finder studies had determined that significantly new visions were necessary for this corporation's long-term survival and success. The company was comfortable with the concept but could not afford to invest in expensive trial-and-error efforts. Risks had to be calculated, and changes built on the fine traditions already established in the organization. Therefore we certainly didn't want to clone a bunch of insistent–Quick Start specimens and let them go off on too many tangents. We had to build an Innovation Team that utilized diverse approaches. We had to produce results.

BUILDING THE TEAM

ASSEMBLING THE INNOVATION TEAM REQUIRED CONSIDERATION OF COGNITIVE, AFfective, and conative issues. Team members had to be part of the company's best and brightest. Strong interpersonal and communication skills were critical because the team was charting new territory for the company and would be under a great deal of pressure to convince others to go along with its recommendations. In addition, organizational and technical issues were a factor. We needed particular skills sets and lots of political power within the organization. The conative mix is just one factor in the demanding challenge of assembling a critical team. Instinct *isn't* everything. But without instinctive synergy in a group, you can have all your other ducks in a row, and they will just sit there.

Without the positive energy generated by the right mix of instincts, the group would contribute to the problems instead of the solutions. We needed many people with the instincts to initiate change, tempered with those who would keep them from getting too carried away. The team's focus on innovation made the Quick Start–instinctive category the most critical to structure effectively. The first step was to find sufficient insistent Quick Starts who fit all the other criteria as well. I've found

Innovation Teams require a range of two to three times the amount of normal distribution in Quick Start insistence, which means 40 percent to 60 percent in that zone.

Insistent Quick Starts naturally seek alternatives. While you're showing them how the system works, they're thinking of ways to change it. While you're giving them the requirements, they're figuring out how to get around them. They originate unique, untried approaches. Lots of them. Too many to be practical. Too many to be integrated into existing programs. Too many for the available space and equipment. Yet insistent Quick Starts must be free to offer them and open to others' refining them.

Approximately a third of the team members naturally responded as a moderating influence, contributing to the probability that changes would be adopted. Those were the accommodating Quick Starts. They worked with unique alternatives without either promoting or thwarting them. "Okay, if you need to try the new system, I'll help with it," a midrange innovator said, "but I'm going to keep the old one available, just in case." By responding to Quick Start ad-libs, brainstorms, and intuitions, these bridge people enhanced the possibility that innovations would become accepted practices. They often became the interpreters between those who originated seemingly off-the-wall methods and those resistant to taking risks, who otherwise would have nixed all consideration of unconventional ideas.

This third perspective, Quick Start resistance, would have been harmful in the early stages of the innovation project, even with people who would have tried to facilitate conflicts in the mode. Yet, before projects were finalized, 18 percent (close to the typical resistance per mode in the general population) with Quick Start resistance were added to the group, which helped it stay on track. By preventing diversions from the changes we were trying to make, the resistant Quick Starts saved the group from reinventing its own inventions, and they became essential to the process. "If it ain't broke, don't fix it," they said repeatedly. This rankled those trying to bring about necessary change because the profit margins were "broke," which meant to them *every* aspect of the business was subject to change. Not so, the resistant Quick Starts pointed out.

Some things were irrevocable, and we had to find a way to work around them. We had to take this into account whenever we altered the status quo. It also was important that these changes be made at the right time. Had resistant Quick Starts had too much power in the early stages of the project, they would have closed off some possibilities too soon. But

Kolbe Management Report
SYNERGY REPORT

For

HARD HIT CO.
INNOVATION TEAM

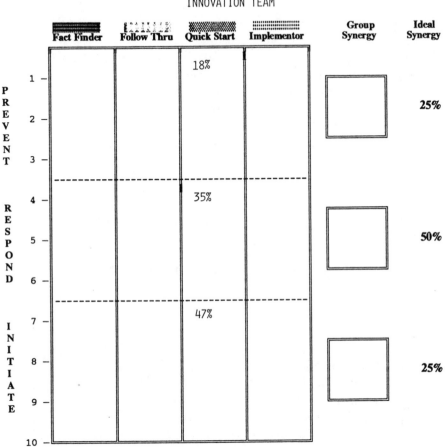

This analysis is based on a total of 15 respondents.

before valuable time was invested in wild goose chases, their help was incorporated into the process. They kept the team from going too far too fast.

The Innovation Team we designed was a success. Within a year the team's recommendations for reengineering marketing strategies and the addition of several new products were accepted by the board of directors and top management group. These innovations increased profitability and vastly improved ratings in financial circles. The company's stock went up 8 percent in the first quarter after the innovations were adopted, and long-term forecasts have improved as well. The changes became shared objectives among the employee groups responsible for producing the new products. The process started by the Innovation Team became part of the organizational culture. By factoring in conative issues when assembling the team, the company harnessed the group's natural energy—and the members' instincts drove it to success. Similar teams are now being formed in a variety of areas, including finance and operations.

THE CHALLENGES OF INNOVATION

Beginning the Process

Honeywell's Ed Hurd (3-5-7-6), president of a worldwide business unit, begins the innovation process in his organization by trusting his insistent–Quick Start needs as they merge with his accommodation in Follow Thru and Implementor. A highly credentialed engineer, he keeps himself from getting bogged down in Fact Finder detail, trusting others to take over in that department. He innovates by instinctively responding to chaos by bringing it into both Follow Thru order and Implementor tangible form. "Until the pieces fall into a pattern, nothing happens," he said. "I let it churn until it clicks, then I mold it into a shape. I have to get the blocks to fit the concept in my mind."

Instinctive risk takers come up with a multitude of new "schemes," as Ed calls them, some of which are impractical. "If people started blindly following everything I say, we'd have trouble," he said. "Most of the time I'm talking, I'm exploring. My success is based on the fact that I'm able to motivate a team. I have to be open with others and have them share in the process." It's clear to Ed that his role in the innovation process is to get it started, which involves selling others on projects. "I put together more sales presentations for an internal audience, for others on the team, than for external customers," explained this born promoter.

Ed Hurd has learned to use his insistent–Quick Start as a positive force for change with his team. He is the initiating force, but he acknowledges and benefits from the instincts of the rest of his team: to move ahead, but in the right direction, at the right pace, and with success.

Shared Commitment, Shared Risk

Innovations involve risk. There are no guarantees or 100-percent probabilities when dealing with unknowns. Members of Innovation Teams have to work in a high-risk environment, often with their professional reputations—if not their jobs—on the line. What if they recommend something that later proves to be more costly than anticipated? What if the technology isn't in place according to their projections? What if they miss the window of opportunity, and a competitor beats them to the punch? And then there's the worst possibility of all: What if they don't come up with anything that's very innovative? Because of the fear of not being "right," not taking risks causes the failure of most efforts to innovate.

The complete commitment of a team creates an environment in which risk is shared equally among the members, with no one withholding the benefits of his instinctive perspective. This can be a difficult assignment. In a deadline-intense situation where insistent Quick Starts are pushing toward change and promoting a now-or-never philosophy, someone who is resistant in Quick Start will need a lot of personal fortitude to speak up as the naysayer. "You've come up with a great suggestion, but I can't see moving ahead with it until we do some marketing research," is a statement everyone in the group expects from the resistant Quick Start who leads with Fact Finder. Some eyes will roll, but he may be right. If the information he needs is not available, further investigation may be necessary. The group can then take advantage of his insistent Fact Finder by charging him with the responsibility to conduct the appropriate study.

If Quick Starts constantly override others' instincts, members with differing insistent modes will lose commitment and may leave the team. "I can't go along with what's happening," Heidi said as she walked from an assignment on an Innovation Team. "I'm not able to make a contribution, so they won't miss me anyway." Yes, they will. Sorely. The team needed Heidi to stay and fight for her perspective. The instinct to innovate doesn't equip people for that part of the assignment. A commitment from all team members to acknowledge and support one another's instincts will lower the risk for people like Heidi, a resistant Quick Start who focuses on marketing research, as well as for others whose intuition is at odds with the team's direction. In the long run, this will actually speed up the process by allowing for a freer flow of ideas.

Supporting the Drive to Innovate

As essential as the other modes are to the group effort, none of them should be allowed to dominate or try to contain Quick Start energy. This is the problem that has caused many traditional R&D teams to fail. The researchers often chaired the group with a firm Quick Start resistance. Risk was overmanaged. Participants on an Innovation Team benefit when they concentrate on working through their various zones of Quick Start before they try to contribute through any of the other Action Modes. As soon as Fact Finder effort defines the objective too narrowly, or Follow Thru forces structure too rigidly, or Implementor becomes too literal, efforts are distracted from the central purpose of creating change.

Nothing kills innovation faster than an insistent Fact Finder demanding proof before experimentation. For instance, the inventor of what became a multibillion-dollar device was told by his employer that the company wouldn't support his trial efforts in the start-up stages because he hadn't researched other alternatives sufficiently. "Until you are sure this is the best possible approach," he was told, "we don't want to move forward." He left the company, got his own patent, and assembled an Innovation Team that pulled off a major coup. Companies that commit to Innovation Teams will support efforts that go against the odds. Others may use the term but deny the process.

Training team members to innovate begins with developing trust in their instincts. If a Quick Start offers an intuitive approach not substantiated by experience, it's important that others don't trounce on it as unsubstantiated and therefore "stupid." A Quick Start recounted how he came to expect his boss to criticize him for having "dumb ideas" any time he acted instinctively. "I learned to ignore her," he said, "and follow my guts. When I realized I trusted them considerably more than I trusted her criticism, I left the firm."

Reward systems must support innovation even when it doesn't work. Conatively synergistic teams that could be successful at innovating won't put forth effort if they're not rewarded for taking risks. A company will benefit from ongoing innovations when its bonuses are shared among those whose efforts create opportunities. Companies put their money where their mouths are when they are willing to reward failure. The worst possible alternative is to criticize risk takers because of a poor result, instead of praising the innovative process. Ed Hurd makes this point when he talks about risk. "I don't punish failure," he said. "If people take on something risky, I won't hammer them if it doesn't work. You can't shoot someone for failed risk, or people will never take one for you again."

Organizations have to be sure that resistant Quick Starts are not in charge of writing policies on innovation. They tend to write statements such as this one issued by a large metropolitan county government: ". . . . Employees are urged to take calculated risks when appropriate during the performance of some job activities and are rewarded if they are successful."

R&D: A TRADITION OF MISTAKES

TRADITIONAL R&D DEPARTMENTS OFTEN DEVELOPED A REPUTATION OF BEING BLACK holes; places where resources, people, and information went in, but nothing ever came out except little pieces of paper that said, "We're working on it." There are many R&D horror stories, such as the one about a supposedly innovative group that rejected the concept on which Xerox later built copy machines. It was originally considered not technically viable or commercially feasible. Often this does nothing more than increase conflict.

The problem in many R&D environments has been conative mixtures that were doomed to failure. Jim Radulski, American Express Mexico, leads the organization that won Mexico's quality award for human resources programs in 1992. He said: "Once our team had KCI results, we understood how to assure ongoing innovation. Now we make sure Quick Starts are given free rein to explore possibilities. But our Fact Finder– and Follow Thru–insistent people have learned when to step in and protect us from going too far." Radulski's KCI result of 4-2-10-3 explains his comment: "Understanding the byplay that comes with various instinctive combinations allows me to go full throttle when necessary with confidence that others will apply the brakes when that makes sense."

As symbolized by the name R&D, such groups have often been polarized in two modes. The *R* side of such task forces were strong Fact Finders who were often risk averse. The *D* side consisted of Quick Starts who inevitably brought the group to the brink of visionary risks while resisting proven remedies.

How could they have accomplished many of their goals, when their energy was directed toward internal battles? Power struggles ensued every time someone made a suggestion. Was it too uncertain? How would you know without trying? Was it the best possible alternative? How could you know without more research? Fighting to control the method of operation was self-defeating, and it limited any possibility for productivity. When their labors did not result in leading-edge products and services, companies lost ground to competitors who were building more effective Innovation Teams.

The classic R&D team, with lots of technical expertise, experience, and seniority, also had heavy doses of Quick Start. That energy often came from upstarts who were thought to have high potential—if they didn't flame out because of introducing copious alternatives others considered off the wall. The result was too many research-driven Fact Finders suffering strain by trying to act like Quick Starts, and too many intuitive Quick Starts equally frustrated by trying to justify their hunches. In such scenarios, conative stress destroyed the team's effectiveness. Even as giant steps were being made in technology, the marketplace saw a slowdown of innovation within American corporations because of faultily structured R&D teams.

Depletion of mental energy in R&D teams cost many companies productivity in an arena in which they could ill afford to fall behind. Management's requirements were unrealistic, since developing new products and services was impossible under the circumstances. R&D team members could not satisfy demands, causing the Meltdown of entire projects. From a conative perspective, the differences between available talents and team members' self-expectations was too great to sustain. People burnt out trying to make things happen that they were never going to make realities. The organization chart for one R&D team indicates 40 percent of its members were suffering from self-inflicted strain. Each place on the chart that has a block filled in under the title

Kolbe Management Report
SYNERGY REPORT

For

TRADITIONAL R&D TEAM

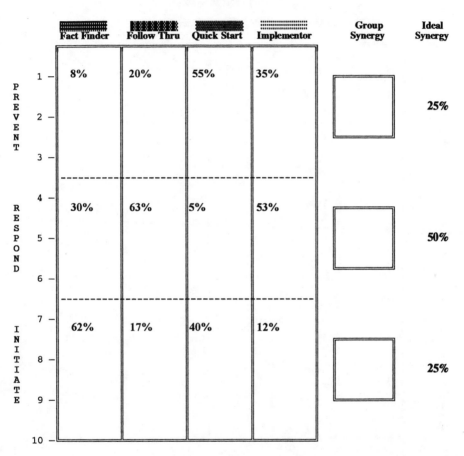

This analysis is based on a total of 17 respondents.

Kolbe Management Report
SYNERGY REPORT

For

TRADITIONAL R&D TEAM
KCI-B RESULTS

	Fact Finder	Follow Thru	Quick Start	Implementor	Group Synergy	Ideal Synergy
1	0%	10%	0%	30%		
2						25%
3						
4	30%	55%	18%	40%		
5						50%
6						
7	70%	35%	82%	30%		
8						25%
9						
10						

(Left axis labels: 1–3 PREVENT, 4–6 RESPOND, 7–9 INITIATE)

This analysis is based on a total of 17 respondents.

Kolbe Management Report
SYNERGY REPORT

For

TRADITIONAL R&D TEAM
KCI-C RESULTS

	Fact Finder	Follow Thru	Quick Start	Implementor	Group Synergy	Ideal Synergy
1	15%	25%	25%	25%		
2						25%
3						
4	40%	50%	25%	50%		
5						50%
6						
7	45%	25%	50%	25%		
8						25%
9						
10						

(Left axis groupings: rows 1–3 = **PREVENT**, rows 4–6 = **RESPOND**, rows 7–9 = **INITIATE**)

This analysis is based on a total of 17 respondents.

indicates a person operating out of sync with natural abilities. This 40 percent depletion pinpoints one of the causes of lost productivity.

Another indication of costly misalignment of talents on an Innovation Team is management's assumption that everyone in the group is responsible for initiating change. The example below highlights the places on another organization chart where the KCI-As and KCI-Cs are vastly different. In each highlighted role, the problem is a manager's failure to understand the importance of accommodation. The team's inability to meet management's demands, as shown in the KCI-C results, leads to tension throughout the group. The end result is a department filled with unproductive, stressed-out employees. Yet when they go to the company cafeteria and complain about the stress in their jobs, others often respond, "What have you got to be stressed about? Your deadline isn't until the next century!"

Today's solution to the old R&D impasse is often a focus on Innovation Teams. Their goal is also made clear by their name, but the same lack of instinct-based synergy makes it every bit as difficult to get things done as in the old R&D days. Innovation Teams are generally led by a strongly insistent Quick Start who promotes the need for innovation with great determination. In hopes of overcoming the problems of the past, the team is further stacked with more kindred Quick Start spirits. Now we have the inertia of a team tripping over its own energy, loaded with ideas but never hovering on one long enough to get results.

Making innovation work requires reducing conflicts between research and development, and tempering risk with planning, demonstrating, budgeting, and overseeing, and, most important, preventing too much of any of these elements from overrunning the process. It's a team effort that requires a unique kind of team, one with conative synergy, in which Quick Start initiative is more prevalent than usual.

INNOVATION SUCCESS: CHOOSING THE RIGHT LEADER

As with any striving process, developing and marketing innovations requires the right instincts in the right combination, properly managed, carefully nurtured, and committed to the effort. Though innovation or change requires Quick Start drive, an Innovation Team can be led by a Fact Finder who sets priorities, a Follow Thru who conceptualizes, or an Implementor who demonstrates. The only MO that would naturally limit an innovative approach is one with a resistance in Quick Start.

Kolbe Management Report of Organizational Strain

R&D TEAM

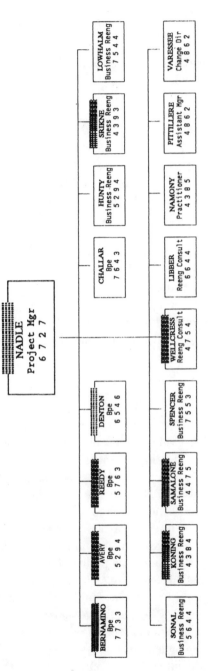

The Insistent Quick Start

Ed Hurd, with his insistent Quick Start, supported by the accommodating Implementor and Follow Thru, leads toward innovation with confidence. "I don't need to spend time disapproving specific directions. I approve and disapprove concepts," he says.

A Quick Start like Ed or American Express VP Jim Radulski can be good leaders for the innovation process, as long as the person also has insight into the ways leadership has to rotate as needed, regardless of official titles. Both are receptive to others' warnings. "We go through a correction process; agree on the grand scheme of things without interrupting the process," Ed says. "I have to create space for complementary modes."

Ed explained how his leadership approach garners innovation similar to the Japanese model: "The person who puts forth the straw man is the Quick Start. You give it to the team, which needs to tear it apart. The team owns the project. During the buy-in process, you keep sending ideas back to the drawing board, until there's comfort. . . . Frustration comes when I can't control something that impacts me. I'd like to influence to the point that we get renegade things into the puzzle."

The Insistent Fact Finder

Insistent Fact Finders have a positive effect on innovation by pushing for new methods, forcing alternatives onto the agenda, and making the group accountable for diversifying programs. An insistence in Fact Finder can also lead the Innovation Team by determining that change is the most practical approach to satisfying a need.

The finance director of a tool-and-die firm, with a KCI result of 7-6-4-2, was an expert in his industry. He knew foreign competitors were killing the company's profitability and recognized the only way to meet the challenge was to "get out in front" on product development. "We've got to set aside more funds for innovation," the strategist said. "It won't happen if we don't target it as a specific responsibility for some of our best people. Let's make it a priority over the next two years to shelve the outmoded approaches and get back into the forefront of this industry." He didn't say he would come up with the changes himself, but his statement began the innovation process.

The Insistent Follow Thru

Through ensuring that the team allots sufficient time and space to explore innovations, insistent Follow Thrus increase the probability that new products and programs will be introduced.

One insistent Follow Thru triggered diversification in an effort to ensure security and continuity. "We've got to find new outlets for our products," a systems-intense manager warned. "Otherwise we're going to have leftover inventory we'll have to warehouse and insure. We've got to find a way to get it off our hands." The call for new outlets pushed toward change. "We've been toying with some of these possibilities for months," the insistent Follow Thru added, "and there are too many items left dangling. A decision has to be made one way or the other so we can get on with it. I can't arrange for all the contingencies if we aren't even sure we've covered every potential." She pushed the innovative process toward decisions.

The Insistent Implementor

Implementors can influence innovation by offering concrete images, taking into account spatial and mechanical considerations. The insistent Implementor may lead the innovation process by presenting an opportunity for change.

A Hollywood special-effects artist who initiated tangible solutions showed his producer a prototype for a new method of manipulating body parts and changed the direction of their project. His uniquely grotesque creatures gave the film a new twist, as well as desired publicity. Props, costuming, set construction, makeup, and hair styling all turned out to be Implementor-dominated aspects of the production.

This particularly successful flick could not have been pulled off without the involvement of the hands-on contributors. "Look, I was just doing my job," the special-effects guy said. "If the writers and producer wanted to make my creatures into central characters, that was up to them. My part is to be sure I'm pushing the technology as far as it will go. I want to make sure I get things moving in all the ways they can. I can't always see how they're going to use the stuff I create. That's up to them. They take it the next step."

The Mediator

A Mediator, a person with no insistences, is an especially good choice to lead an Innovation Team. Without any particular way of having to get the job done, the Mediator is a crucial bridge between polarized conative factions on the team.

The Resistant Quick Start

Everyone involved will suffer conative stress if the group leader views his role as preventing change. Every other resistance helps move toward innovative results by keeping the process from getting mired in past or present considerations. A resistant Quick Start as the leader of an Innovation Team will need to use that energy to ensure the group does not stray from its goal to create change.

TRUSTING OTHERS' INSTINCTS

TRUSTING OTHER TEAM MEMBERS' INSTINCTS COMES FROM WATCHING THEM SUCCEED during times when they trusted their own natural drives. When a Follow Thru says, "Trust me, I'll work your project into the program," and then *does* it, you begin to believe he'll commit his operational talents successfully. When another team member says, "Watch, I'll make something that will show them how the deal works," and then *builds* a working model, you trust her to do it in another situation. With all the unknowns of the innovation process, the instinctive talents of others need to be clearly understood, accepted, and appreciated.

If a team member has been badly burned by false promises from a person with a particular MO, others with similar MOs may have to go through hurdles in order to be trusted. One Fact Finder encountered disbelief when he said he'd scour the literature for supporting material to assist an Implementor–Quick Start inventor in protecting his intellectual property rights. "Yeah, sure," the inventor said. "I've been down that road before. You Fact Finder types are all alike. It'll be six months before I hear anything from you, and by then somebody else will have ripped me off, and I'll be left with nothing but your lengthy memo."

Some people have experienced Quick Start efforts that were "ditsy," "scatterbrained," or came from a person they considered "a flake." An uncommitted insistence in Quick Start can be a flavor-of-the-month type who jumps on a bandwagon only until the next fast-buck opportunity comes along. It takes only a few experiences with such people to become leery of trusting the next highly insistent Quick Start on the team.

It's as easy to build stereotypes around instinctive makeups as anything else. Yet each person deserves a chance to build trust without conative bias. Any method of classifying behavior can be abused by those unwilling to give people a chance to succeed. Especially on Innovation Teams, such biases need to be discouraged. Otherwise nothing new will be developed.

Eliminating judgmental attitudes and biases is a primary goal of training for the Innovation Team. Attempting to place a value, whether positive or negative, on one MO over another will inhibit contributions. Brainstorming stops as soon as one person criticizes another's ad-lib. Developing and marketing innovations is a team process, so the entire range of performance modes must be recognized for the value each one adds. This is best accomplished in team meetings that reinforce the strengths of each participant, not by pointing to a star who is probably insistent in Quick Start.

In one such situation, cohorts in a fast-food marketing operation were astounded to discover that their manager was a resistant Quick Start. "He can't be!" one friend and coworker claimed. "I see him push for innovation all the time. He's intent upon our coming out with the most creative marketing plans in the history of the company." These statements gave some clues to the source of confusion. Don, the manager, had given the impression he was a Quick Start because he *wanted* innovation. Close questioning revealed that he pushed *others* to come up with novel solutions. In other words, he was good at encouraging the Quick Start contribution, but not good at providing it himself. His strong suit was keeping outrageous suggestions in check by comparing them with past failures—a Fact Finder approach—and creating Follow Thru plans that integrated diverse options into a unified program.

BUILDING AN INNOVATION TEAM
AGAINST THE ODDS

A PHARMACEUTICAL FIRM IN THE NORTHWEST WAS PUTTING TOGETHER A TEAM TO develop new products for the health-care industry. It required technical experts from a variety of disciplines, along with administrators, clerical people, and marketers. Armed with a large number of qualified candidates in terms of educational requirements and experience, the field was narrowed according to conative capabilities.

The company's recruitment efforts had led to problems. Given the level of scientific expertise required, it was inundated with Fact Finder–intense people, those who naturally gravitate toward research-oriented fields of study and deal well with the complexities of scientific investigations. At first the company believed this was appropriate. After all, the KCI-Cs, which were completed by managers, ended up requiring insistence in Fact Finder for almost every job. They had overlooked the need for people like Ed Hurd, an engineer who operates within a highly technical engineering company yet uses his Quick Start push to start the innovation process. Without someone like Ed in the mix, this company wouldn't get innovative results. If *everyone* became immersed in the specifics of research, who would get things moving? Insistent–Fact Finder energy will delve deeper and deeper into research, sometimes indefinitely. Those who prevent in the mode interrupt, so people will stop staring at their spreadsheets and move on.

The inertia of a bunch of insistent Fact Finders caused this team to repeatedly get caught up in debating esoteric details. The director needed to search for people with the right professional skills *and* the right balance of conative MOs.

Recruiting Change Makers

None of the applicants for one of the technical positions fit the company's conative criteria. Candidates' KCI results indicated they would all take insignificant risks and resist trial-and-error methods. The recruiting techniques were obviously not adequate, and they had to try again. There was a concern that headhunters often get fixated on résumés with relevant experience, completely overlooking the instinct-driven dynamics of team projects. The company decided to recruit for Quick Start talent. An ad was placed in a professional journal. As Quick Start bait, it used terms such as: "unique project" . . . "break-thru opportunity" . . . "pioneering effort" . . . "leading-edge program" . . . "experimental process."

The need couldn't be ignored, even though it was difficult to find the right combination of knowledge, interest, and instincts. The director understood he'd be setting up the group for failure if he didn't immediately address the conative issues. They had to have a team that could bring about change. In fact, so much effort was spent ensuring the input of Quick Start, the resistant Quick Starts in the group grew concerned that a bias existed against their method of operation. The word *synergy* had been used only as a catchword, so it didn't mean much to anybody. When it was defined for them in instinctive terms, it was more palatable yet still disconcerting. The point was clearly demonstrated through Glop Shop.

I used this exercise to show how three different teams would approach an innovative assignment that had some parallels to the company's goals. Each had similar skills and expertise. To get the diversity of MOs for three types of teams, we had to bring in employees from other parts of the company. Based on conative mix, two of the teams were designed to perform poorly, while one was balanced, having all the necessary conative elements for success. Each consisted of three members.

Team X was polarized in two modes. It included either insistent or resistant Fact Finders and Quick Starts, with no one having the middle-ground accommodation in either mode.

$$X1 = 3\text{-}4\text{-}8\text{-}7$$
$$X2 = 8\text{-}8\text{-}2\text{-}2$$
$$X3 = 7\text{-}3\text{-}9\text{-}4$$

Team Y had inertia in Quick Start, with all three members insistent in that mode, and no one with an insistence in Fact Finder.

$$Y1 = 3\text{-}4\text{-}8\text{-}5$$
$$Y2 = 2\text{-}2\text{-}8\text{-}8$$
$$Y3 = 5\text{-}7\text{-}7\text{-}3$$

Team Z was synergistic. It was designed with a balance of insistence, accommodation, and resistance in each mode.

$$Z1 = 7\text{-}3\text{-}8\text{-}7$$
$$Z2 = 6\text{-}7\text{-}3\text{-}5$$
$$Z3 = 3\text{-}4\text{-}5\text{-}7$$

I asked each team to use the Glop Shop materials to build a prototype that would explain the importance of the Innovation Team's mission. Team X had the person with the highest drive to innovate. X3 tried to find a unique way to meet the criteria. X2 attempted to slow down the process until the participants had discussed the merits of one possibility before moving on to others. Meanwhile, X1 disrupted X2's sorting of materials and began experimenting with some newfangled constructions. Conative conflicts kept the group from interacting productively. They were polite to one another, but the polarized effort caused a disruptive push-and-shove effect. This example illustrated the typical problems of failing R&D teams.

Team Y, with all its Quick Start energy, was overwhelmed with initiators of innovation, all trying to find unique solutions without building on one another's prototypes. Y2 immediately took charge of the materials and began building something that hadn't been agreed upon by the others. Meanwhile, Y3 tried to put together an inventive plan that met some of the criteria, but to no avail. Y3's attempts to discuss priorities and organize the materials were rejected by the others, who were off and running in different directions, each trying to use the one-of-a-kind objects.

The realization that these same problems could surface if these were real project teams made the group shudder. It's rare for Glop Shop to receive as much committed energy as on-the-job responsibilities. So it's a good bet that real-life, highly determined teams that are polarized or have inertia suffer from even more frustration than was reported by the members of teams X and Y.

Team Y's activities were stressful for both participants and observers. There was no interplay of conflicting approaches; just three individuals off on their own tangents. The team members who suffered through four minutes of inertia declared they were done before time was up, even though they hadn't accomplished any of the goals. These three Quick Starts had rushed to the first things that came into their minds. Too many Innovation Teams start off with this unfortunate mix. Early agreement on low-level accomplishments puts them out of their pain. There's no joy of true accomplishment of goals.

Team Z had the greatest probability of producing an innovative prototype. There was insistence in each mode. Innovations began with and were self-edited by Z1. Z2 offered the vital element of structuring the effort so it was completed on time and presented in a comprehensive way. Z3 built the model to demonstrate the workings of their prototype.

There was no runaway initiation unchecked by editing or prevention. There was someone to respond to each striving effort. This team successfully carried out an assignment that required it to innovate.

The Glop Shop exercise isn't just a way to see what *might* happen. When I predicted how they would behave, I wasn't guessing, I was absolutely certain what would happen and why. Because the outcomes of polarized or inert teams can be predicted with such accuracy, the Glop Shop exercise was an effective way of proving to everyone involved that sticking to the right instinctive mix on each aspect of the project would help them achieve results.

Tolerating Intolerance to Change

Few management issues caused the director more headaches than calming the concerns of the resistant Quick Starts. He couldn't live without them because they kept the team from going off on impractical tangents. But they also slowed down the innovative process. The one thing he had to ensure was that they were not put in positions of power *over* others. This was where the true team effort came into play. Everyone had to contribute without cutting off others' avenues for success.

Lorenzo, whose KCI result is 9-5-2-5, offered a terrific background on the scientific issues and participated in field studies for which he kept thorough records. But the intense Fact Finder tied up meetings when sharing the details of his findings. The insistent Quick Starts had too much on their plates to sit around and listen to what they found to be a tedious compendium of information without a bottom line to it. Lorenzo had to learn to summarize; no one had been able to get through to him previously about this issue. But his Fact Finder was vital to the team's productivity, so the director made a commitment to helping Lorenzo learn how to function well on the project.

Lorenzo had to be accurate, and to him accurate meant thorough. The group needed those qualities from him, but not on *every* issue. The director asked him to select the three points that were most crucial to the project and explain the key issues relating to them. His Fact Finder energy was good at such evaluative processes, so he was able to help the team focus on the drop-dead concerns. Having Lorenzo commit his recommendations to paper provided an opportunity for him to tell others all the information he'd gathered without taking meeting time to do it. He used his Fact Finder talents to provide a cover sheet for his report, outlining the most important findings and giving recommendations in rank order. Then he pared that page down further by highlighting with a yellow marker the most significant words and phrases.

This process wasn't as frustrating for Lorenzo as it would have been for less insistent Fact Finders. When team members with the greatest initiative in Quick Start jotted off bulleted recommendations on a single sheet, attached to something torn out of a magazine, and covered with a Post-it note or two, Lorenzo marveled at how that person could "get away with" doing it that way. "It would keep me awake at night," he said, "if I hadn't done my homework. I have to compare all the options before I can think about making a recommendation." Clarifying his priorities helped Lorenzo contribute more to the innovation process.

Yet if Lorenzo interrupted other team members for more clarification, it frustrated them. He didn't get far asking those who don't share his need for facts to submit written documentation. As a result, Lorenzo found ways to probe behind others' assumptions without slowing them down. Taking time to read the original proposal and talk with those insistent or accommodating Fact Finders who had been around since the inception of the project helped. "Why are we trying to innovate in this arena?" was an issue he raised that helped the group focus its energy. He turned to Maxine, a resident Follow Thru, for help in putting together the historical pieces to the puzzle.

Maxine, whose KCI result is 5-8-4-3, wasn't inclined to tell Lorenzo everything he needed to find out, but she did direct him to the relevant files. Maxine's Follow Thru talent had the place organized so that insistent Quick Starts could get their hands on bottom-line information even when they didn't use the exact title for the reports. Lorenzo used her as a source for starting his in-depth study—and learned early on that he'd better return anything he borrowed from her files. His information needs couldn't interfere with her need to keep it catalogued for everyone's use. As issue after issue requiring different instincts came along, having KCI results tacked up near their desks helped remind all the players of the mutual benefits of their mix of methods. "I know now that people didn't leave meetings when I was talking because they were being rude," Lorenzo said. "They were doing me the favor of not interrupting what I needed to say. I used to be insulted by things I now understand are not judgmental. I'm thrilled to be part of a team that's going to change the way this company does business; especially knowing my contribution is going to make sure it'll actually work."

Innovation as an organizational process is essential for growth and development. It cannot be stereotyped as the domain of only insistent Quick Starts, nor can it be pulled completely away from innovative striving to operate through other instincts. It is an arena in which the conative dimension has proved to play a crucial role. Without accurate assessment and management of conative talents on an Innovation Team, a company puts its future at risk.

CHAPTER THIRTEEN

INFORMATION SYSTEMS

DO-OR-DIE OPERATIONS

Have you ever tried to make an airline reservation, only to be told "the system is down"? Or have someone trace a mail-order item that's "lost in the system"? If so, you know why Information Systems (IS), which uses technology to enhance the speed and accuracy of information, have become critical to meeting customer needs. IS is also critical in improving management capabilities, because good management decisions rely on thorough and timely information. This reliance on technology has turned IS from a support function into an area that can be a distinct competitive advantage—when it works. When it doesn't, we wonder how we ever allowed ourselves to be at its mercy.

An IS system is only as good as the creativity of those who build it and only as useful as the end user's talent for operating it effectively. An Information System is developed and maintained by people striving to meet the needs of customers who run the conative gamut. "I could do it faster manually," says the frustrated accounting manager who once did payroll without the computer, but now has no way of retrieving overtime information, absentee records, and other essential data without the system. He's reliant on it, like it or not. Some customers, like this accounting manager, won't take time to figure out how it could help; others seem to lose data on computers just by striking a key. There are users who intuit its capabilities but forget to make backup copies. On the other hand, the computer greatly magnifies others' productivity. To meet these varied and constantly changing demands, teams that design, maintain, and manage information systems need a full conative spectrum of talents, each coming into play at just the right time.

Today's companies rely on accurate, current information in order to succeed, and Information Systems have become the primary conduit. The technical demands of IS have created a focus on bringing together people with specialized skills. Outsiders often perceive IS as an area where instinct is useless. "After all," said a personnel manager, "computers are all logic. You should think solutions through, not 'go with your gut' like you can in marketing." This attitude is part of the reason IS is sometimes perceived as an "essential albatross": having value, but heavily weighted down with unnecessary information, and not always responsive to customer needs. Yet when IS teams trust their members' instincts, this image is unfounded.

REDUCING CYCLE TIME

GOING THROUGH THE MANY PHASES OF AN IS PROJECT CAN BE LONG AND ARDUOUS, especially when the system's user needs everything done yesterday but doesn't want to take the time upfront to provide the information necessary for ultimate success. Trusting and properly utilizing instincts can help improve the situation. Jack Spurgeon, vice-president of information systems for Eastman Chemical, said, "We've gone through so many different attempts to find the right way to get people to work together on IS projects. Never before have we gotten down to the heart of the matter. Even though our projects are complex, what people need is to relax and contribute their instinctive energy. Doing so has helped reduce the cycle time on IS projects, and a by-product of that is reduced stress.

"Just knowing each others' KCI results cuts planning time," said Jack, whose KCI result is 6-5-8-3. "We know who to count on to contribute in certain ways." This chemical company's operations are so complex that its IS group includes over three hundred people. He calls the first step of using the KCI with his direct reports the "kidding stage." Jack added, "It brings people in a work environment together productively, so they can tolerate each other's differences."

After his managers completed a Kolbe TeamSuccess seminar, Jack had each one route his or her KCI result to the others. "The IS team needs to understand the dynamics of how it works," he said, "which can only be done when they understand each other's MO." The Eastman Chemical IS team has learned to start the design phase of a systems project with Fact Finders hammering out strategies. Then they count on Quick Start–insistent people to brainstorm alternatives. As Jack remarked, "I want innovation on the front end; on the back end I use Fact Finder and Follow Thru again, to tie the ribbon." In other words, Jack sees IS projects as going through a series of phases, each requiring a slightly different conative emphasis. Throughout the project, the team has to recognize how and why various talents come to the fore.

The biggest problem Jack had encountered in the past was being able to quickly assess the source of an IS problem. "We've traditionally spent an inordinate amount of time trying to figure out if we had all the data," he said. "We spent days, weeks, months, with projects that went down the tubes. There's a point in time when you have to move on, particularly when customers have to be satisfied. With the right mix of instincts we can shorten that time, even create synergy rather than inertia." He reviews team members' KCI results prior to meetings so he can better understand the needs of that group. "It's knowledge I can leverage to help the group," he said.

THE CONATIVE NEEDS OF IS

THE TOP PRODUCERS IN BUSINESS TODAY REALIZE THEY WILL NOT BE ABLE TO respond to changing economic conditions without a flexible Information System. This requires the right balance of creativity through all the Action Modes, as well as technical expertise. When these instinctive requirements are not taken into account, IS's bright and highly trained minds will not be enough to produce the desired result. IS is a data-processing function that relies heavily on accuracy in gathering and disseminating details. That would seem to be a job for Fact Finder and Follow Thru energy. But, one or two modes cannot dominate a team if it is to accomplish significant results. While Fact Finder– and Follow Thru–insistent contributors are essential to the specialized process of designing information systems, people with these insistences have to refrain from dominating the environment. They must not let their conative biases handcuff the contributions of other instinctive modes.

"All I wanted was a simple tracking system for purchases, one where

I could look up a supplier quickly and find out what we bought from them, and when," stated Amy, the purchasing manager for a medium-sized hotel chain. "Instead the IS department created *more* work for me. Now I have to fill out extensive forms every time I buy something and jump through hoops just to retrieve information that would have taken me two minutes with my old filing system. I wish I'd never asked for their help." In their eagerness to develop a complete system, this IS group lost sight of the original request, which had a relatively simple solution. Instead it provided Amy with much more information than she had asked for or needed. The IS department was so focused on the cognitive that the conative, or common sense, was lost.

Such ever-changing variations in the conative needs of its end users influence the necessary makeup of the IS team as it cycles through the development-delivery process. IS requires a wider variety of conative approaches than most business groups, since innovation and systems design lead to the need for maintenance and troubleshooting. The changing needs of the customer base require diverse talents.

The IS team must be carefully crafted to find the right allocation of both the required skills and the balance of conative talents. To do it right the first time, each step in the life cycle of an IS project should be assessed according to company and team objectives. As projects move through the various phases, leadership and project groups must be adjusted to meet those goals. To illustrate this, let's look at all the phases of an IS project in a small mail-order company.

PROJECT LIFE CYCLES: CHANGING NEEDS

Phase One: Problem (Opportunity) Recognition

The instincts of every employee were drawn toward the use of computers. No one doubted technology's value in maintaining mailing lists, tracking inventory and orders, monitoring financial data, and updating prospect lists. In the 1980s the benefits were apparent, but neither the money nor the expertise was available. So the company moved slowly, buying some personal computers, some software programs off the shelf, and using vendors for large projects such as maintaining mailing lists. By early 1990 the company had a serious problem. It was growing rapidly, and its systems couldn't keep up. One software program it used wouldn't talk to another, so there was no integration of inventory data with sales and no easy way to convert sales into an automatic billing system.

Computers weren't linked together in this company, so information entered on one machine couldn't be called up on another. Productivity was often held up because people were waiting in line to use the computer. The more information added to the primary data-base, the slower it functioned on all transactions. The machines' memory was used up faster than anyone expected. Equipment was replaced with whatever was on sale rather than planning properly for hardware needs. The mishmash of marginally useful machinery was costing more to maintain than it was worth. Productivity was dropping; something had to change.

The president of the company called a meeting. "We've got a problem," she said, "and an opportunity. We've taken a haphazard approach to managing our computer needs, and that approach is clearly failing. I think it's time we joined the world of Information Systems. We need to find out how to get all our PCs talking to each other, and how to manage our information more efficiently. Who wants to be in charge?"

There were no takers. Everyone recognized there was a problem, but no one had the expertise to deal with it. She ended up choosing two people—an insistent Quick Start and an insistent Fact Finder—to take over the next step.

Phase Two: Feasibility Analysis

Mix Quick Start ingenuity with Fact Finder practicality, and you have a good balance for a *feasibility study*, or assessment of the costs and benefits of developing an integrated information system for the company. Quick Start energy plays the "what if?" game, pushing possibilities to the limits. Quick Start instincts have always been crucial to Information Systems; without them, the technology wouldn't have exploded into as many new and amazing applications. To have a complete feasibility analysis, the Quick Start "what ifs?" had to be answered with well-documented arguments that came from the Fact Finder mentality. It was more than a question of technical knowledge. The insistent Fact Finder instinctively turned to experts, researched complex possibilities, and compared the benefits. "We *could* do that," the Fact Finder typically answered, "but we'd better find out if it's *really* what we need." Enter the next phase.

Phase Three: Analysis

The Quick Start should step out of the way at this point and let someone else study his wish list in great depth. The Fact Finder instinct is the best resource to determine the comparative benefits of various options. For example, if the mail-order company linked all its computers, entry-level computer operators would have access to corporate financial records. Fact Finder analyses determined that would be dangerous. They backed off and took time to figure out exactly which PCs would have which level of communication available. Would any or all of the off-site operations be able to transmit information by modem? What if they all tried to communicate at the same time? These were issues for strategic planners, people with a combination of Fact Finder expertise and the Follow Thru nose for smelling out systems. They tracked transactions from inception all the way through the process. Using the right instincts, they took the necessary time to conduct a thorough analysis before moving on to the commitments of the design phase.

Phase Four: Design

If designing an information system simply involved establishing a pattern, Follow Thru talent alone would be able to get the job done. Instead this phase requires a balance among the modes. The mail-order company gave an insistent Follow Thru the leadership role here, so he could most influence the outcome. But an insistent Quick Start was also needed to seek alternatives when plans reached dead ends. Opportunities to engage this troubleshooting mode were plentiful because of a series of unforeseen problems. Fact Finder energy was necessary in design as options were reevaluated. Implementor instincts also became critical when dealing with the physical layout of facilities, handling the network design, and hardware issues.

Phase Five: Construction

The term *construction* in IS is possibly misleading. This is not the type of activity for which Implementors are well endowed; it is strictly Follow Thru and Fact Finder work. Construction is the programming phase

during which minute instructions are fed into the machines in a pains-
takingly systematic process. A minor omission could result in a major
problem. A few wrong keystrokes while constructing the inventory-
control program could lead to the mail-order company being told it had
hundreds of musical shoes in stock in a range of sizes, accepting money
for them, then discovering it had only three hundred pairs of size 9 AA,
forcing a return of the money for all orders in other sizes, and within the
time frame demanded by government regulations. The possibilities for
error in constructing any Information System are always present. You
definitely want to avoid the "once over lightly" approach of the speedy
and distractable Quick Start, which could bring about a disaster. People
who prevent in the mode are needed at this stage.

Phase Six: Installation

Getting the system up and running—setting up the equipment—requires
Implementor talent. But the wiring must be done exactly to plan, so don't
let the Follow Thrus off the hook. This stage requires a team effort
involving the handiness and spatial-relations knack of Implementor and
the pattern consistency of Follow Thru. The partnership is so key at this
point that neither will be able to succeed without the other. Someone has
to read the map while the other is driving.

Phase Seven: Operation

Day-to-day operations for a system entail accommodation in every mode.
Too much insistence in Fact Finder explanations would delay data entry.
Highly intense Quick Starts try to jimmy the system to get it to do things
it wasn't set up to do, causing malfunctions. However, the ability to
accommodate others' sense of urgency is a necessity. Too much Implementor focuses on technology instead of applications. Even the consistency of a dominant Follow Thru can be troublesome if that person is
overly insistent on runing things sequentially. It is difficult to find operators who are all Facilitators, so it is important for management to
promote people's use of their insistent and resistant energies.

Phase Eight: Maintenance

If everything in the maintenance phase has gone like clockwork, monitoring the system would be a Follow Thru task because of the need for consistency and regularity of the function. However, Information Systems rarely run smoothly for long, and there will be crises with any IS project. Therefore the full Creative Power of all four modes is necessary for ongoing success. The mail-order company finally had its new system in place, the bugs worked out, and was discovering the benefits from it. Then the system crashed. No one knew why. By this point, the company was dependent on the system, and the work of the entire operation was on hold. A team effort was needed to get it back up. An insistent Quick Start brainstormed the possibilities, while a Follow Thru reviewed all the procedures to see if anything was amiss. The Implementor-dominant team member tackled the hardware end of it, checking out wires, phone lines, plugs, and the guts of the machines. A Fact Finder got on the phone, seeking expert advice, and assessed the priorities for diagnosing particular problems. Every instinctive mode made a direct contribution to determining the problem and discovering a timely and workable solution.

Leaving any instinctive need out of the IS equation is a guarantee of trouble: communication systems on long-term hold, for instance, or inventory controls out of control. If a Fact Finder mind isn't present during the design phase, important specifications will be overlooked. Without sufficient Follow Thru effort, transitions between the phases will be bumpy. Quick Start involvement is crucial to challenge the team to provide the greatest possible flexibility. Installation without Implementor contributions can cause ongoing malfunctions because all the efforts to create an effective, intangible software system are wasted when they don't interface properly with the hardware.

RESULTS-DRIVEN PROJECTS

THE PROBLEMS CAN BE GIGANTIC WITH IS PROJECTS, BUT SO CAN THE OPPORTUNIties. Striving Instincts have proved an effective forecaster of success—and regret—in the high-stakes IS world. The following case studies show the practical applications of instinct in different results-driven phases of Information Systems efforts.

Case One: Designing an Innovative System

A Fortune 500 company pulled thirty-five high performers off other tasks to compile a leading-edge information system for its global operations. Their design would become the first application of new software to completely integrate all of the company's worldwide data and communications. Sophisticated systems were essential to track inventories, sales, cash flow, and customer service. Determined to get it right the first time, decision makers incorporated the Kolbe ABC approach in selecting and managing the team. By doing this, many problems were avoided and others corrected during the delicate design phase.

Zelta Company (obviously a pseudonym) escaped many problems that often occur when technical wizards are brought into a project, by check-out out conative issues *before* making assignments on its high-risk–high-reward IS design team. Organizations in the design stage are often so busy forming a team and getting everybody trained, they put off dealing with issues of instinct. They bring in people with the skills but wait to evaluate the conative mix until *after* pulling people off other jobs, uprooting them, and disrupting former teams.

Eight team managers with conative synergy (see chart) were led by a project coordinator whose individual KCI (6-5-6-4) and Job KCIs (B = 6-6-7-3, C = 6-5-6-5) indicated he was well suited for the necessary role of keeping conative peace. As a Facilitator, he was an excellent choice in a situation with reliance on all four forms of initiation from managers, and thus a strong probability of conflicts. He would be a natural at bridging the differences.

This Facilitator was also an introvert who could bring consensus without making others overly aware of his involvement. During the first meeting with the managers, he sat back as the others discussed their fears concerning deadlines, user cooperation, and potential technical difficulties. Once they'd drawn a dreary picture for the probabilities of success, he noted they had an advantage that would help them overcome seemingly impossible odds: their instincts.

Each manager's conative strengths were validated when KCI results were shared within the group. They readily agreed that they had vastly different ways of operating. After a team-building seminar in which I emphasized the equality of their conative talents, they opened up with stories on one another. "Yeah, Ted's no better than the rest of us," Horatio, a Quick Start, said teasingly of a Fact Finder–Follow Thru manager. "He just thinks his facts are better than ours. Turns out he's

Kolbe Management Report
SYNERGY REPORT

For

ZELTA COMPANY

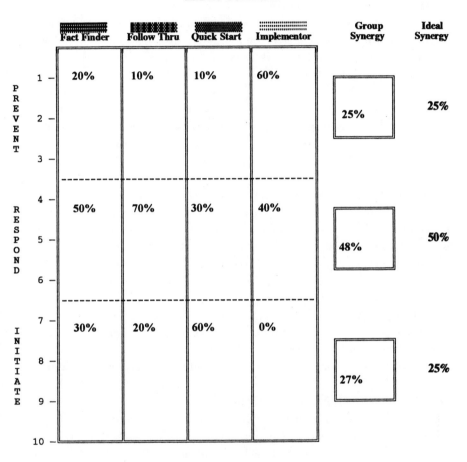

This analysis is based on a total of 8 respondents.

right! But the last time he pointed that out to me, I wasn't very receptive. He told me he'd gone over the word-processing needs five times, so he had to be right. I figured anybody who had to go over it that many times must not know what he was doing. We Quick Starts do it once over lightly and take our chances."

Understanding their equal conative footing helped when it came to responsibility for cooperative efforts. They also realized they needed diverse talents to get their work accomplished. They had discovered that together they had what it took.

The Facilitator encouraged others to initiate proposals. His management approach was to build on the energy within the group. The resistant Fact Finders sought specificity without apology. "I feel a sense of relief," an insistent Follow Thru explained, "because I don't have to explain why the flowcharts have to be sent back to me on schedule. It's as if there's a shorthand way I can explain why it matters. Others now know I *need* Follow Thru, and they now know *they need me to need it*."

The full team met as a group so every participant's instinctive strengths could be shared. This confirmed the broader synergy of the total group, as well as the appropriate selection of particular people for specific roles.

One key player (7-5-6-3) had been added to a task force working on *scripting*, or the documentation for programming. As far as his skills were concerned, he seemed an unlikely choice; it had been years since he had done much programming. However, he knew enough to serve as a good conative bridge between the Quick Start manager and the predominantly Fact Finder/resistant–Quick Start task force. As long as he was willing to commit to that role, he would be an important moderating force.

The issue was put directly on the table. "Will you interpret Ellen's bottom line demands so the resistant Quick Starts don't rebel over them?" he was asked. "Of course, I've done that for a lot of Quick Starts over the years," he said. Then, turning to his manager, he added, "Ellen, I empathize with your sense of urgency, but you do-it-yesterday folks can be unrealistic. The way I see it, my job is to explain why it has to get done sooner rather than later, not just make demands that are perceived as unreasonable and unrealistic. It's better if you'll let me deal directly with this issue, so others don't get frustrated by the deadlines and cause errors along the way."

Communicating conative methods without standing in judgment of one another's MOs became a significant part of this IS group's competitive advantage. They were discovering they could leverage one another's

Kolbe Management Report
SYNERGY REPORT

For

ZELTA COMPANY

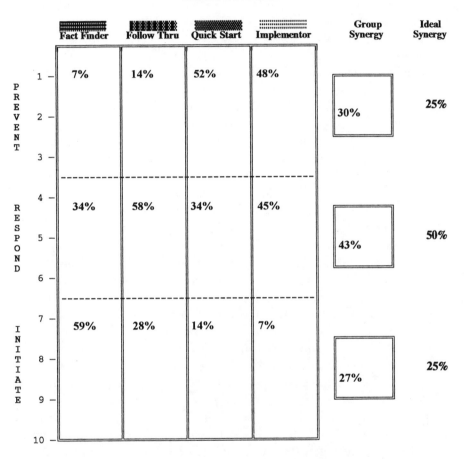

This analysis is based on a total of 35 respondents.

mental energies to increase productivity on complex problems. It took time, of course, and reminders. One subgroup was put together according to its members' experience with the issues involved; they immediately got waylaid on perfecting solutions for a programming problem. While every other benchmark was reached on schedule, this subgroup was consistently behind. "What's the problem?" the Facilitator asked. "They're all capable of doing what needs to be done. But it's not happening."

The Facilitator's wake-up call occurred when he looked closely at the MOs of the people in the group. Everyone was resistant to Follow Thru. And they'd gone off on several Quick Start tangents, trying to break new ground with innovative solutions. They'd let their Fact Finder instincts run to the point that they were authorities on the issues involved. Those who accommodated in the Implementor mode had chosen to pound away personally at the keyboard to enter data. The problem wasn't that they hadn't committed the talents they had available, nor that they didn't understand the assignment. They had conative inertia, and it was costing them dearly.

Keeping that in mind helped Zelta Company's IS design group to consider how both internal and external customers would be using the system conatively. They had to provide in-depth information for Fact Finders that allowed printouts of extensive backup data. Follow Thru users demanded that the system be streamlined and efficient to use, with ready accessibility of the most used functions, and none of the deviations that make information retrieval difficult. If the system would automatically reject anything out of order, it would suit them especially well. A good system also had to address the on-line speed essential for Quick Start use. "I don't need pounds of computer sheets dumped on my desk," said a business-unit director insistent in Quick Start, "I have to have data summaries that I can call up on the screen. If I have to go back and forth between menus or scroll through a bunch of pages, the system's too cumbersome."

The best way to ensure that the instincts of all users are considered is for the design team to mirror those needs. By analyzing historical problems, exploring currently available technology, and imagining every possible opportunity, Zelta's project team proved it could satisfy the conflicting priorities of a global operation. As of this writing, every milestone has been successfully reached, and the system has been enthusiastically incorporated into the company's global operations.

Case Two: Operating Against The Odds

TGL, a medium-sized high-tech company, develops and markets advanced-program applications to outside customers, but it had lousy internal communication systems. Putting on a brave face cost it months in the split-second world of its competitive market. When the company finally took a hard look at the problem, it became clear that its fast-track technology was being broadsided by people problems. Kolbe Management Reports pinpointed where strain caused by unrealistic self-expectations, and tension from supervisors' requirements were hurting productivity. Confronting these issues, as you'll see, helped force a reconciliation between objectives and conative options in the ongoing operational phase.

TGL was owned by three computer geniuses who marketed sophisticated programs to retail stores for sales and inventory controls. Its market share of the previous year fell 12 percent with the introduction of a new system from a competitor. First-quarter results for the current year indicated another major setback. Panic set in as everyone wondered how they could possibly work any harder to regain TGL's edge.

The firm's three partners were good friends who'd left a Fortune 500 corporation to begin their own company. TGL grew rapidly over the first five years, based primarily on the specialized programs two of them, Ted and George, had designed for the retail industry while moonlighting. Their mental energies had been invested in this project long before TGL was even a bona fide business. The third person, Louie, was the business partner, brought on board as an equal partner to give the company the management experience Ted and George knew they lacked.

The conative profiles for TGL's owners were: Ted = 8-5-4-4; George = 6-8-3-4; and Louie = 6-2-8-3. As the business grew, all three got caught up in marketing and operations. They developed an Information System for retail chains, for which they provided technical support. Their well-paid service division handled that aspect of the business. They saw the operating stage of the process, once designed, no longer required their attention. As highly accommodating or insistent Fact Finders, Ted, George, and Louie believed their thorough documentation and user's manuals on the program's applications more than adequately met the ongoing requirements of their customers. None of them saw a need for a less complex approach, and this hurt them in the marketplace.

"TGL's got a great product," one of their customers said, "but only a handful of my managers use it to capacity. We're paying a lot of money to license a product that has much more stuff than we can use. On top of that, I can't make heads or tails out of the documents they send. If you have to be a rocket scientist to get your dollar's worth from it, it doesn't make any sense for us anymore. Not now that there's a program that's more adaptable to our needs." The user had stuck with TGL only as long as its technology was ahead of the game. Ted and George knew they should get in front of the competition, but they didn't have the time or energy to start all over. Even Louie's Quick Start was maxed out. But they didn't *need* to start at the beginning. The problem wasn't so much with the product but with customer interface; their ability to satisfy the end user.

Louie was so busy selling customers on the benefits of their system, he wasn't hearing complaints. It was natural for him to overlook the trend that was building because of his resistance to Follow Thru. This preventative talent kept him from getting bogged down in routines, but it also kept him from seeing the pattern to the complaints. He could have trusted his Quick Start intuition, but when he tried to do so, his partners knocked him off stride by demanding he back up his hunches with specifics. Louie knew customers were using TGL's system because nothing could compete with it, but they didn't really *like* having to use it.

When Louie tried explaining this to Ted, he got a patronizing response. "Computers scare most people," Ted said. "But what's the big deal? The world is becoming dependent upon them anyway. Our customers need the system, and the longer they have it installed, the more comfortable they'll get with it."

People resistant to Implementor are unlikely to ever become completely at ease with machinery. As long as everything works without a hitch, they can coexist with it, but the moment a hard-drive warning flashes or some strange noise emanates from the "monster," these people are likely to retreat as far as possible from the situation.

Resistant Fact Finders' instinctive reaction to the TGL product was to avoid it in the first place. The complexities were too great. District managers who either weren't insistent in Fact Finder or who didn't view the software issues as a priority would eagerly delegate all responsibility for its applications. Store managers with the same conative makeup would do likewise. So the connection TGL had with its clients was usually through a low-level employee. None of the partners in the software firm used their Fact Finder to monitor training or to adapt the system to users' needs, so when cracks appeared in customer loyalty, it took them a long time to recognize the problems and react.

When they finally retraced the problems associated with the client training function in their company, they found a department that was conatively polarized. Its several insistent Quick Starts were focused on winning internal battles instead of accommodating customers' needs. The resistant Quick Starts had lobbied for standardized training videos and on-line interactive programs. These would cut the presentation possibilities for the promotion-oriented Quick Starts, who were increasing their take-home pay through sales incentives. Videos and on-line programs would cut back on customer interface, giving them fewer opportunities to sell more products.

Louie, the Quick Start, had introduced the bonus plan for trainers, and initially it injected some additional cash into the business. But it also distracted the intuitive trainers from reading the needs of their customers, a cost that was far too great. The trainer sales-bonus plan's short-term focus frustrated the long-term security needs of Follow Thrus such as George, as well as the Follow Thru trainers. George could identify with those who had tried to structure the training process and make it more accessible to users. Of course, their suggestions of alternative techniques were geared to Follow Thru users who would go through the entire program at the established pace. The Quick Starts were right about their kindred spirits tuning out.

TGL exemplified the multitude of problems that can arise when user training and ongoing adaptations are not properly addressed. It takes conative energy to use a data-processing system. If the system doesn't allow operators to use their talents, it won't be used to its fullest capacity. People do not adapt their manner of working for machines, so technology has to adapt to people's instinctive approaches.

The solutions began when the internal conative stresses at TGL were identified and methods for reducing them were established. Once the company developed a project-team approach, it began to maximize the variety of conative talents at its disposal. Addressing user needs through a synergistic team increased customer retention dramatically. George used his Follow Thru talents to begin monitoring customer satisfaction and found a direct correlation between the conative balance on the interface team and the rating levels. Training was also reorganized with a team approach, mixing natural inclinations together. A separate development task force—again, with a good conative balance—worked on a multimedia approach to augment face-to-face training. These measures made all the difference. TGL held firm in its market share for three quarters, then began to regain its competitive position.

MANAGING INFORMATION SYSTEMS

MANAGING INFORMATION SYSTEMS (MIS) HAS BECOME A SPECIALIZED FIELD. MY client data, with over three hundred senior managers of Information Systems, show a clear conative difference between their talents and those of the people they manage. The highest levels in IS are achieved most of the time (70 percent) by people highly accommodating or insistent in Quick Start. Only 52 percent of the people they supervise fall into that range in the mode.

Perhaps one of the reasons for this is the almost constant state of crises in which people manage in an IS environment. As Lani Spund, chief systems architect at Apple Computer, Inc., put it, operating in an IS world causes you to develop "a habit of anxiety." Not too many resistant Quick Starts would choose to be in charge of such risky, chaotic situations.

Because of their Fact Finder expertise, sometimes IS specialists get trapped in the individual-producer role and are not available for leadership roles; they're considered too vital doing what they do. They use their energy as specialists and have none left to manage others. One of the challenges of MIS is to keep technological needs from encroaching on people's ability to advance within the organization.

When computer experts become caught up in the cognitive functions of the technology, they may have to be relieved temporarily of team responsibilities. They want *one more* answer, or to test *one more* hypothesis when there's no time to do it, yet they take the time. Separating cognitive curiosity and motivation from conative effort helps refocus energy. "You may want to know more about how this function works and where it will take you," one manager had to caution a state employee, "but we're under the gun now. You're not holding up your end of the bargain if you don't put your energy into doing the work that *has* to be done."

Ron Silacci, systems test supervisor for quality assurance for AT&T Bell Laboratories, is a Follow Thru initiator and resistant Quick Start who suffers during the crunch period of an IS project. "When we're in the middle of change," he said, "I feel like we will never get through it. I'm too hurried and unable to put in enough time to get on top of the situation. It's always in the back of my mind that I have to finish this part of the project, close the door on action items, or there will be trouble later." But there's light at the end of the IS tunnel for this supervisor. "Others around me depend upon my Follow Thru and play to my

Kolbe Management Report
SYNERGY REPORT

For

IS SENIOR MANAGEMENT

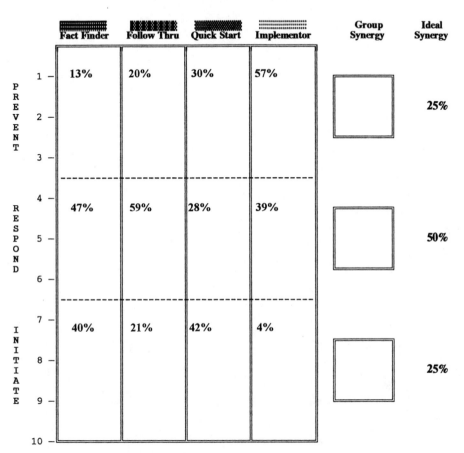

This analysis is based on a total of 153 respondents.

Kolbe Management Report
SYNERGY REPORT

For

IS NON-MANAGEMENT

	Fact Finder	Follow Thru	Quick Start	Implementor	Group Synergy	Ideal Synergy
PREVENT 1	6%	14%	48%	45%		
2						25%
3						
RESPOND 4	34%	49%	35%	48%		
5						50%
6						
INITIATE 7	60%	37%	17%	7%		
8						25%
9						
10						

This analysis is based on a total of 254 respondents.

strengths. Since I'm recognized and valued, it helps me get through the chaotic periods. As situations settle down and I can get control over them, there's the thrill of knowing you've delivered on a commitment." That, he said, is what makes managing in IS worthwhile. "Once you do one of these leading-edge technology projects, and you get to the new version, and the system is working, you feel proud of the team, amazed at what you've produced, and thrilled for the customer. It's such a good feeling, it's addictive."

OUTSOURCING AND CUSTOMER SATISFACTION

KATHY HUDSON, WHO BECAME KODAK'S CHIEF INFORMATION OFFICER, PIONEERED the notion of *outsourcing* in IS: turning to workers outside her company to provide IS functions that didn't add value to its product or service. It is important, however, for those outsourcing Information Systems to manage the process internally. You can't give up the influence over setting goals. It's also important to look at the phases at which outside instincts could help or hinder.

Many companies lack the technical expertise to design their own computer systems. They're forced to turn to systems-design firms or consultants. Information Systems is so integral to a company's operations and growth potential that the mental energy of in-house staff also has to be allocated to supporting the design efforts. Customer satisfaction requires this interface early in the design phase, which magnifies problems and opportunities. How does a person who doesn't understand the options influence the outcomes? Poorly. Yet most small companies are in that boat.

The best bet is to have people with as wide a conative diversity as possible work in conjunction with the external design team. Don't leave it only to the people who understand IS language. Learning a few buzz-words and gaining an understanding of basic processes will save your staff from untold traumas. If all a company does is go on-line with a financial system or an inventory control system, it can withstand the inevitable problems along the way. But a firm that undertakes a major shift by converting research and development efforts, administrative and financial functions, and marketing and sales in order to take advantage of technological advances must have a wide range of instincts targeted on the project.

Conversion from some off-the-shelf programs into a full-service system was made the responsibility of a Fact Finder/Follow Thru–insistent executive whose KCI result is 8-7-3-3. He labored over the details of the company's requirements, carefully researching all the past problems to ensure it would be covered by the program being designed for the company. He interviewed department heads to ascertain their desires and concerns, and communicated those to the program designers. Regular meetings and checkpoints were established, which he made sure representatives of each user function attended. His thoroughness was commendable. People were comfortable with the thought that everything would be fine. Everything worked without too many glitches for about a year. Then all hell broke loose. The system had maxed out. An investment that had been expected to meet the company's needs for six years had to be replaced after about eighteen months.

The Quick Start entrepreneur had stayed as far away from the design and interface processes as possible, which had seemed sensible at the time. The conflict in Quick Start between the CEO and the in-house IS project coordinator had been the effort's downfall. The resistant Quick Start had failed to assess the potential for rapid growth and dramatic changes the business experienced due to the insistent Quick Start's drive toward development opportunities. "It became a different situation," the coordinator lamented. "But how could I have anticipated what happened?" Easily, if he had understood the instincts of the CEO. Even though she resisted the Fact Finder details, she should have been dragged into the process. The past and present orientations of those on the design committees forced a lopsided approach that did not deal with future needs. It was a preventable nightmare. The CEO-customer could have been satisfied had she been more a part of the process.

Functions that do not add value to your product or service can be outsourced only when they are managed with the same combination of instinctive talents as would be necessary internally. With IS, the customer has to be part of the solution. To do that, customers have to contribute their instincts and actively participate as part of the team.

CHAPTER FOURTEEN

CUSTOMER SATISFACTION

SALES AND SERVICE THAT MEET CUSTOMER NEEDS

Customer satisfaction can be achieved only when the customer's instinctive needs are met. Whether a customer seeks Fact Finder contracts, Follow Thru money-back guarantees, Quick Start immediate delivery, or Implementor test drives, those conative urges must be satisfied. They require action.

As any experienced real-estate salesperson can tell you, showing customers what they say they *want* doesn't always do the job. "There's something so unconscious, that my clients don't seem to be able to describe it," a midwestern realtor said. "It's as if they're drawn to a certain house even though it doesn't match their stated criteria. They know it when they see it. I have to guess what that might be."

An auto dealer remarked: "Someone walks in who looks for all the world like a staid business type, yet he'll buy the bright-red convertible. It's taken me years to look behind the physical facade and personality type to really get into their heads. There's something going on in there that drives the decision. If I can figure out what that is, I don't have to work at closing the deal. I just give them what they need."

SELECTING SALESPEOPLE:
INSTINCT OVER PERSONALITY

A SUCCESSFUL SALES TEAM IS A SYNERGISTIC GROUP THAT TAKES ADVANTAGE OF ALL the instinctive insistences. The most familiar member, the front-line salesperson, "rides point" for the sales team of any company. Sales recruiters spend a lot of time and money finding candidates with the right "sales personality," which they describe as outgoing, high-energy, and driven—often by greed. If they were right, and these were the qualities that determine success in sales, the widespread use of personality tests for picking salespeople would have improved their abysmal record for identifying and retaining high producers. Instead, based on standard turnover rates for salespeople across industries, 80 percent of these hires fail. The problem is that intelligence and personality don't predict a person's ability to promote, negotiate, or handle any of the other challenges facing salespeople. Successful selling requires creativity. It's a matter of pure instinct.

Being smart or friendly is a plus, but those qualities are an advantage in any career; they don't make you any more suited to sales. Being an introvert, turning inward for motivation rather than deriving it from others, does not decrease effectiveness in sales. When personality tests are used unfairly, they discriminate against introverts (who aren't the type to sue, either). You don't have to be the life of the party to have sold the host on hiring your band. However, most sales roles do require taking a risk, perhaps to call strangers or to be able to respond spontaneously to objections and unexpected opportunities. These conative characteristics are linked directly to the job's requirements. That's why the KCI can be so accurate in identifying high-probability hires for sales positions.

Companies often compound hiring mistakes with sales-training errors. The popular sales-training programs on the market teach people to manipulate the selling process. One national sales-training program conducts seminars such as "How to Control with Questions" and "Emotions, the Triggers of Selling." Through the use of motivation, or desire-based, issues, salespeople learn to latch onto and mirror customer *personalities* in a way that gives salespeople a false sense of rapport. They may be able to control how a person feels through affective manipulation (often fear based) long enough to make a one-time sale, but soon a customer's innate needs will surface, perhaps leading to buyer's remorse.

One top American automobile executive expressed concern over the

Kolbe Management Report
SYNERGY REPORT

For

SALES
Commissions Equal to 50% or More of Compensation

	Fact Finder	Follow Thru	Quick Start	Implementor	Group Synergy	Ideal Synergy
PREVENT 1	14%	30%	7%	48%		
2						25%
3						
RESPOND 4	64%	62%	20%	49%		
5						50%
6						
INITIATE 7	22%	8%	73%	3%		
8						25%
9						
10						

This analysis is based on a total of 760 respondents.

quality of his sales force. "We have the product. People like our cars. Our marketing plan is first-rate. The ads work. People walk into our dealerships excited, really wanting our cars. Then the salesperson walks up to them, and by the time they're through it's become an experience they want to forget." It doesn't have to be a contentious process.

The situation can be changed by using conative issues to select and train salespeople. To succeed in sales a person has to begin with the right stuff, the raw talent necessary for the approach required by a particular sales role. Successful transaction-based salespeople for most companies tend to fall into one specific conative pattern: insistent Quick Start, accommodating Fact Finder, and, generally, resistant Follow Thru. The insistent Quick Start allows people to thrive on the challenge of building a strong client base and introducing new clients to the products. Accommodation in Fact Finder supports the need to provide information on products and to gather information from clients without getting too bogged down in detail. If the product is tangible and hands-on, salespeople benefit from an accommodation or insistence in Implementor. Resistance in Follow Thru helps in sales situations that are sporadic rather than those that adhere to a consistent sequence.

If salespeople take full advantage of their instincts every step of the way rather than feigning rapport, they will be perceived as more authentic and believable. Consumers instinctively sense when another person is putting on an act. When salespeople don't engage their instincts, they can come off as the kind of superficial, pushy people who give sales a bad name. A salesperson who is acting instinctively will succeed even if the instinct engaged is different from the customer's. There's humor in negotiating with a Quick Start who obviously thrives on cutting the deal. There's disgust with phony lines learned in sales training.

SELLING WITH, NOT AGAINST, INSTINCTS

IF YOU RAISED EXOTIC MUSHROOMS, YOU *COULD* SELL THEM TO WHOLESALERS BY explaining in Fact Finder detail that they weren't poisonous, offering Follow Thru guarantees of availability, providing Quick Start fast delivery, or conducting Implementor tours of your growing fields. But you wouldn't personally do all four things as the salesperson any more than you would need all four to make a buying decision as a customer. For the salesperson to communicate effectively with a potential customer, both parties have to be able to trust each other's inclination. For successful communications in sales or any other process, both parties have to have the freedom to be themselves.

If you're not at least an accommodating Implementor, for instance, it would be silly for you to conduct the tour. A client who needs a demonstration would sense your resistance and be turned off. Your best bet as a salesperson is to follow your natural inclinations. A resistant Implementor horse breeder confided she usually doesn't even see, let alone touch, the animals she buys. "I wouldn't have the foggiest notion how a good horse *feels*," she said. "I'm just amazed at the people who run their hands over a horse's body and actually tell something from that. I run my finger down the page of statistics to set the price." It works for her. She's made several million dollars through her paper transactions.

The salesperson has to meet the instinct-driven needs of customers without compromising his own inclinations. Closing a sale requires a true meeting of the minds, with the salesperson finding the customer's path of least resistance and greatest need, then accompanying the buyer through the process until the shared goal—customer satisfaction—has been reached.

Barry, whose KCI result is 5-3-8-4, sells medical supplies. Most of his customers are insistent Fact Finders who crave more specifics than he is inclined to provide. So he jokes with them about his "handicap" of not being able to explain anything but the bottom-line benefits, as he hands them written materials, which they benefit from more than a speech, anyway.

Barry's clients describe his self-admitted lack of expertise as "endearing," so long as he finds other ways to satisfy their Fact Finder urge. His Quick Start makes him so intuitive that he senses when to call in authorities. Like the time he took one client to lunch at a restaurant next door to a potential customer with unanswered questions and got them together over dessert. "If it were anyone else that did this to me," said the client, who was accosted as he went by the restaurant window, "I'd kill 'em. But Barry always seems to get away with it. I like his tenacity. But he better not do it again." He would. But not without knowing just how far he could stretch it.

Barry met a potential customer's need by using his instincts to find alternatives that provided satisfaction. The existing client obviously had enough Quick Start to ad-lib, and it helped to reconfirm his buying decisions to have him handle the prospect's objections. The sales process ought to be a win-win situation in which people aren't manipulated to act contrary to their best interests. When instinctive needs are met, there's no procrastination, no buyer's remorse, and no customer dissatisfaction.

These examples show sales at its best, meeting the conative needs of both seller and buyer. But the reality is that many salespeople are trained to use methods of selling that go against their own grain; much sales "talk" is artificial communication; and buyers' instincts are often ignored in favor of a do-whatever-it-takes-to-get-the-order mentality. Until this changes, the vast majority of salespeople will continue to fail, and customers will have to continue to jump through hoops for the privilege of spending their money.

BUILDING A SUCCESSFUL SALES TEAM

BUILDING TRUST WITH A CUSTOMER BEGINS WITH THE SALESPERSON, BUT CONTINUED satisfaction depends on the entire sales team, including service representatives and clerical staff. For many products and services, making the sale is only the first step in the process. A true-to-conative-form salesperson saying "trust me" is more likely to be believed, but what happens afterward cements that trust and turns a one-time buyer into a long-term customer. After insistent Quick Starts complete a sale, they move on to the next conquest. It's the service-oriented people on the sales team who then have to meet the promises the salespeople made. The challenge is to build a team that can work together to both sell to and satisfy the customer.

As indicated on the following chart for the insurance industry, Quick Start insistence predicts success in this endeavor. Quite the opposite conative initiatives are necessary among service-oriented administrators. The high producers in this study are members of the Million Dollar Round Table, the top 5 percent in life insurance sales. Average producers make a good living, while low-performers' incomes are under twenty thousand dollars annually.

Wise executives often compensate top salespeople more than they do themselves. Finding people who can get and keep customers is so imperative, companies will do almost anything to keep good salespeople happy. Unfortunately, most companies have little understanding of what makes these people tick. One midwestern bank was so alarmed at the high bonuses trust-department salespeople made that it changed its compensation plan to a larger percentage coming in preestablished salaries. Most of the high-producing Quick Starts resigned. The actions

KCI™ RESULTS AS PREDICTORS OF PERFORMANCE
IN THE INSURANCE INDUSTRY

	Percent Insistent	Percent Resistant
FACT FINDERS		
High Producers........................	13%	26%
Medium Producers....................	14%	30%
Low Producers..........................	37%	4%
Administration.........................	54%	5%
FOLLOW THRU		
High Producers........................	5%	50%
Medium Producers....................	13%	32%
Low Producers..........................	23%	19%
Administration.........................	51%	3%
QUICK START		
High Producers........................	68%	5%
Medium Producers....................	59%	13%
Low Producers..........................	27%	27%
Administration.........................	8%	57%
IMPLEMENTOR		
High Producers........................	5%	47%
Medium Producers....................	5%	38%
Low Producers..........................	2%	42%
Administration.........................	3%	46%

N = 1,067

required of a salesperson include primarily Quick Start behaviors such as:

- finding prospects
- promoting benefits
- overcoming customer objections
- negotiating deals
- closing sales

Marketing is often confused with sales. It differs greatly because it requires the talents of insistent Fact Finders to strategize, price goods, and write marketing materials. The Fact Finder marketing method is more judicious and practical than that found among Quick Start–inclined salespeople, who, without the marketers, might give away the store. A team effort, with marketing people analyzing costs and setting prices, provides a conative balance that protects the company. The Quick Starts can't get away with offering unprofitable deals, and the Fact Finders are pushed to the limits of what's possible. The following Fact Finder methods distinguish marketing needs from sales issues:

- researching customer needs
- studying demographic data
- identifying target markets
- measuring competitive opportunities
- quantifying pricing and profit issues

Marketing might also oversee advertising and public relations, which usually require a combination of Quick Start ingenuity and Fact Finder tactfulness. These functions serve as a strong bridge between people who are out in the field selling and the marketers back at the office crunching numbers.

In some companies, the sales department also delivers the product and provides ongoing service. In such cases, insistent Follow Thrus are essential to back up assurances and guarantees, and to provide dependable service. When sales and service contracts have offered terms that are irrevocable, the resistant Quick Start is an ideal person to protect those terms. The insistent Quick Start will never stop trying to negotiate, whereas his resistant counterpart will adhere to the letter of the agreement. The service-oriented responsibilities that require these conative qualities are:

- recording transactions
- following up on promises
- coordinating schedules
- handling logistics
- tracing and retrieving information

Customers don't remain customers without receiving consistent service. The one objection that cannot be overcome is inefficiency. There is no excuse for it. Because the sale depends upon quality service, the salesperson depends upon the instincts of the service rep. The two functions are as interdependent as they are different. When a service technician is needed to repair or replace products, those with service contracts will be lucky if a person with a dual insistence in Follow Thru and Implementor walks through the door. When he leaves, the machine will be in working order, *and* he'll clean up after himself.

For any sales team to be successful in the long-term, it is critical to have insistence in all the modes, yet those differing approaches can lead to conflicts within the group. The team *can* come together, with the right synergy, the proper trust in differing methods, and an understanding of how much they rely on one another to succeed. The insistent–Quick Start salesperson achieves success when landing a critical account. Marketing gives that person the brochures and sales material, including product background and information, that clinches the sale. Unless the insistent Follow Thru ensures the ongoing service, problems with delivery could lose the sale. Without an Implementor handling installation of a copy machine, problems could arise that cost the sales team future business. An appreciation of the instincts of the others can free team members to be themselves, and succeed.

AVOIDING BUYER'S REMORSE

Affective issues, wants and desires, motivate people to take action but do not predict *how* they will make a decision or whether the buyer will be satisfied. A resistant Quick Start may want to buy clothes that are "a bit crazy," but her instincts generally overcome her desires, except for the time she really got carried away and bought the gaudy dress she never wears. She blames that purchase on the salesperson who encouraged her to go against her instincts, even though she wanted to make the purchase. Anytime a salesperson plays on emotions rather than a customer's needs, it can backfire in this manner.

Why does a customer say one thing and do another? Because, affectively, we often want to step out of our own skin for a little while and be different just to see how it feels. But we won't do it for long. We always revert to form. Sometimes we let ourselves make an out-of-character decision for the fun of it. If it's a major decision, we usually regret it. When the sale engages instinctive energy, product returns are minimized.

Cognitive issues also play a role in buying decisions, which involve the triad of wanting, awareness, and willingness. The person who *knows* a lot about tropical fish may not fall for the pitch that they're easy to raise. The one who is *aware* of fluctuations in interest rates may be determined to refinance his house as soon as possible. Knowledge contributes to the process, but it is instinctive need that moves the sale from mere desire to buy, or interest in the product, to the act of purchasing. You have to engage people's Striving Instincts to get them to make a decision and stay with it. Top salespeople satisfy instinctive urges and match customer needs with product or service benefits. By doing this they gain customer satisfaction.

This book is not a sales-training manual and does not explain the many ways in which salespeople can use their instincts to discern the instinctive needs of customers. There are general principles, however, which help define the opportunity to improve sales and customer service through an understanding of the concept of instinct-based sales. First, the product-sales-service system has to be designed around the instinct-based needs of the customer, rather than forcing the customer to live within artificial parameters. These needs relate to resistances as well as insistences. If a product or service requires that a buyer use it through a resistance, it will be underutilized. If the sales process were to require such effort, it would cost the sale.

OVERCOMING RESISTANCES

THE SALES PROCESS WILL NOT WORK UNLESS EFFORT IS MADE TO OVERCOME CONATIVE resistances. The customer's inclination to avoid certain sales situations because of a conative resistance can end a sales opportunity mysteriously if buyer and salesperson are unaware of the influence instincts have over the decision-making process. Even if a potential customer wants to buy a car, something "interferes." While it's unrealistic to think a salesperson is going to be able to KCI every potential customer, it is possible to increase a salesperson's sensitivity to the issue of instinct. If nothing else, the salesperson who knows that a force beyond disliking him or his product may interfere with a decision to buy has an advantage. He can address all four instinct-based reasons for avoiding a purchase or just the ones that seem most likely. He can also give himself a break, recognizing some people will not make a particular purchase no matter how hard he tries. Even without KCI results, salespeople trained to consider instinct-driven needs increase their sales. They accomplish this by removing as many of the frustrations caused by conative resistances as possible and by paying attention to any clues for what the customer needs to have happen in the sales situation.

For many people, shopping is a necessity, not a desire. They strive to avoid taking up too much of their time or spending too much money, impractically or impetuously. The exceptions—the ones who wear Shop Till You Drop sweatshirts—use insistent modes to initiate the process. The Follow Thru die-hard shopper has a plan of action and hits every store in scheduled sequence, knowing whose specials will be sold out if not purchased before noon. The Quick Start initiator is more likely to go on shopping sprees, spontaneously buying up unusual bargains. Those who shop for the sake of shopping don't require a salesperson. Generally, however, these people aren't buying aluminum siding, septic tanks, freight cars, insurance, or other essential items.

Since most buying is nondiscretionary and is done because a product or service is necessary, the first step in the sales process is to overcome natural resistances. The preventive zone of any instinct is part of the buyer's internal protection system, and it kicks in when a buyer is committed to spending as little as possible.

To Overcome a Resistance in Fact Finder

Don't get bogged down in minutiae. Don't ask a lot of questions if the buyer gives short answers or resists filling in details. Provide big picture or global benefits, with summaries of the fine print. Highlight competitor comparisons, so the customer doesn't have to seek them out or read copiously to feel adequately informed. Don't force history and verbatim quotes on the buyer. Instead give assurance that it's not necessary to become an expert to benefit from the product or service, and offer to provide a shortened version of any training manuals or instructions that may be necessary. Sell the expertise of the service department as a substitute for energy the customer would have to expend to maximize the use of purchases.

A resistant Fact Finder needed a new fax machine, so he got a recommendation from a friend. He called for the price ranges, assuming he'd be able to order one over the phone. The sales company's receptionist asked for his zip code and whether the purpose was business or personal; then she wanted to know the size of his company. After checking out his situation so he could be assigned to the appropriate commissioned salesperson, he was told that person wasn't available until the next day. When the salesperson called back, she asked for an appointment to explain the various options. That was too much fact finding for the buyer, who called elsewhere and placed his phone order.

To Overcome a Resistance in Follow Thru

Help cut through red tape and eliminate any bureaucracy in the sales environment. Prefill forms whenever possible and don't keep the customer waiting for completion of your company's procedures. Skip standard operating practices, so the customer doesn't have a sense of being boxed in. Provide variations rather than requiring prepackaged formats. Give buyers considerable latitude in terms of when, where, and how they meet with the salesperson or try the product. Let them take a sample home, stop by after hours, or order outside the predesignated quantities. A sale to a resistant Follow Thru requires flexibility. Don't tell customers what they can't do, even if the policies exist for good reasons. Figure out how to get around obstacles. Any sense that they are being herded through the process or made to conform to standardized practices will hurt the sale, even if buyers want your product.

A resistant–Follow Thru bride wanted to try on the "dream gown" she saw in the window of a bridal shop. The only way she could get information about it was by making an appointment to go through an established program designed "so every bride has an opportunity to see all the options before making the most important fashion decision of her life." She resisted being scheduled. Her decision was to move on.

A resistant–Follow Thru international sporting-goods executive was about to order four suits in the men's department of an upscale department store when the sales clerk explained the fitter wasn't in the store that evening. The customer was asked to make an appointment, which had to be scheduled on certain days between certain hours. He resisted having to plan around their structure, walked out of the store, and never went back.

Another resistant Follow Thru was considering buying a condominium in Hawaii during a vacation trip to the islands. He'd seen one he really liked, but he wanted to make some changes in the exterior entrance if he bought it. The saleswoman suggested he would have to submit his plan to the owners committee. He didn't have time to arrange for the design and dropped all consideration of that purchase.

To Overcome a Resistance in Quick Start

Don't tell resistant Quick Starts that everything is negotiable. Some issues need to be irrevocable for them. Emphasize the low risk involved in the purchase, especially how future needs can be met without having to make drastic changes. Stress availability of parts and ability to reorder existing items. Explain long-term benefits and why the item is not part of a passing fad. Show how the line of products or the type of service has a record for not having to be reinvented every few years. Do not create a sense of urgency in making a decision. "If I have to decide today, the answer is no" is a statement that reflects the needs of a resistant Quick Start. Anything that rushes them, demands immediacy, or gets to the bottom line too fast will lose the sale.

A highly successful designer of traditional marketing formats rewarded herself with a large addition to her home. "The builder must have been used to working with Quick Starts, because he told me how fast he could accomplish the work," she said. "I told him to slow down and do it right. I doubled the time he said it would take and told him that was the earliest I would pay him the final amount, so he'd better not try to speed it up and do it wrong."

Another resistant Quick Start was told how lucky he was to get the last inventory available on office furniture he liked. In fact, the floor samples were in like-new condition but still came at a specially discounted price. "I'll wait," he said. "I never buy closed-out items. You never know what will happen. They might go out of style next week, or a chair might break, and I couldn't replace it."

A travel agent helped a company arrange a trip of a lifetime for its president's retirement gift. Lots of effort went into finding a unique experience, something he and his wife never would have been able to do during their working years. His family and coworkers were excited the night the couple was surprised with round-the-world tickets for a magical trip that included a variety of exotic locales. He was extremely appreciative of the gesture, but the next day he told the travel agent, "I've been looking forward to retirement so I wouldn't have to go places like this. I'd like to visit my family and friends around this country over the next few years. If only they hadn't felt they needed to surprise me, I could have told them better than to do this to me." He canceled all the reservations.

To Overcome a Resistance in Implementor

Do not ask a potential customer to make, fix, build, or in any other way physically manipulate goods. Even test-driving a car with a salesperson makes some resistant Implementors self-conscious. While a product may be made with the finest materials, avoid burdening buyers with feeling and touching them unless they pick them up naturally. Certainly don't ask them to put parts together to see how smoothly they join, since some customers could break even the best-built system. If sturdiness, endurance, and other issues are important to the sale, show a video of crash tests or ask for volunteers to jump on the unbreakable watch. Do not suggest customers need to try it themselves in order to make a good buying decision. Even handing a resistant Implementor a blanket and saying, "Here, feel how soft and light it is," can be a mistake. She might have decided it is practical, matches her sheeting, and solves her immediate problem, but then she'll back off.

A food-services manager resistant in Implementor had decided to interview produce suppliers to select the one who would supply the corporation's eating facilities. One vendor invited the buyer to visit the warehouse so he could see for himself the quality of the operation and how carefully the produce was selected, stored, and transported. "Who does he think I am?" the food-services manager said. "I don't see myself as having to go down there and watch them handle fruit to know whether the quality will satisfy us. What a waste of time for me to meet with him if he couldn't convince me without my having to go to that trouble." As a result of the buyer's resistance to Implementor, the supplier lost out, even though the same invitation had converted several other companies into clients.

A father went to the toy store to buy his young son a train set for Christmas. He watched with delight as one ran along the tracks set up in the store, banking past a make-believe village and easing down a hill, past a farmyard. He became so engrossed, he was startled when the salesperson handed him the controls and suggested he could get it to back up or switch tracks. He allowed as how he was "just looking," left the store, and ordered a train set from a catalog—one that emphasized that any five-year-old could operate it without assistance.

ENGAGING INSISTENCES

IF RESISTANCES ARE OVERCOME, THE SALES TEAM CAN MOVE TOWARD ENGAGING insistences. An insistent Quick Start who wants to buy a product over the counter needs fast-paced service. If the salesperson is tied up on the phone, the potential customer will keep on walking. An insistent Fact Finder, on the other hand, might get annoyed at a salesperson who sets too fast a pace and doesn't explain things in detail.

Sam sold training programs to a customer who was an insistent Quick Start but had an insistent–Fact Finder boss. Sam soon learned to send one-page proposals summarizing the highlights, but attached support information with all the facts and figures in easy-to-access form. The insistent Quick Start was satisfied with the summary and had the backup information ready in case his boss wanted to see more detail. The relationship is ongoing because, in large part, Sam accommodates the needs of both decision makers.

Customer requirements reflect the full range in each Action Mode unless the buying population is narrowed by conative issues such as career groups, types of businesses, or buying behaviors. With nursery growers, for example, the primary mode of operation is likely to be Implementor. This can't be assumed; after all, you may be dealing with the insistent–Fact Finder son who inherited the business. It would be best if you knew his KCI result. But since that's not always possible, I recommend offering customers a variety of options regarding the way in which they make decisions. The sales process can be set up to meet most conative needs.

Engaging Fact Finder Buyers

To win over insistent Fact Finders, give them indisputable data that proves your offer compares favorably to what they are already using, and they'll be inclined to further investigate your product or service. Put it in writing. Give them time to study the alternatives, making your comparisons as direct as possible. Use statistical information, quote experts, and provide references. Footnote or document your claims. Ask insistent Fact Finders enough specific information about their needs and experiences so that they will be satisfied you have sufficient background to make a recommendation. Provide evidence of your qualifications, which will let them view you as an authority.

The decision maker for an electronics firm had to select a new phone system for the company. Her secretary requested information from several vendors. Four of the packages contained the kind of material necessary to engage her insistent–Fact Finder instinct. The others were either too glitzy or made what she considered unrealistic claims. "I'm not drawn to fancy marketing pieces that only sell sizzle," she said. "Four-color brochures with lots of pictures but not much explanation get tossed. They don't give me what I need."

She eliminated another company in the next round, which included presentations by sales representatives. One person showed up dressed inappropriately and presented herself unprofessionally. "I may have been unfair," the executive said, "but I just didn't want to work with her. She didn't even try to figure out why we were unhappy with the system we have before she launched into her pitch." The winning bid compared costs for this company with unnamed competitors. Industry averages were provided, along with an analysis of what costs would have been had the company been using the new phone system for the past two years.

Engaging Follow Thru Buyers

Insistent Follow Thrus will turn down a bargain if the item isn't on the shopping list. They will also make a planned-for purchase even if it's out of season, out of style, or out of stock. One Follow Thru explained he *always* makes salads with tomatoes, paying the high off-season price even when the quality is poor. Another searched for the type of slippers she had always worn, even though they had to be special-ordered at a two-month wait and a premium price. If a person comes in with a neatly drawn list, the salesperson would be foolish to try to offer a substitute without making every effort to accommodate this apparent Follow Thru need. Of course, you could be fooled into believing you were dealing with a Follow Thru, when the customer is really a forgetful Quick Start. Again, be careful of assumptions, and provide options. The first option, whenever a list is presented, is to go to as great a length as the person seems to need to get an exact match.

Follow Thru insistence pushes for the fully coordinated set of furniture, clothing outfit, or service provider. Offering them a smorgasbord can cause frustration. They don't need to mix and match—just match. They also sense what will work with what, so it can be insulting to make suggestions. Instead of showing them a scarf you believe goes well with clothes they are trying on, ask if they would like you to bring out a selection. Intense Follow Thrus will often add to an initial purchase in order to complete a set or a look. If they buy a breakfast table and chairs, they're likely to purchase placemats and napkins that go well with it. Providing accessories for large purchases will enhance the average size of an order when dealing with this instinct.

The best way to engage the energy of a dominant–Follow Thru office manager is to call for an appointment. Don't just walk in and expect to get her attention. Find a time when she won't be distracted with other activities and present information clearly and sequentially. Begin with an overview of what you will be explaining, whether it's an intangible service or a product you are selling. A peel-the-onion approach works best, moving from the general to the specific. As you turn the pages in a well-diagrammed marketing piece, ask if she has any questions and do not move on until they are answered. This may seem like advice that will work with anyone, because so much sales training advocates Follow Thru behavior. It is not. It is the need of a buyer who has to have an orderly integration of a new tool into a present system. By the time you have gone from the overview applications to the precise benefits for such customers, their heads will be nodding, and you'll likely get a yes. Others may be nodding off. Those are the insistent Quick Starts.

Engaging Quick Start Buyers

Go right to the bottom-line benefits with the insistent Quick Start. "Try it, you'll like it" and "What do you have to lose?" work well with them. Engage their sense of urgency. Don't let anything interfere with an immediate decision. If you don't have an answer for one of their questions, get on the phone and find out. If they want changes of any kind, find out how soon they can be done—and try to make it faster than usual. Negotiate on the spot rather than sending out a written proposal later. If something has to be confirmed in writing, send it by fax—with their permission. *Never* tie up an insistent Quick Start's fax. It'll cost you.

Highlight information, preview films, and fast-forward to key places for these folks. Emphasize unique and visionary aspects of the sale. Use a variety of bright colors to get their attention. Get them involved in finding unusual applications or variations. One-of-a-kind goods and customized programs intrigue them more than anything off the shelf. Let them lead in negotiating terms or any other aspect of the sale that allows for pricing, packaging, or other variations.

It's easier to sell to salespeople because they're probably Quick Starts and are quickly drawn into negotiating, sometimes before they know enough about the product or service to make an informed decision. "I'll take one! How does it work?" seems like a backward approach to anyone but the insistent Quick Start. You have to sell to these people by assuming the order and then avoiding anything that "unsells" them.

Lisa, an insistent Quick Start, walked into an art gallery and immediately became entranced with a brilliantly colored abstract. She already had her checkbook out when the salesperson walked up and began an involved explanation about how the picture had a "hold" on it and wouldn't be available until the next day. As the salesperson got deeper into the story, Lisa literally began backing away. The gallery manager, seeing the problem develop from a distance, rushed over. "If you will give me two minutes, I can get an answer on the painting," he explained. "In the meantime, why don't you sit down and decide where in your house you want to put it. The picture is so wonderful, it will brighten up any room." This response worked for Lisa, who ended up buying the painting for her living room.

Engaging Implementor Buyers

You've hooked the insistent Implementors once they start playing with the goods you have to sell, as long as the quality is up to their standards. Don't try to get them to read material, discuss benefits, or communicate in any other way until you see them manipulating your wares. If you're trying to sell them a service, give them props to show you their needs.

Photographs and videos are poor substitutes but better than anything else when a finished product or a service is involved. If possible, meet them outside the office, preferably in their plant, shop, or place where purchased items will be used. If they're deciding on a training program, meet them where it will be held and bring along any notebooks or other materials that will be used in the process. The least desirable option would be to have to close a sale with an Implementor over the phone. A face-to-face in the office is preferable, unless she's on the car phone driving somewhere that suits her needs—the effect may be just right.

Marty, an athletic-equipment store owner, noticed that some of his customers weren't comfortable with a purchase until they had a chance to try it out. After several customers took apart his store displays so they could try out the equipment, he set aside a practice area for customers to experiment with his products before they bought them. "Sales on my most expensive lines have hit the roof!" Marty exclaimed. "Now that my customers can actually use the equipment, a lot of them can feel the difference the top brands make." Another advantage Marty discovered was fewer returns. "Many buyers are so pleased with the chance to use something before they make a purchase, they don't even bother to shop anywhere else." Marty stumbled onto a way to engage the instincts of his insistent–Implementor customers, and his store has reaped the benefits.

Engaging Facilitator Buyers

Facilitators are willing to listen to a sales pitch, watch a demonstration, or accommodate any other method of presenting benefits. But that doesn't mean they are pushovers when it comes to buying. A product or service has to sell itself, or they won't buy. They're not inclined to initiate a purchase and don't move naturally toward a close. They may seem to be sold because they're nodding in agreement with most of the possibilities.

The salesperson has to create the sense of urgency or do the price comparisons for these shoppers. They expect to be *sold*. As much as they may desire a particular purchase, Facilitators will make salespeople do the work of presenting the case. If they are not convinced intellectually, they find it easy to walk away. When a sale forces them into an insistent stance, such as having to initiate service calls, they will abandon the effort. A salesperson who is trained to ask for a great deal of information won't face resistance and may incorrectly interpret this as a sign that the customer is an insistent Fact Finder. But the response was actually that of an accommodator, which ought not cause a presumption of a sale.

"The guy answered my questions," an auto salesman said, "test drove the car, even looked under the hood, and read the service manual. I couldn't believe it when he did all that and then left without even taking my card." He may have disliked the car, or he may have been waiting for the salesperson to ask for the order. Quick Starts have a hard time becoming engaged in the auto sale that doesn't allow them to negotiate a deal. When all prices are preset, it frustrates their urge to try for a better bottom line. Facilitators have a hard time when they have to begin the negotiating process. They need a salesperson to identify the negotiable items and start the bidding.

The general manager of a wholesale distributorship was a determined Facilitator. She wanted the best possible deal on warehouse space. So she accompanied an industrial-property salesman on a tour of several possibilities. When he asked for her specific needs, she gave him a list; when he queried her about price, she gave him a range. She let him know that her company had a deadline for making a decision. He felt certain he would find a suitable property within her parameters. But her willingness to accommodate his schedule and look at everything he wanted to show her sent a mixed message. She didn't appear to be in a hurry, but she had a deadline to meet. He didn't narrow the field and present her options in the order in which they met her needs. She didn't push, so he had to do the pushing. She bought a building from a more conatively assertive person. The salesman lost out because he reined in his insistent inclinations.

INSTINCT-DRIVEN CUSTOMER SATISFACTION

To satisfy customers, you need a product they value, accessible in a way that works for them, and follow-up service that meets their needs. Many products on the market are designed, sold, and serviced in a way that may be convenient for the seller but work against the instincts of his customers. This gives those companies that *do* discover a way to accommodate the conative needs of their buyers a competitive advantage and makes them look like lucky stars when their sales "unexplainably" skyrocket.

One good example of this is the burgeoning success of the mail-order market and home-shopping TV networks. They can appeal simultaneously to every instinctive insistence while compensating for resistances. Insistent Fact Finders appreciate the product information provided. Resistant Fact Finders can ignore the words and focus on the product headlines and pictures. Insistent Follow Thrus can turn to the order form and get a clear idea of the procedures involved in the order process. For resistant Follow Thrus, ordering by phone is the solution. The unusual products many catalogs offer, combined with twenty-four-hour toll-free numbers, are perfect for insistent Quick Starts, who need to place their orders *now*. Resistant Quick Starts can take their time making buying decisions, hanging on to the catalogs for months or watching a repeat of the show. Insistent Implementors appreciate the clear pictures of the products and benefit from watching them demonstrated on TV. It also helps if they can return them if the merchandise doesn't meet their sense of quality. Resistant Implementors appreciate others packing and shipping gifts they order through catalogs and telephone. Catalog and home-network shopping can be user-friendly product-sales-service systems. No wonder they are the fastest-growing segments of the retail business.

Just as companies work better when employees have a chance to achieve using their individual talents, engaging the instincts of both the seller and the buyer makes the transaction process smoother and more successful. Meet the conative needs of your customer, and you've taken the first step toward a positive, long-term relationship.

CHAPTER FIFTEEN

GUMPTION

YOUR ULTIMATE DEFENSE

Productive people are frequently perceived as stubborn. They act with *gumption,* which is to the Creative Process what turbo power is to a car's engine. It's the intensity that keeps the Striving Instincts from being overpowered by either motivation or reason.

As a painfully shy child, I was often labeled obstinate; a designation I wore as a badge of honor. Perhaps it's not surprising that as a parent I was determined to rear obstinate offspring, the kind who know their minds and are unrelenting in their pursuits. They are the last people on earth to join some cult, and wouldn't let themselves be controlled by others—physically, spiritually, or emotionally—without a knock-down, drag-out fight. You see, I consider obstinacy a life-saving quality. Whether parent, manager, or teacher, we must be prepared to support tenacity, even when we receive the brunt of it. We must advocate gumption.

Those who don't need to control you will revel in your conative persistence. They want a tough-minded employee, spouse, or coworker. Persistence in trusting instincts is a desirable form of stubbornness, and being adamant about doing things your way is certainly not a personality flaw. It shows strength of character. A conative cop-out, on the other hand, means that a person has given in to demands and is trying to change the natural way she functions.

Danger signals arise whenever someone refers to our instinctive needs to prevent as a "negative attitude"; or when our instincts to accommodate are viewed as an "emotional hang-up"; or when an insistence is simply called "stupid." Being conatively obstinate provides an armor to be used in defending oneself against any obstacle.

CONTROLLING MISUNDERSTANDINGS

WINIFRED, A SUPERVISOR WHO CONSIDERS HERSELF A CARING PERSON, SAT IN A staff meeting and passed judgment on Jeff, a highly insistent Quick Start, by labeling him an "incorrigible scatterbrain." Even though she said this in a teasing tone, her remark wounded Jeff. It hurts when we are teased about a form of initiation or are told to "improve" in a mode lacking insistence. Had she poked fun at his prevention of Follow Thru order, they might have had a mutual laugh over his foible for not finishing everything he started. Jeff may even have told some stories on himself. But Winifred had seriously miscalculated when she made fun of his Quick Start talents; she'd hurt Jeff to the core.

Winifred later told me that she just couldn't stand the way Jeff forced their team into constant turmoil. "It's as if he isn't happy if he's not disrupting the systems that are in place," she complained. "He's a good man, and I guess he means well, but it's no help at all when he gets everyone stirred up the way he does." In turn, Jeff said he was considering quitting. "I've given this place my all," he sighed, "but rather than thanking me for sticking my neck out to make improvements, I'm considered a troublemaker."

Winifred felt threatened by Jeff's take-charge approach to presenting alternatives to the company's long-held systems and procedures. Her natural response as an insistent Follow Thru was to defend the status quo. The conflict could have been healthy for the organization (and others in the group would have acted as sufficient buffers) had the differing conative points of view been the real issue. Instead, Winifred's fear that Jeff would one-up her prompted her ridicule. Both acted with gumption, and it heightened the conflict.

As a consultant to the organization, I was determined to convert their gumption from a source of conflict to one of contribution. I knew Jeff was serious about leaving his job, so I decided it was worth the risk to have him put on special assignment. For sixty days he did not attend group meetings or problem-solving sessions. At first Winifred was glad Jeff wasn't around. "It's a relief to have him out of my hair," she said. "Our meetings go faster without his interruptions. I think people give me more respect when they don't see me hassling with him."

Within six weeks, however, she was asking when the experiment would end. Jeff's absence had made his contribution clear to her. She missed not having anyone to question her desire for consensus or to suggest alternatives she had overlooked. In other words, there was no combative energy bringing her mind into sharper focus. I made her wait it out.

Two months with no sparring partner also provided a good lesson for Mr. Quick Start. "Much as she bugs me," Jeff said, "I think she sometimes brings out the best in me. I just hope she won't do it with such a vengeance anymore." Both of these erstwhile adversaries discovered how much they needed each other.

Gumption can be a double-edged sword. As Jeff and Winifred came to understand, the more persistently you contribute your innate abilities, the more your creativity will flow. Yet gumption makes you more susceptible to nonconstructive criticism. "Don't be such a damn equivocator," an adamant Fact Finder hears when delaying a decision until all the evidence is available. "Are you incapable of make a decision without hedging your bet?" You bet she is, if she stays true to her instinctive self. Would you blame such a person if she no longer chose to give her best effort and practical compromises to such a critic of her tenacity?

It's equally devastating for a persevering Follow Thru to be labeled "obsessively" rigid. Ron, a diligent Follow Thru, asserted, "I just can't stand it when things are out of kilter." Ron was trying to explain the problems he was having with his coworkers. "I just don't understand how anyone could actually get angry with me for putting things away where they belong or for keeping neat records," he continued. "God knows, no one else is going to do it!" Some of his coworkers mistook his cleanup routines as criticism that they hadn't returned shared supplies. They were indignant because the time he took to be tidy drained the group's momentum. "We're forever having to wait while Ron gets his act together," one fellow staff member griped. "It wouldn't bother me no matter how much of a neatnik he is, but we depend on him to meet deadlines. This is ridiculous."

Yes, ridiculous it was—on both sides. Ron was spending too much of his Follow Thru on minor matters, when his talents were needed for more important things. His energy was consumed protecting petty procedures. The company had begun using CAD (computer-aided design) but hadn't trained him on the programs. He felt useless. He added only "finishing touches," as he called them, to computer-generated documents instead of working with the software to create the documents from scratch. Management was so pleased with the technology, it had neglected to retrain this experienced, resourceful contributor. A shy person who felt intimidated by his boss, he saw no alternative but to turn his excess energy to reforming messy and disorganized coworkers. He had too much gumption to let his Follow Thru talents go completely unused, so Ron wound up contributing his talents in counterproductive ways.

Deciding that a person such as Ron, who acts with instinct-driven steadfastness, is impervious to improvement often fixes the person into an unyielding, defiant stance. Instead of using energy to make a constructive contribution, he's likely to put his effort into counterproductive maneuvers, often by playing politics in the organization, looking for others to take sides, and creating an us-and-them mentality.

ACTING WITH RESOLVE

PEOPLE WHO KNOW EXACTLY WHAT THEY WANT AND UNRELENTINGLY PUT THEIR instinctive efforts into accomplishing their goals exude energy. They're decisive. They lay it on the line. Their drive is riveted, unwavering.

Virginia Tierney is an excellent example of someone who acts with gumption. Prior to her retirement, Virginia was the director of personnel at Boston University. She had also served as the business manager at Harvard's College of Business Administration and was once the assistant dean there. Now in her late seventies, she's both classy and feisty, a strategic planner whose KCI result is 8-6-4-2.

Virginia hasn't let up one bit over the years and is working tenaciously as an area director for AARP (the American Association of Retired Persons), an organization that sends you a membership greeting the day you turn fifty. She travels the country to attend and conduct seminars, develops issue papers on controversial public matters, works with other volunteer leaders in the six New England states that report to her, and keeps abreast of the concerns for two million national members in the chapters she represents.

Experience is vital to such an indomitable Fact Finder. Virginia maintains that having experience in a field lessens her fear of being judged harshly and gives her the confidence to assert herself. There are a tremendous number of programs in AARP, and Virginia demands that she have "sufficient information on each one." She uses her Follow Thru back-up mode to sort through documents and structure background material. "I have to set priorities so I'm not running in so many directions," she explained, adding that her greatest stress comes from "wondering if I have the whole picture; questioning whether I'm concentrating too much on some aspect. I'm a volunteer now, so I don't have to do anything, yet I can't withhold my full commitment. I'm using my talents, experience, and values, just as I always have. Continuing to pursue goals releases my creative energy."

Does gender or age discrimination slow Virginia down? "They don't really apply to me," she said, "because I'm going to do it my way regardless. Instead of letting it frustrate me, it becomes a part of my drive." Does she notice any changes in the way she approaches problem solving now that she is older? Her answer was true to her instinctive self: "I keep hoping as I age, if I begin to be forgetful, that I'll hone in on the important things." Virginia has served for seven years in the Silver Hair Legislature, an advocacy group of citizens over sixty who are elected by their peers in legislative districts to draft and propose bills for regularly elected legislators. As speaker of the house for the Massachusetts Silver Hair Legislature, she was her unhesitating self. "If I was going to be a senior citizen," she said, "I wanted to know what was being done for them. The ground rules in my actions haven't changed. I still have the same kind of drive; it's just about different things. I'm operating in a different sphere, but I'm still me."

THE BUY-IN COP-OUT

A *BUY-IN*, OR AGREEMENT ON IDEAS AND VALUES, IS HIGHLY DESIRABLE FOR ANY organization, but agreement on a single conative method is artificial among people with diverse talents. Such a contrived consensus won't stand up over time, so, at best, it brings false hope. Those who contribute to the problem by going along with unrealistic demands are guilty of copping out, or a lack of gumption. Uniform processes among conative clones are bad enough; when they result from people denying their different strengths, the self-betrayals cause personal and organizational harm. Asking insistent Fact Finders to conduct in-depth investigations before giving opinions on a merger is actually unnecessary. You're giving them permission to do what they would do anyway. Asking resistant Fact Finders to go along with the same process is detrimental. They can support others' needs to work in that manner, but their contributions will be eroded if they have to perform so contrary to their instincts.

Rather than praising those who quell conative conflicts by buying into misguided means of reaching a goal, organizations benefit by encouraging people to have the gumption to fight for their natural ways of achieving results. Asking people with instinctive differences to all work in the same way is poor management. If they agree to such a standoff, it is a cop-out. It means they have decided to withdraw effort but aren't admitting it.

We all have equal instinctive energy, but we don't all have gumption. Some people in very high places—presidents of corporations, media stars, and the like—talk about what they had to give up to get where they are. The usual sacrifices are their families and themselves. They gave up time with people they love, and they gave up fighting for who they are. When Ruben was a candidate for a senior position in his firm, he agreed with the search committee that he needed to try becoming less rigid and to ease up on his typical concerns for systematizing everything around him. "All they wanted," he said, "was for me to be less of a Follow Thru than I am. At the time, that seemed reasonable. After all, if I wanted the promotion badly enough, I could stifle some of my 'Mr. Clean' tendencies. The bigger problem, I thought, was that they also wanted my guarantee that I would become more 'progressive,' which meant more open to change. I can't believe I actually told them I would work on that. Now that I know my KCI result, in hindsight I see that I caved completely. I told them, 'If that's what you want, you've got it,' as if I had it to give."

Ruben didn't have what they demanded, but because he had made a promise he couldn't keep, the months he spent trying to make good on it robbed him of his confidence and his energy. "I read books on how to become more risk oriented, I went to seminars, I listened to motivational tapes," he recalled. "I thought I had the intellect and the integrity that would allow me to do things any way I'd agreed they had to be done. I was dead wrong. So wrong, it almost cost me my marriage and my health. What I couldn't do naturally I tried to do by working harder. It was a cycle downward until I went in one day and laid it on the line." He finally acted with gumption, telling his boss he could do the job that needed to be done, but he had to have the freedom to do it his own way.

I wish I could tell you that Ruben's boss saw the light and that everything ended happily ever after. Everything didn't end up working out. He lost his job. But he saved his marriage, his self-respect, and his conative integrity. When Ruben walked away from the job he had worked hard to get, he was not discouraged. "I felt as if the weight of the world had been removed from my shoulders," he said. "I stood up for everything about me that really matters—finally. I didn't care if I never earned as much money. I earned the admiration of my wife and kids, and the friends who really care about me. The job I have now is a breeze, because I took one where my Follow Thru is appreciated. My work is getting recognized, so I'll move up. I feel good about myself again."

BUILDING UNREALISTIC CONSENSUS

Self-directed teams are often confused when someone attempts to get them to operate by consensus. Instead they work best when the leadership rotates naturally from one conative talent to another as the situation requires. Even if no formal leader is named, the person most persistent in using his instinctive approach functions as the actual leader of the moment. In such situations, I've found those with the greatest conative intensity will set the tone. If there's an equal portion of two different modes represented in the group (say one person is an 8 in Fact Finder, and another is an 8 in Follow Thru), the Fact Finder will almost always dominate because this mode sets the agenda by defining the priorities. Therefore, in such groups you don't have to appoint a leader, because the natural one will emerge. After Fact Finder, Quick Start is the next dominant, and then Follow Thru. This natural pecking order, or *Theory of Dominance*, forecasts outcomes when you put together groups without otherwise identifying leadership roles. Had I realized this relationship between the modes when I first placed them on the KCI results chart, I would have put them in this order.

When a group seeks a conative buy-in, gumption on someone's part is easily viewed as a problem. People taking a stand for their conative insistence may be tagged obstructionists. To duck such labels, highly insistent people may try to repress their inclinations and not initiate action. Because strong resistances can seem like nay-saying when a group is trying for a buy-in on methods, those who naturally avoid the chosen approach may feign a willingness to go along with it. They won't be deemed negative or uncooperative, but they also won't make as much of a contribution as they could have.

Consensus sounds so good. It has the ring of togetherness, of a united front. But when a buy-in insinuates conative actions upon people unrealistically, it differs from a buy-in based on a cooperative attitude. If you are asked to work contrary to your instincts, it's always preferable to use gumption and refuse to buy in. Highly productive people are confrontational when it comes to their creativity. But they walk away from confrontations over conative methods. Generally, the only way to win an argument over *how* something must be accomplished is to have the gumption to go do it.

The buy-in cop-out creeps into organizations every time the door is opened to "getting agreement before we move forward." That's another way for a so-called decision maker to say, *I won't put myself on the line.* Few acts destroy credibility faster than seeking a buy-in to one method of action. It's not easy to manage conative diversity, but it's impossible to succeed by trying to enforce conformity. Of all the factors that discredit otherwise high performers—especially in the minds of their associates—it is dawdling over what should be put forth with gumption.

AVOIDING THE BUY-IN COP-OUT

To avoid the buy-in cop-out, do not hesitate when your guts tell you to act. If you have an insistence in Fact Finder, your instincts will tell you when you have enough information to make a decision. For a Follow Thru–insistent person decision time comes with having all the pieces to the puzzle and being ready for closure. Whatever your methodology, trust your instincts when it comes to timing. Don't wait for conative consensus when the next step is obvious to you. If you stall, you will have lost the moment—and perhaps the momentum.

It takes gumption to go the limit for your methodologies. It requires the full use of your mental resources, your powers of persuasion, and your conative talents for communication. When you could offer a better solution, feigning commitment is tantamount to abdicating your responsibility. Through the forcefulness, directness, and mental stamina you exhibit, you will be an example of personal enterprise and professional courage.

THE CONATIVE STALEMATE

When obstinate people butt heads over opposing approaches, the situation often leads to a conative stalemate. It happens when natural conative conflicts pit opposing creative forces against each other, and each tries to change the other's method. The impasse can also stem from the actions of opportunists with a divide-and-conquer mentality. The result is that efforts grind to a halt, and the problem-solving process stalls.

When a company asked its budget analysts, all heavily insistent in Fact Finder, to determine whether or not to move forward with an undercapitalized acquisition, the answer was a predictable no. Meanwhile, another group of employees was sent off to negotiate the best terms possible and to consider all the advantages of cutting a deal. Not surprisingly, the people chosen for this duty were insistent in Quick Start. Both sides worked feverishly to accomplish their goals within a narrow time frame. The more they exercised their conative prerogatives, the more entrenched they became in their diametrically opposed camps. When the time came for a showdown, the Quick Start contingent fought for an innovative but admittedly risky approach. The cautionary Fact Finder number-crunchers opposed the acquisition and countered them at every corner. The factions engaged in internal warfare to the point of mental exhaustion, and the opportunity passed without either a yea or a nay. They lost by default, not by decision. A conative stalemate between two groups of talented, normally productive people ensured that nothing was accomplished.

TO AVOID STALEMATES

Stalemates won't occur without a conative obstinacy. They only happen when a person or group of people stubbornly insists on using one particular conative way to get things done. One party's stepping aside would remove the cause of the deadlock. Such a resolution is usually sought, but ultimately it's detrimental because it inhibits synergy. If you're the party who retreats, you've withdrawn your creative resources. You're no longer in the game. If the other party bows out, you are deprived of talent. Rather than blocking that contribution, you must recognize this predicament calls for an immediate halt in activity. Stop incapacitating each other and immediately seek a conative referee (or referees).

Facilitators and other conative bridge people do not necessarily have to bring expertise to the situation, nor must they be in positions of authority over you. They will be able to act as interpreters and Mediators, but do not expect them to resolve the cause of the stalemate. When an ongoing bridge person is not available, a temporary go-between can help divide tasks so that each party will be able to work toward a commonly shared result without hindering the other's efforts. When no one can run interference for even a short term, your mutual purposes are best served by working separately until individual results can be shared.

One married couple found third parties within their co-owned midwestern farm to be very helpful in mediating their conative differences. Jane and Steven Alevizos tried to work cooperatively. Her KCI result of 6-2-8-5 and his of 2-8-1-8 meant their only mode without stress was Implementor, and that wasn't exactly a fit. They both recognized that an important motivation for their hard work was to be financially able to travel and explore nature together. Although their business relationship worked well in the beginning when each of them was busy in his or her own area, as their business grew the work-related problems between them increased as well and eventually affected their marriage.

The Alevizoses' large farm took every ounce of Steven's Implementor in the early phase, when he had to repair much of the equipment, plot acreage, and plant on his own. As for Jane, handling finances, managing the office staff, and negotiating with suppliers and customers absorbed her energy.

As the farm took off, he no longer had to be out in the fields, having turned over those duties to a foreman. And a full-time bookkeeper and office manager had taken over many of her duties, especially because Follow Thru wasn't her forte. These employees added so much to their overhead that the Alevizoses couldn't just take off for weeks at a time, as they had dreamed of doing. They were committing as much energy to the business as ever. Only now he was underfoot, questioning her lack of systems, and she was frustrated that his greater involvement with customers wasn't closing enough deals. By the time they contacted me about problems with their son coming into the business, these two wonderfully obstinate people were at loggerheads.

It would have been convenient had the son been the conative bridge, but no such luck. As demonstrated by a KCI result of 8-3-7-4, his proclivities resembled his mother's more than his father's, so his coming aboard was only going to add to the frustrations. Some employees were bridges in Follow Thru and Fact Finder, but we had to separate the roles of wife and husband when it came to Quick Start and Implementor efforts. The office manager (with a 5 in Follow Thru) interceded by establishing systems that accommodated the husband's needs without insisting on routines that locked his wife into them. He stayed out of the day-to-day fact finding, which accommodated the bookkeeper's needs. The wife instituted marketing studies that the staff summarized for him, because his eyes would glaze over when his partner went on and on about all the details. He took over formulating company policies and procedures, which had been sorely missing.

We got them both to agree that, especially with the arrival of the son's Quick Start, the sales end of the business was being well covered without the husband's participation. While he desired to stay in touch with customers, he was convinced to let the deal makers work their magic alone. He no longer took offense at being excluded from that process, because he saw it not as a personal rejection but as a productive approach, pure and simple. Meanwhile, his wife conceded she had no talent for determining the condition of crops and agreed to keep out of that area of the business. In addition, she promised not to personally complete all the office procedures, nor undermine them with the staff. The stalemate was overcome without anyone having to compromise conative abilities. Natural conflicts between Jane and Steve haven't disappeared; they've been managed productively.

ACTING IMPULSIVELY

Some people are driven toward achieving results no matter what. they act impulsively, using their instincts without reason.

Many heads of corporations and other businesses act impetuously, especially in tough economic times. They have plenty of gumption, but rather than influencing goal setting as a selective process, they rally people together to take action on an abundance of initiatives—which diminishes their effectiveness. The group spreads itself too thin and goes in too many different directions, all for the sake of being "proactive."

An industrious computer-software executive fell into this trap when responding to news that a group of his former employees had gone off to form a competitive organization. "Let's cut back on prices that they won't be able to match," he began. "And let's move up the in-store dates for the new product line." Then, building up steam, he added, "We'll have the marketing department design a more aggressive print ad; be sure our vendors know they'd better not be working both sides of the street." He sounded like a take-charge type, but that was a veneer. True high performers don't get caught up in the pyrotechnics of decision making, because they recognize that's how people—and companies—flame out.

A so-called doer such as this executive can have a negative influence by taking action solely on instinct, without using reason or emotion to temper his impulses. By defining the conative dimension, we're able to explain why intelligent, caring people approach situations differently. It's the integration with the mind's other faculties that helps us control our gut reactions. This executive wasn't thinking clearly about what was possible, or necessary. Even the most insistent risk taker won't go off half-cocked if she *knows* her professional life is in danger. A by-the-book person may back down on some regulations if he feels the pressure to do so. A hands-on person may stop tinkering for a while if he knows he's driving you nuts. "Think about what you're doing!" isn't a bad admonition for guarding against the just-do-something mentality.

To avoid impetuous decisions, don't confuse conative actions with the Creative Process, which incorporates the checks and balances of the full scope of mental elements to produce reasoned, responsible actions. Actions have consequences. Determination does not replace the reasoning aspect of the Creative Process. To avoid getting detoured by the false standard of the "doer," remember that substantive actions, reactions, and interactions require thoughtful editing.

CREATIVE QUAGMIRES

AN OFFICE THAT'S CAUGHT IN A *CREATIVE QUAGMIRE*—COMPLETELY BOGGED DOWN in uninspired make-work activities—is a boring place to work. There's no determination, no zest. When people *refuse to initiate and act only through their resistances*, they create quagmires. "I don't do word processing," a corporate-account salesperson told her supervisor. "If I don't have a secretary, I just won't get all the records filed."

The list of won'ts dominates discussions, employee reviews, and management meetings. Barry, a resistant Quick Start, won't make any cold calls, or attempts to sell to people who are not prequalified as potential customers. Susan, resistant in Implementor, won't travel anymore. Bart, who resists Follow Thru, won't punch in every day. Marion won't come up with Fact Finder recommendations in time. These employees drag everyone's energy toward avoidance behavior, which isn't countered by the give-and-take of conflicts. Decisions are based on how to get around the quagmires instead of how to advance toward goals.

Listlessness is an empty feeling. No one wants to fight to keep his eyes open on the job as the minutes tick by slowly and the afternoon drags on. Unless illness is a factor, listlessness, indifference, and passivity indicate a mind that's unwilling to make an investment. Achievement is elusive without motivation and the forcefulness of instinctive energy. Determination by itself will not help you reach goals. All you're doing is going through the paces without reaching your destination.

To avoid creative quagmires in a group, you need to gain people's active participation. Watch what happens to a concert audience that claps in rhythm or, better yet, sings along with a song: It applauds the loudest and longest for those songs. Employees are more enthusiastic about projects they have helped initiate. Their attention becomes riveted when they are invited to dissent. They don't wallow in inactivity when their contribution is both sought and rewarded, and the absence of it is a recognized loss. "We really missed your thorough proofreading when we had to turn in the report before you got back from vacation," signifies much more to the person than "We really missed you" or "Hope you had a good time."

If your initiating and accommodating instincts are disengaged by a creative quagmire, you may find yourself spending most of your energy avoiding work. In order to achieve goals, you need to engage instinctive energy. This can happen by giving yourself an assignment that has positive implications in each Action Mode. Even if you don't know your KCI result, requiring yourself to use all your energies will get you unstuck. Try making demands of yourself to act through each mode, even though one or two may seem awkward to you. Think of it as running water through a tube to flush out debris. If your energy is clogged in one of the channels, using it for short-term, high-spurt efforts will do the job. An insistent Implementor caught in a quagmire might try turning her energy toward fixing her office phone that's been making funny sounds all week. An insistent Follow Thru who's stuck in a rut could reorganize the files. If you don't know your MO, you can explore options and see what cures your apathy.

"GUMPTION IS ME"

Ed Hurd, head of one of Honeywell's rapidly expanding global businesses, described himself as "relentless in trying to reach consensus." This insistent Quick Start doesn't view consensus as everybody agreeing, nor as others taking the rap if initiatives don't pan out. "I work toward a consensus of *understanding*, not of agreement," he explained. "You have to have the guts to go out on a limb and the initiative to make things happen. I'm relentless when I get a cause, pushing until I think everyone understands the concept. Then if they present reasons it won't work, I'll back off."

Uniquely articulate in describing his conative process, Ed is able to describe his use of Follow Thru structure using the concrete vocabulary that also stems from his Implementor talent. These two accommodating modes shone through clearly as he described his leadership role.

"This whole thing is like a big puzzle that's always in the back of my mind," he said. "A whole lot of the blocks [Implementor imagery] don't fit. If the puzzle is not complete [Follow Thru issue], it feels uncomfortable. There may be an offshore oil-drilling project we could tackle in the North Sea, or some gas plants in Russia that need to be controlled. Individually, we wouldn't pursue the job, but putting the pieces together represents a tremendous opportunity. Finding that unique common thread is my talent. I develop a concept in my mind and take it to a bunch of people and see if it sells. If I get people excited, it's a go. The details don't matter to me. [But then, we knew that.] The in-betweens are not important except as showstoppers. If people agree on the big-picture concept, I'll make decisions quickly in that direction. I trust my instincts.

"I recognize that I have a limited amount of brain power," he continued, "which means I have to block out details and sort through things in my head to eliminate confusing data; create space. I like to have a team around me that keeps my feet on the ground, because I can get too conceptual. My ideas need modification. The bottom line to the business is the numbers. I'm a gear-and-tooth kind of guy. I can see intuitively where the costs are. I can go into a factory and don't need a lot of data to sense where the P and L [profit and loss] will come out. I need others to boil the numbers down to the essence so I can zero in on areas of concern. I trust my instincts to pick the areas we'll focus on."

Ed Hurd is someone others describe as having extremely high energy. He describes himself by saying "Gumption is me."

ASSERTING YOUR CONATIVE SELF

GUMPTION IS YOUR ULTIMATE DEFENSE AGAINST ANYTHING THAT TAKES YOU OUT OF your instinctive stride. By caring too much or rationalizing solutions, you can pull yourself off course, but acting with gumption will get you back on track. Asserting your conative self takes personal fortitude and great confidence in your ability to create solutions. It's well-placed confidence: If you have the gumption to use it, you have the creative power to succeed.

CHAPTER SIXTEEN

LEADERSHIP

INFLUENCING COOPERATIVE EFFORTS

The last letter I received from my father was in 1979. It came attached to a book, *The Art of Leadership*. He knew I was searching for clues to explain why some people become leaders and why some leaders are effective and others disastrous. As he was ending a lifetime of assessing people's capabilities, he passed on to me this treasure that had helped form his own thinking on the subject of whether leadership qualities were innate or could be taught. This 1935 work by Ordway Tead contains a definition of leadership that remains the best I have ever read or heard: "Leadership is the activity of influencing people to cooperate toward some goal which they come to find desirable."

Leadership is an *activity*. That means it is neither a skill, nor an attitude, but conative. By distinguishing leadership from learned behavior (skill) and personality (attitude), Tead offered what he termed a "unique emphasis." That was true in 1935, and it is still true today. He pointed out, "The leader . . . is unquestionably one who can make us aware of impulses and aspirations in ourselves which we had not known were there . . . with [an] end result [that] has reality and meaning only as the individual finds satisfaction through this process. The criterion is always in terms of a reaction which says, 'Now I know myself and am myself more fully than was before possible or even imagined.' " In other words, a leader's actions are directly tied to identifying team members' instinctive capabilities and finding ways of putting them to productive use.

Leaders who functioned as both influencers and enablers were novel in Tead's day, and they remain all too rare today despite much discussion of empowering employees. But this is an idea worth promoting. Now that we can identify the Striving Instincts, it is possible for leadership to be both effective *and* ethical. It entails:

- influencing the goal-setting process
- gaining cooperation toward achieving results
- gumption

Influencing the goal-setting process isn't simply a matter of asking "What do we want to have happen?"—though that is a good start. It also involves influencing the chances of success for both participants and programs through effectively selecting, placing, and directing conative talents. It means being able to dissuade when a team isn't equipped with the right instincts for a project, such as convincing a group of resistant Implementor people not to go down the rapids in a raft without a trained guide. And it assumes a willingness to put your own talents on the line for what you believe is right.

Getting people to cooperate with one another to achieve a goal requires leaders' commitment. They can't stand by and watch a team muddle through. They have to commit themselves to assure results. Some modern-day executives deny their leadership responsibility by becoming too passive and indecisive. When they demur, saying the group has to come to its own decisions, they withhold their influence at their own peril. The void they create is bound to be filled by someone willing to step into the breach.

Some leaders cajole the troops with Fact Finder analogies, others with Follow Thru charting of possibilities, some use Quick Start metaphors that encourage decision making, and others turn to Implementor models to show how problems could be solved. Every conative method can be used to influence others, but the most effective approach is when the leader is true to her own instincts. Trust develops between leader and team members when neither withholds the instinctive self. When leaders use their own instincts to gain the commitment of other people's instincts, goals become more attainable.

True leadership builds on participants' motivation, Striving Instincts, commitment, reason, and talent—the entire Creative Process. Anytime someone needs to control people's methods of contribution, it signals a lack of leadership qualities.

Leadership training is detrimental when it assumes leaders have to be assertive and authoritarian. Influences don't demand *how* people perform, they encourage others to accomplish *what* needs to be done. Leadership programs are most effective when they help people understand there is more than one way to achieve results. A leader's responsibility is to help people discover the way that works best for them and then give them opportunities to adapt their tasks to their instinctive needs.

When you contribute your form of instinctive energy to a group, you become a high producer; perhaps a star performer. When you manage other people's instinctive drives, you are a leader. Effective leaders accept the obligations of stewardship, of overseeing the process of attaining goals. They accept responsibility for selecting teams with the right mix of instincts, skills, and experience, and for guiding conflicting natural energies. Leaders act as a catalyst for freely given conative commitments and give direction to the variety of problem-solving methods that a conatively synergistic group will suggest. And they manage to do this without inhibiting anyone's participation. They bring out the best in people, drawing forth and focusing instinctive energy toward cooperative efforts.

THE FLASH OF A STAR AND
THE FORCE OF A LEADER

THE DIFFERENCE BETWEEN A LEADER AND A STAR IS THAT THE LEADER STRIVES TO increase others' performances toward group goals, and the star strives toward individual achievement. We're all capable of being stars. All it takes is being in a situation where one's conative talents are most necessary. The lone Follow Thru among a group of workers designing an inventory-control system can become an instant hero. The only preventer of chaos among Quick Start pioneers can shine by halting incessant commotion.

Such important contributions differ from directing others' efforts. The star generally initiates activity, whereas the leader uses all three zones of instinctive energy to help a group succeed. That often includes preventing problems that would be caused by people interfering with one another's methods, and responding to others' needs.

A Quick Start leader will use his energy to promote innovation from a team; the Quick Start star originates her own solution. The leader stays with the project as it develops; the star bows out once a start-up program is off and running. Both the stellar performances of the star and the guidance of a team leader are important to reaching goals. But we dare not confuse the two roles. Rewarding stars by trying to make them leaders can be costly.

THE GUMPTION OF A LEADER

Perseverance is an essential characteristic of leadership. It takes backbone, grit, and strength of mind to influence the goal-setting process and to gain the cooperation of others. A common trait among leaders in business, government, and education is their decisiveness. Their tenacity singles them out; they have gumption.

When gumption is missing in executive offices, we're left with ineffectual people trying to exert power over others and how they use their instincts. Rather than steering the striving forces within an organization, these inhibitors of the creative cause either delegate the basic duties of leadership or ignore them altogether. It's as if they say, "I do only the important things, like meet the press, decide about brick and mortar, equipment and money—oh, yes, and set policies that our people have to abide by." Policies ultimately won't matter, not if the people side of the business is in shambles. The best-financed operation in the world will survive only if it has a leader or leaders directing its workers toward ongoing productivity. We've certainly seen examples of money being frittered away when a government lacks leadership.

A case in point is a venture-capital group that had five principals, all recent MBAs with top grades from major American universities. It was given $20 million by Japanese investors, with only one instruction: "Make good investments and let us know the results at the end of each year." Unfortunately there was no leadership or cooperative effort among the partners. In fact, a few of them were in conative conflicts with one another—which they did not address—and one of them was in conative transition. This was passed off with the comment "That comes with the territory." With no leadership, each person went his separate way, seeking his own advisors and clients. They duplicated efforts, and, not surprisingly, within just two years they'd run up expenses and debts that put them out of business.

Lack of leadership exists in many organizations. It often happens because of a desire for equality. Since everyone is equal conatively, and therefore has equal talents to give a team, the leader does not have *more* to give the team. The leader's equal amount of instinctive energy is committed to greater responsibilities. Expecting everyone to assume equal responsibility for a group is wishful thinking.

In most professional partnerships and many university environments, the desire for collegiality causes people to defer to others instead of assuming leadership. Without a leader, the people involved fragment into their individual worlds.

An example of the absence of leadership occurred when the founder of a previously profitable family dry-cleaning business passed away. The next generation certainly knew the business and cared about it, but the company failed to prosper because it lacked the tenacity and the passion of a leader who was able to keep the group's mental energies focused on company goals. It wasn't long before squabbling became incessant. When the founder was alive, the company worked as a team. With him gone, it was like a basketball team with each player trying to improve his own statistics at the expense of winning the game.

MANAGING CONATIVE DIVERSITY

IT IS POSSIBLE TO INFLUENCE HOW PEOPLE FEEL AND WHAT THEY THINK, THEREBY motivating them to act, but it is ineffective to dictate *how* someone else will actually perform. Because diversity of conative talents is essential to a team's success, its leader has to be able to manage a variety of methods without bias toward any one of them. Yet many managers criticize unique processes of problem solving, especially those that vary greatly from their own. They reward their conative clones with high evaluations, not necessarily because these workers achieved group goals, but because the effort was made the way the bosses would have done it. Managing conative diversity is as much an issue of fairness as is any other form of bias. Handing out the plum assignments only to those with a narrow band of conative abilities is prejudicial treatment that limits individuals' opportunities and the group's effectiveness.

Another challenge for leadership is to make assignments that do not stereotype particular conative abilities. There's a tendency to burden efficient Follow Thrus with mundane, repetitious jobs just because they'll stay with them. This assumes the person who initiates a pattern will also operate in the accommodation zone and continue to follow the system as it was designed. To take advantage of insistent Follow Thrus' structured nature this way is unfair—and likely to backfire. The dissatisfied person will add layers to the system, making it increasingly cumbersome for anyone else to use.

Managing conative diversity so people cooperate is undermined if a leader singles out any Operating Zone for particular praise. Initiating activity is important, of course, but so is accommodation and prevention. Those who build on someone else's ideas, or find weaknesses in them, contribute just as greatly. While brainstorming solutions, insistent Quick Starts have to be encouraged to keep adding alternatives. Yet other, less verbal team members also need to be given a chance to contribute. Shutting out any form of instinctive talent is detrimental to the dynamics otherwise derived from conative diversity. The role of the leader is to keep team members' mental energies from going down contradictory paths.

Dealing with conative conflicts is among the most challenging aspects of managing diverse instincts. Imagine a situation in which one person uses Quick Start intuition to eyeball a result, while another, resistant in that mode, gets disgusted with the off-the-top-of-the-head mentality and practically shoves him out of the way. Or a case in which a resistant Implementor's dabbling with repairs insults the artisan's need for crafts-manship. As discussed earlier, when two people have a gap of four or more units in an Action Mode, their perspectives on how something should be done are drastically different. Preventative behaviors will not be viewed positively, just as contrasting insistences won't be seen as contributions. "He's so egotistical," a resistant Fact Finder will say about someone insistent in that mode. "He just thinks he has all the answers." Maybe he does and maybe he doesn't. All we know for sure is that he will share the facts and figures he has researched. The leader's job is to see that he gets the opportunity, without the leader imposing his Will on others.

Management training on the Kolbe Concept prepares leaders to gain cooperation among people with vastly differing needs. The very synergy that gives an organization its greatest advantage can bring management its biggest headaches. It opens the door to conative conflicts. For in-stance, as a team leader in the office-equipment business was readying a position paper on gearing up for the year 2020, a couple of conative sparring partners took off after each other outside his office. "I couldn't believe it," he said. "The Follow Thru was practically screaming about how the other guy had disrupted his work, again. And the proverbial slob got so mad he started throwing the paper clips he'd borrowed. I felt like I was managing a kindergarten." Yet these same two people were major contributors to a crucial project. He could have separated them and told them off, but he knew better. It was leadership's responsibility to direct them toward constructive outlets for their differing instinctive energies.

Workers are likely to goof off when their striving energies lack direction. The manager's preoccupation with his individual writing efforts kept him from his leadership responsibilities. He had to reconfirm that the Follow Thru's initiative was needed to sort through the many options gathered by his unorganized coworker. Their need to contribute cooperatively to reach joint goals then took precedence over the aimless display of their differences.

If leaders realize that instinctive energy is an urge or necessity to act in certain ways, they will be more likely to find productive roles for each participant. Otherwise instinctive energy can seem—and often is—a nuisance. A leader would have converted the two sparring workers' negative energy into appropriate conative assignments. By finding ways to involve every team member in the problem-solving process, no one's energy distracts or subverts team goals. Finally, a leader has to assess whether a team has the right mix of talents, and if not, take action to acquire those missing elements, or subdivide the group into more synergistic project teams.

HOW LEADERS SET THE TONE

BEING A LEADER USUALLY ALLOWS YOU TO SET THE TONE FOR A TEAM. IF YOU'RE an insistent Quick Start who must get right to the bottom line, you'll be much less frustrated if you chair a committee. You can keep it moving at a fast pace. However, resistant Quick Starts might accuse you of steamrolling things through if you don't allow them sufficient time to raise issues that would prevent acting too hastily. Setting the tone ought not to imply that you tune out other conative points of view.

If a resistant Fact Finder has to sit through sessions chaired by someone who insists on sticking to a detailed agenda, frustrations could build. The chairperson gets annoyed because the participant proposes ideas without prior consideration. Since they haven't been studied by a subcommittee, the chair considers discussion of them premature. The participant is frustrated by an atmosphere that makes it difficult to overcome the status quo. The chairperson needs to set aside time for introduction and discussion of new items *before* sending them back to subcommittees.

In the case of Yoshi, a highly insistent Fact Finder who heads a telemarketing firm, techniques such as management by objectives set a corporate tone compatible with his instincts. He orchestrates the organization through lengthy management meetings, for which he expects well-documented fact sheets, thorough background papers, and detailed agendas. Though Yoshi's decision-making process is well defined in advance, those around him are encouraged to add their talents. He's willing, almost to a fault, to hear all points of view, even from those who prolong already extensive discussions.

Yoshi's staffers have found they can miss a meeting only if they're checking out more facts, making sure nothing is overlooked. In fact, they're better off not showing up at all than arriving without having done their homework. In typical Fact Finder fashion, Yoshi relies heavily on available resources such as last year's budget drafts, comparables in the industry, and standard measurement-supporting projections. He also uses outside consultants to provide objective critiques of his operations and gives credit where credit is due. Yoshi never forgets an IOU, whether outgoing or incoming. Fact Finders keep score, all right; not just the hits and misses, but the foul balls, stolen bases, and unearned runs.

Harriet, an equally insistent Follow Thru I found heading up a franchise operation, leads with the efficient tenacity of a queen bee. Consistency among her staff is crucial to her, so the company's daily schedule is more like a ritual, complete with checklists. Omitting a step is tantamount to treason in her book. Her persistence has paid off, because she operates without loose ends. By following procedures, her team can predict its rate of accomplishment, in everything from its orderly progression of raises to the assurance that meetings will end on time. Under her Follow Thru form of leadership, the group's tasks are meted out in a methodical manner, and a steady cadence permeates the environment. She doesn't demand a lock-step approach but offers a sufficiently synchronized pattern so that people can anticipate progress.

Harriet encourages commitment to the system, to safeguards against glitches, to results that stick to a routine. Her company profits from her knack for meshing gears, sorting out discrepancies, and establishing maintenance checkpoints. It works like a well-maintained machine because of the order she brings to it. She constantly comes up with designs that establish cost-saving patterns. No wonder others can so successfully prosper in franchises fashioned after her formulas.

An entirely different environment has been created by Russ, an intense innovator who runs his own advertising agency. I've watched Russ buzz around his place, his fingers in all the pies, changing tempo so often that others find it difficult to keep up. He calls meetings on the spur of the moment, without an agenda. They're for brainstorming, not giving reports. He counts on those around him to provide structure and carry out the details, and doesn't pretend to plan the particulars. He just has to be sure his employees are excited enough about their roles that they'll fill in what's needed, like musicians at a jam session. And from the parts he often gets a magnificent whole. That's what they all count on.

Megan, a dominant Implementor, leads her aeronautical-parts business by marching to an entirely different drummer. Her concern is for substance. She's a shirt-sleeve executive who communicates with her staff while literally on the run. She changes into jogging shoes *after* she gets to work because she stays informed by walking the full building complex, often several times a day. Words don't mean as much to her as being shown situations on site. Building quality products is of the utmost importance to her, so she inspects materials, personally tests machinery, and maneuvers equipment. It's tough to keep her behind a desk. She handles the packaging and transporting of metal parts as if they were raw eggs, going to extraordinary lengths to ensure they arrive undamaged.

Short on words and long on examples, Megan works well with apprentices, who find she doesn't specify exact requirements but has a knack for judging space requirements, weight, and other physical factors. She's not someone you should count on for thorough paperwork. Her forte is dealing with the tangibles.

These leadership styles are often a combination of personality and instinct. The introverted leader may not *choose* to be out front with the media, but if he's a Quick Start, he'll naturally jump in during the Q&A session. He won't be able to stop himself from taking on the verbal challenge when he's on the spot. Regardless of how a person prefers to perform, instinctive proclivities will set the tone when he leads a group.

NATURAL LEADERS

EVERYONE HAS THE POTENTIAL TO BE A LEADER. REGARDLESS OF THE PARTICULAR tone set by a leader, the basic objectives remain the same. All leaders have to use their instinctive power to gain the cooperation of others toward achieving results. Different forms of leadership are needed in different stages of a project, a company's growth, or a country's development. No one person can be a leader in every situation. Effective organizations allow the natural leader to emerge as needs require. The natural leader is the person with the right instincts to influence the group at a certain time. The following are some clues to how various modes manage to get the job done.

Fact Finder—insistent leadership offers explanations of the nuances behind decisions, backgrounding on the pros and cons of specific tactics, and written proposals that build the case for complex strategies.

Fact Finder—resistant leadership will prevent a group from getting mired in micromanagement to the detriment of reaching goals. It will avoid reliance on time-honored but perhaps shopworn alternatives.

Follow Thru—insistent leadership can be counted on to seek secure alternatives that ensure the team's ongoing strength. Team members will receive a comprehensive overview of objectives from this mode of leadership, complete with charting progress and worse-case scenarios.

Follow Thru—resistant leadership provides limitless options with lots of room for restructuring goals. It's an approach that doesn't confine team members to regular meetings, practice sessions, or programs, but has a strong project orientation.

Quick Start—insistent leadership drives toward growth and development of new directions with unending possibilities. It pushes the team toward visionary goals that demand experimentation and remain negotiable as better deals come along.

Quick Start—resistant leadership will keep growth from getting out of hand. It protects members from being pulled off task by distracting flavor-of-the-month options, and fights to identify the unalterable "givens."

Implementor—insistent leadership sees to it that goals are carried out with more than once-over-lightly. It transforms abstract notions into concrete, readily demonstrable objectives with the use of technology. By taking nothing for granted, this mode of leadership literally forces the quality issue.

Implementor—resistant leadership pushes past the day-to-day realities toward unseen possibilities. It doesn't get bottled up with a need for literal translation of goals into tangible goods, but makes moves based on intangible perceptions.

The Facilitator's method combines all the Action Modes in midrange intensities, without any need to be the initiator. It's well characterized by Del Webb Corp. CEO Phil Dion, whose KCI result is 6-4-6-5. Phil, a strong manager, is actually dismayed when he has to play a starring role. "It's superficial, and I don't feel I'm contributing," this natural facilitator said about opportunities when he has to grandstand. His goal is to juggle a group of high performers—including entrepreneur Joe Contadino, whose home-construction company was acquired by Del Webb—to keep them from killing one another off. Phil naturally responds in each Action Mode, so it wasn't surprising when he described himself as accommodating others.

"I'm pretty balanced," Phil explained, "good at empowering other people and delegating. I'm damned determined that this management team work together," he said. "I want us to grow old together. I want to be seen as a leader who could bring a diverse group together—and keep them together." How does he do it? "For me," said the instinctive Mediator, "leading is all about building consensus."

Dick Weden, CEO of American Express Mexico, also exemplifies the benefits of a Facilitator approach to leadership. But he says that it's usually not until after he has left a management role, and conflicts arise, that people realize he'd been the glue that kept it together.

SELF-DIRECTED WORK GROUPS

WHEN PEOPLE WITH THE RIGHT INSTINCTIVE DYNAMICS ARE BROUGHT TOGETHER, they click. Leadership on such a team can come from within, from every contributor. When self-managed teams don't work well, it is usually because the group lacks instinctive synergy or suffers from high levels of impossible expectations (Depletion) or misdirected requirements (Meltdown). An imbalance of instincts makes for a poorly constituted team. When those same energies struggle against the odds for success, adding the responsibility for self-management becomes untenable, unfair, and unproductive. Only when team members have the authority for self-selection should they have the responsibility for self-direction.

A dentist's office in the Northwest operated as a self-managed work group. The dentist was a hands-on Implementor who chose not to get involved in setting goals, assigning roles, or any other aspect of staff management. He figured everyone knew the work that needed to get done and would divvy it up according to skills and experience. The people he chose for his office were friendly and outgoing. They were also uniformly resistant to Follow Thru. Not surprisingly, bedlam ensued. He was losing patients because of double-booked appointments, long waits, mistaken past-due notices, and the shabby appearance of the place.

It wasn't that the group didn't *want* to be self-directed, or that they didn't try. Until obvious inefficiencies eroded their confidence, they had enjoyed working together and given their best effort. The problem was that they all misfired on the same cylinder. With no control over how they were selected, all they could do was live with the stress or leave. Self-directed teams excel when given the authority to add people with necessary instinctive talents. If the dentist's staff had sufficient information about one another's modes of operation and were fully aware of the impact such a combination had, they could have added the missing talents. Unless self-directed teams can also be self-selected, they do not have the authority necessary to accomplish their goals.

Conative clones may love being left alone to manage themselves, but such a situation can also be potentially disastrous. In the early stages, the players don't believe they are suffering. Only later, when everyone on the team tries to download the "undesirable" work to nonreceptive others, will they all feel the frustration. However, a person at the helm could inject some outside contractors into the equation or determine when team members need to work independently to keep the operation moving forward. When a group suffers from Depletion because of an abundance of false individual expectations, someone in a leadership position should reduce the stress by refocusing energy. Outstanding managers recognize that participants will get discouraged, tired of trying, and fearful of mediocre showings. Management must be able to redirect energy toward doable goals by clarifying for workers how they can do the job through their Striving Instincts. Those in the midst of strain-filled situations don't have the energy to help one another out of it.

LEADERSHIP AS RESPONSIBILITY

LEADERSHIP IS A RESPONSIBILITY, NOT A PRIZE. IT OUGHT NOT BE GIVEN AS A reward for individual achievement unless the person expresses a determination to fight for the Will of the group. Shepherding the Creative Process is an awesome assignment that succeeds most often when there is an understanding of instinct-derived needs and capacities. If leadership were merely a matter of making demands, of telling people what to do and rewarding them when they did it, then oppressors would rule, and ultimately fail. The human spirit will not be "led" away from its innate intents and purposes for long. Rebellions occur when leaders misread the instincts of those they presume will follow. We sense when a leader has our best interests and needs at heart and acts on our behalf.

Workplace leadership that nurtures employees' instinctive strengths is rewarded with high employee job satisfaction, as well as high productivity. Jobholders who indicate on KCI questionnaires that they feel a lack of freedom to operate instinctively will work best with managers who make decisions based on the employees' MOs. Team members are pleased when leadership intervenes in conatively stressful situations, whether they be conflicts, cloning, unrealistic self-expectations, or misguided requirements.

ARE MANAGEMENT AND LEADERSHIP THE SAME OR DIFFERENT?

WHILE I GREATLY RESPECT THE THINKING OF HARVARD'S DR. ABRAHAM ZALEZNIK, I differ with his belief that management and leadership are always two different qualities. He recognizes the importance of instinct. In the March–April 1992 edition of the *Harvard Business Review* Zaleznik states: "Leaders . . . are often temperamentally disposed to seek out risk and danger. . . . For those who become managers, a survival instinct dominates the need for risk, and with that instinct comes an ability to tolerate mundane, practical work." But he confuses Quick Start behavior with leadership and Fact Finder–Follow Thru actions with management. This professor of leadership, who is also a psychoanalyst, states:

> A crucial difference between managers and leaders lies in the conceptions they hold, deep in their psyches, of chaos and order. Leaders tolerate chaos and lack of structure and are

thus prepared to keep answers in suspense, avoiding premature closure on important issues. Managers seek order and control and are almost compulsively addicted to disposing of problems even before they understand their potential significance. . . . It is the instinctive move to impose order on potential chaos that makes trouble for organizations.

My observation is that leadership is not limited by instinctive makeup. People with any MO can influence others to reach shared goals. It's true that not all managers are leaders. Nor are they all so intent on providing Follow Thru order that they impose their process on subordinates. Those without a Quick Start visionary approach often use their conative talents to influence others to contribute *their* visions.

I've found most large companies are led by Fact Finder–insistent people who have a second suit in Quick Start and usually a resistance or low accommodation in Follow Thru and Implementor. Entrepreneurial companies are usually led by those with Quick Start insistence. Small companies with a tangible product, sports teams, agriculture, the military, fire and police departments, are where you will find Implementors rising to top spots. Follow Thru–insistent people often head government and service-oriented groups, as well as those related to fashion, furnishings, and education.

It's important to select and train people for the most suited roles on a team that's balanced to achieve conative synergy. But if a team does not have a leader who takes responsibility for influencing its members to strive toward achieving common goals, the rest of the process can be for naught. Every team needs a person or people who are willing to contribute instinctive energy toward leadership efforts, often forsaking the opportunity to use their personal resources in ways that are more likely to make them star performers. That's the sacrifice of leadership. The benefit of leadership is in helping a team reach its greatest potential.

CHAPTER SEVENTEEN

FINDING FOCUS AND REENERGIZING THE INSTINCTS

I feel as if I've failed to help Dr. Ryan Thomas. He's a brilliant lawyer, also a Ph.D., university administrator, and statistician who can teach people the Kolbe Concept, convince corporations to use it for the fair selection of employees, and manage a multimillion-dollar program using KCI results to build synergistic teams. If he were merely a workaholic, he might be able to stretch his instinctive talents of 4-2-9-5 across multiple activities, all of which require and receive tremendous commitment. I'd still have to coach him to move some efforts down to an attempt or intention, which is tough with a guy so dedicated to people and causes. Still, it might be possible, because he's smart enough to know he has to delegate some responsibilities.

But Ryan can't delegate his role as a father of six children, or as a husband, or as a highly involved leader in his church. He's built physical stamina through hiking, skiing, and training kids to play basketball. It seems there's not much Ryan can't do—except to do it all. He can't dredge up any more instinct-based energy than the rest of us or produce beyond his mental capacity. Headaches were the first symptom of trouble. Then neck and back pain. I'm not a physician, but I do know conative burnout when I see it. And it almost always leads to pain—of which we are most aware only when it manifests physically.

Ryan was hurt and insulted when I told him he was a case study in overcommitting. In the past it had been okay to tease him about taking on too much. A particular example, such as staying up all night analyzing data for someone else's presentation (when he had to be "on" for his own speech), was open for discussion. He'd say he understood why he had to allocate his mental energy more appropriately. What he had never confronted was the necessity to conserve mental energy over the long haul. He has to focus his efforts. Not just among work-related matters. Ryan has to take into consideration every aspect of his life when he parcels out his creative contributions.

While helping his young son through life-threatening surgery and agonizing physical therapy, it was imperative that Ryan step back from some other activities. But his wife and other kids needed him more than ever. And it was a crucial time in negotiating contracts at work that couldn't be ignored. And church never means more than when prayers have to be answered. Ryan believed he had to tough it out. He couldn't let up in any department of his life. And the next time there was an emergency at work, a friend who needed help, or a cause that required his expertise, he did the same thing. He kept working so hard that he didn't notice the depth of his mental fatigue. When physical problems finally stopped him in his tracks, he had to make some career decisions. Should he step down from the role about which he cares so much at the university? Should he give up extracurricular, entrepreneurial efforts?

"What do your instincts tell you?" I asked Ryan. "I can't *hear* my instincts anymore," he said.

"Then don't make any decisions," was all I could tell him. "Do nothing."

But Ryan has never learned how to do nothing. Of all the lessons I learned in my school years, one that has stayed with me is a kindergarten exercise. A teacher, for whom I am forever grateful, taught us as young school kids how to act like Raggedy Ann and Raggedy Andy. We learned how to do nothing for a little while, and got credit for doing it well. We admired those in the class who became best at letting go of everything and could walk around completely relaxed. If only Ryan could learn how to do nothing, it could help him be all that he is capable of being.

I'd failed Ryan by being another person who wanted and needed his mental energy. I was like many others who valued his intelligence and integrity. On top of that, I validated and helped him find productive outlets for his instinctive qualities. "I love knowing I'm a Quick Start," he once said. "It explains so much." But we spent too much time discussing how he could use his talents and not enough time figuring out how he could relax his mental muscles.

LEARNING TO RELAX

FORTUNATELY, IT'S NOT TOO LATE FOR RYAN TO LEARN TO RELAX. OR FOR ME TO caution you that using your instincts to increase productivity requires learning how to turn *off* instinctive power. The force behind your actions is so strong and ever-present that it can wear a hole in your Creative Process if it operates without your conscious control of it. My advice is going to seem simplistic, which is all the more reason very bright people have trouble recognizing its importance. It ties to the reason I term the instincts behind our actions the *Striving Instincts*. To go into conative neutral, you have to stop striving. By eliminating all three Levels of Effort, you disconnect the Striving Instincts. They are able to relax. You won't achieve anything in such a state of leisure—except mental rejuvenation.

I suspect sleep, daydreaming, and meditation are vital to our creativity because they are periods of total mental rest. Some people escape mental activity with moments in most days when they do nothing. Others retreat to nighttimes of being couch potatoes. Some people relax more readily when they are able to get out of town, or at least away from places—be it home or office—where they have responsibilities. For many people it works best to change the usual environment, so they don't work in the same rooms where they relax. For others, nonstriving physical activity takes their mind off work. A resistant Implementor may spend time weeding the garden or going fishing. As one executive told me, "The last thing I want to do when I'm on a fishing trip is catch many fish. Too much like work. I don't want to land 'em, clean 'em, or have to cook 'em. I just use fishing as an excuse to sit on a quiet lake and do nothin'."

When, where, and how people find downtime varies greatly. And I have not yet done studies to seek a pattern to this nonbehavior. But I can tell you that I have never found the superhuman person who is able to keep going without taking occasional time-outs. And I've learned to anticipate disasters for people who don't take time to do nothing.

REENERGIZING

"I'M AFRAID IF I EVER GET OFF THE HORSE," ONE WORKAHOLIC SAID, SPEAKING figuratively, "I'd be too sore to ever get back into the saddle." Even if you are working according to your instinctive MO, you will tire without rest, and even with rest you have to find new energy in order to get back into the saddle. Rest heals the sores of overdoing. Better yet, it prevents them in the first place. But rest does not replace spent energy, it simply stops the pain of overuse. Reenergizing the Striving Instincts is another consideration.

I believe we renew our instinctive power with the nourishment of the senses. By observing, touching, smelling, listening, and tasting we replenish the urges our instincts emit. The senses cannot replace misappropriated energy. And they can overstimulate a person who, as with Ryan, sees a beautiful mountain and has to climb it. Once he has taken a mental sabbatical, he will be ready to take in beauty as a car takes in oil and gas. His sensory intake will help him be prepared to do what he is otherwise unable to do.

To work at full power, we all need to have taken time to smell the proverbial roses, to have truly listened to the sounds of the city or the fields. The more deeply people take in through their senses, the more they seem able to sustain striving activity. Pity the poor executive who works seven days a week and never basks in the light of day outside the office. How does she keep going? She doesn't. Not over the long haul.

Most of the high performers I have interviewed have understood this need for both relaxation and reenergizing. Intel's Craig Barrett is a long-distance bicyclist—who doesn't do it competitively. If he were out to prove something with his cycling, it would be a recreational activity. Recreation uses conative talent. It takes energy rather than giving back. Craig's Grand Canyon hikes and long bike rides are downtime for him. Sun, wind, birds, wildflowers, husbandly chatter, and friendly campfires remove him from his day-to-day efforts. Kodak's Kathy Hudson plays with her young son on their farm, business being the furthest thing from her mind. Eastman Chemical's Jack Spurgeon sings gospel music "just for the pure enjoyment of it." Accounting partner Jack Henry reads "for pure pleasure." They've all found ways that work, ways that don't sap their already allocated energy, but instead nourish it.

Family members are often mistaken about one another's MOs because they are most likely to be together in leisure and reenergizing situations. I especially enjoy conducting seminars with business groups and their spouses or significant others because there are so many revelations regarding each person's needs and how they are met differently in different settings. A spouse learns to appreciate why a Fact Finder–insistent husband doesn't have the energy to explain everything that happened at work that day. Or why a wife seems less than spontaneous at home yet achieves in a high-risk work environment. It's important for people to give one another time and space to do nothing at home—without being insulted that "you don't care about what I want to do." It's important to consider the underlying necessity for taking time to walk along the beach, or go to a concert or a movie. Time together with those you love ought to emphasize rejuvenating activity. Certainly very few companies' physical environments or work schedules allow for much of it.

In an ideal world, we would all be able to set our own work hours, operate in a setting that's most conducive to our comfort, and do those things that use our talents best. I'm delighted when my corporate clients encourage flexible work schedules, do away with unnecessary dress codes, and give employees the freedom to daydream occasionally, to look out windows, take walks when answers aren't forthcoming, and work from home or other locations when they believe it will help them get more done.

GROUP RETREATS THAT SET THE TONE FOR SUCCESS

THE BEST WAY TO CONVINCE ANY MANAGER THAT CREATING A SENSORY-STIMULATING environment and providing downtime can improve productivity is to prove it. I've found working with a work-group in a retreat environment is most conducive to assuring long-term results from team-building programs. It not only gets them away from telephones, it gives them a taste of how energizing such an atmosphere can be. Furthermore, I encourage the retreat to include personal partners, be they spouses or significant others. Then we can deal with the majority of influences on how creative energy is committed to sometimes conflicting purposes.

In a two-to-five-day retreat, I confirm each participant's talents in a work-group setting and provide all the benefits of a comparison of the A, B, and C KCIs in meeting team goals. Meanwhile, the personal partners participate in a program in which their MOs are also explained, and their individual efforts are shared in small discussion groups. Great camaraderie usually develops among the personal partners, who now have something a lot more meaningful to discuss than the all-too-typical flower arranging many spousal programs offer. For once, husbands are as involved as wives.

At such retreats, I meet privately with each couple. These usually are fun-filled opportunities to share ideas for how they can reduce conflicts between them, support each other's conative needs more completely, and communicate more openly about why they act the way they do. When appropriate, these discussions also involve issues of designating child-rearing responsibilities according to each person's natural way of interacting. These sessions often solidify the otherwise fragmented information regarding work-related and personal uses of time and energy. When we can deal with the total picture, the directions in which a person's energy is pulled, we can help prevent some of the problems Ryan faced before they became overwhelming.

I don't have a magic wand, and if I did I wouldn't use it to solve people's problems. The quest or journey is the joy. It's the process of problem solving and decision making that brings people closer together and helps them find a sense of accomplishment, as individuals, members of teams, and in personal partnerships.

Nothing I have discussed in this book is as easy to do as it may seem on first reading. As a resistant Fact Finder, I'm still trying to figure out how I can follow my own advice and write books in the future without feeling as burnt out as I do at this moment. The time has come for me to set this aside and plant flowers for next season.

HISTORICAL PERSPECTIVE

Aristotle starteth" the question that has led to a discussion of instinct and its companion principle of "will," according to a seventeenth-century treatise by Ralph Cudworth. "What is it that first moveth in the soul and setteth all the other wheels on work?" he paraphrased Aristotle as having asked. "What is that vital power and energy which the soul first displayeth itself in, and which in order of nature precedes all its other powers, it implying them, or setting them on work?"

Such philosophical discussions on the nature of instinct gave way to heated debate two hundred years later, as the new field of psychology attempted to define instinct in scientific terms. "Actions we call instinctive," wrote William James in 1890, are "as fatal as sneezing." He argued against the notion espoused earlier that century by Lindley Kemp that "unlike animals, when it comes to man, we find ALL is actions placed under the control of reason. Man is, indeed, devoid of instinct. . . . He observes and reflects, and acts in accordance to the decisions of his mind." Although James, Freud, Jung and others brought the issue of instinct into the hallowed halls of academia, their lack of "proof" of the existence of this unconscious energy weakened their theories.

Modern psychologists could have written Kemp's nineteenth-century book on instinct. There is a current contempt among academicians for those suggesting instinct as a source of human activity. James hadn't softened such opinions by saying that, "the older writings on instinct are ineffectual wastes of words, being their authors never came down to this definite and simple point of view [that behavior is energized by instinct], but smothered everything in vague wonder."

Both those in agreement with and those who oppose a human instinct model to explain unlearned behavior have used the same simplistic argument. Lack of proof to the *contrary* was assumed as evidence for both sides. The battle over instincts' power to determine human action has raged since the eighteenth century, when philosophers in the Age of Enlightenment turned to reason as the sole basis of human action.

James's protestations seemed to give encouragement to philosophers and psychologists of the late nineteenth and early twentieth century who rejected the notion that human beings were purely rational creatures. Freud, for instance, identified sex and death (or self-destruction) as instinctual. Jung added the herd and nutritional instincts. William Mc-Dougall, the foremost social psychologist of the early 1900s, identified twelve urges, including seven primary proclivities: fear, repulsion, pugnacity, curiosity, self-abasement, self-assertion, and parenting. The momentum built as H. W. Warren offered twenty-six instincts, and Woodworth threw in one hundred and ten, under the general headings of organic needs, responses to other persons, and play instincts.

By 1926, Luther L. Bernard had enough. His criticisms were instrumental in turning modern scholars away once again from the study of instinct. "There is scarcely any conduct employed in the social sciences about which there is so much diversity of usage and uncertainty of meaning as there is concerning the term instinct." He enumerated the problems as:

1. There was no agreement on the nature of true instincts.
2. The discussions of instinct were too vague and conceptual.
3. Instincts weren't visible and therefore couldn't be a part of scientific study.
4. There were no accurate methods for classifying instincts in terms of overt manifestations.

Bernard was writing at a time when IQ testing was beginning to allow behaviorists to study the cognitive part of the mind in quantifiable terms. In the 1890s Alfred Binet had discovered the measurable qualities of intellect and IQ testing followed within the next few decades. The abstract notion of instinct couldn't compete. By the time the United States had entered into the Second World War, the federal government had nationalized my Dad's Wonderlic Personnel Test to help determine who would be foot soldiers and who would be trained as officers. Since intelligence could be quantified, it became a method for distinguishing among candidates for battle, just as it was beginning to be used to determine workplace roles.

Instincts could be inferred only from observable actions, so they were overlooked as a criterion for selection. Thus, McDougall hadn't been able to substantiate his belief that instinct was the only accurate predictor of human performance. A scientific community caught up in the nature-verses-nurture argument wasn't willing to listen to discussion about an internal energy source not tied to genetics (nature) or to learned behavior (nurture). He ended up severely criticized for his lack of scholarliness and left Harvard in the 1930s.

In 1929, George Binney Dibblee, a lecturer at Oxford and Fellow at All Soul's College, put science's problem with instinct into perspective when he wrote that the term "instincts" was "bandied about so carelessly they have sometimes become nothing but familiar tokens, good coin perhaps originally, but now debased and clipped and worn out beyond recognition . . . [yet] there is generally a true ring in the weight attached to them. . . . The task lies in unraveling the doubt as to whether the words are loose conversational expressions and rhetorical terms . . . or whether their philosophic, scientific, and common use is a genuine phenomenon representing mental facts of importance."

The task he noted as essential went undone. Wiley's 1984 *Encyclopedia of Psychology* states that ". . . the concept of instinct is now largely ignored."

Why? Sir Oliver Lodge, in a 1927 lecture at Oxford, gives a glimpse into the emotion that led to the retreat. Instinct, he said, is "not accessible to our systematic methods of scientific exploration. [Therefore] science . . . [is] apt to despise instinct or to suspect the intuitive apprehension of truth not founded upon ascertained and formulated data." These strong words forecasted the abandonment that took place. A. J. Riopelle's book *Instinct* (1967 edition) explained scientists' rejection of innate mental energy. "With the development of quantitative psychology, the study of natural behavior was abandoned in favor of responses in T-mazes, Skinner boxes and discrimination learning devices. This strategy implied or assumed that behavior was mostly learned."

In other words, now that we could statistically study the cognitive faculty, it was presumed to be the only mental faculty that mattered. Researchers came to believe human behavior was premeditated, that we acted only according to learned patterns. If there was any discussion of instinct, they tried to connect it with motivation, since both remained nonquantifiable components of the performance equation.

There have always been a few learned voices who have realized the limitation of a scientific approach to understanding instinct, for whom this has not lessened a belief in instinct. I like to refer my academically oriented friends to a statement by the philosopher George Berkeley, who said it took "a mind debauched by learning to carry the process of making the natural seem strange, so far as to ask for the WHY of any instinctive human act."

APPENDIX II

DATA
SUMMARY
AND
DISCUSSION

T he following data summary illustrates practical business applications of the KCI. Studies were done in accordance with *Standards for Educational and Psychological Testing.*[1] Specific standards are referenced where applicable. This material is not intended to summarize the entire body of research on the development of the KCI.

VALIDITY STUDIES[2]

THE KOLBE SYSTEM IS BASED ON THE THEORY THAT AN INHERENT PART OF THE human mind, in concert with an individual's knowledge (cognitive), desires (affective), and determination, defines creative effort.[3] Conation,

---

[1] American Educational Research Association, American Psychological Association, National Council on Measurement in Education, 1985. Hereinafter referred to as "Standards."

[2] Standards 1.1—Evidence of validity should be presented for the major types of inferences for which the use of a test is recommended. A rationale should be provided to support the particular mix of evidence presented for the intended use.

[3] Kathy Kolbe, *The Conative Connection*, Reading, Mass.: Addison-Wesley, 1987.

the behavioral reflection of instinct, forms a person's modus operandi, or ways of striving. Three operating zones have been identified that indicate whether a person initiates, responds, or prevents particular patterns of action.

Although many psychologists and philosophers have acknowledged the importance of instinct to human performance, it has been perceived as unmeasurable, and consequently it has not previously been utilized in any form of psychometric testing. By discovering a method to measure the conative reflections of four specific Striving Instincts, instinct can now be utilized as a predictor of behavior. Conative measurement is premised on classifying observable behavior into four distinct Action Modes, identified as:

1. Fact Finder (FF), associated with the instinct to probe,
2. Follow Through (FT), associated with the instinct to pattern,
3. Quick Start (QS), associated with the instinct to innovate, and
4. Implementor (IM), associated with the instinct to demonstrate.

The foundation for the classification of striving behavior into these four Action Modes was derived by doing statistical factor analysis on 200 behavioral questions hypothesized to be predictive of and related to conation. A sample of 250 subjects representative of the general population was chosen. The subjects were tested on this original 200 item conative questionnaire and were also given the Myers-Briggs Type Indicator test and the Wonderlic Personnel Test. If these responses are correlated with results from the Myers-Briggs and Wonderlic tests and any of the 200 items that showed a significant correlation with these affective and intelligence measurement instruments are eliminated, the remaining items are ensured of being independent measures of the striving instinct. Further refinement and statistical analysis showed that the 72 responses that comprise the KCI fall naturally into the four Action Modes described above. They are independent of any affective or intelligence elements of mind and reflect the instinctive behavioral patterns of the individuals' conative actions.

Conative Measurement[4]

The KCI asks subjects to choose two of four possible responses reflecting how they would be most and least likely to act in 36 single-sentence problem-solving scenarios. The 72 individual responses are scored with a complex algorithm used to determine a numerical score between 1 to 10 for each Action Mode. The scores are normally distributed across the general population with a mean of 5 and a standard deviation of 1. Each scale is equally weighted and the four scores are not combined to give a total or overall score because the pattern of the four combined results is an ipsative measure. Action Mode results are, however, comparable between individuals because scale scores are based on a normal distribution.

This reflects the fact that everyone is endowed with some measure of talent in each of the four striving instincts. The four integer scores that represent the four Action Modes are always given separately. The composite of these four Action Modes represent a pattern that is called an individual's modus operandi (MO) and is a conative reflection of the individual's instinctive strengths or creative talent.

Individuals may have modes in which they insist (a score of 7 or above) and others in which they prevent (a score of 3 or below). There are some individuals whose KCI scores reflect accommodation (a score of 4 to 6) with no insistences in a mode. This may either be because they are Facilitators who instinctively mediate between insistence or preventive behavior of others, or because they, due to some form of pressure, are experiencing a conative transition in which their instinctive responses are being thwarted by significant stress.

Scale scores are meant to be used as a shorthand way to identify which of the three behavioral operating zones (insist, accommodate, or prevent) an individual tends to use in each of the four Action Modes. In any given Action Mode about 20 percent of the general population will be insistent, 60 percent will tend to accommodate, and 20 percent will prevent or resist behavioral action. The operating zone percentages are not normally distributed because 10 percent of the general population are in conative transition at any one time. The results of those individuals are expected to change significantly upon retest. Once through the transition period, their KCI results will reflect their true conative nature.

---

[4] Standards 1.3—Whenever interpretation of subscores, score differences, or profiles is suggested, the evidence justifying such interpretation should be made explicit. Where composite scores are developed, the basis and rationale for weighing the subscores should be given.

While scores are normally distributed across the general population, ranges of success in each mode are specific to certain professions and work titles. To establish the ranges for a specific job title, employers analyze the conative makeup of high and low performers within a job title. Comparing these ranges allows the employer to identify the conative ranges within which employees operate in the most productive manner.

As the following research studies illustrate, successful employees in similar jobs tend to have results on the KCI that fall within a well-defined range of success. These ranges, in turn, tend to be consistent with the conative or functional expectations of the job identified by the employee on a companion test, the Job-KCI (B), or supervisors and cohorts on another companion test, the Job-KCI (C). Such ranges have proven to be valid predictors of employee success in job-related criteria, and employer and employee satisfaction.

Illustrative Distribution of Conative Energy for Specific Professions

A database of 40,000 individual KCI results was used to identify the conative energy distributions that match high performance in given careers or jobs within companies. While range of success studies are required when applying the Kolbe Concept for selection purposes, only group means will be used in the following examples. This simplification will help illustrate the point that the KCI is a highly predictive tool in career development and human resource management. The following examples are illustrative of the many studies of this type completed by KolbeConcepts.

Electrical Engineers[5]   The U.S. Department of Labor profile of engineers is closely aligned to the KCI studies completed by KolbeConcepts. The DOL identifies engineering as a career that requires attention to detail, the ability to design practical, technical solutions to problems,

---

[5] This study and the other studies cited in this research report comply fully with Standard 1.11. A report of a criterion-related validation study should provide a description of the sample and the statistical analysis used to determine the degree of predictive accuracy. Basic statistics should include number of cases (and the reasons for eliminating any cases), measures of central tendency and variability, relationships, and a description of any marked tendency toward non-normality of distribution.

and the talent to analyze overall effectiveness, cost, reliability, and safety.

In 1990, a multinational semiconductor manufacturer selected 86 electrical engineers to complete the KCI. The majority of the subjects held master's degrees in electrical engineering, and all were selected for the study based on their success in the company. The KCI results reflected disproportionately high rates of insistence in FF (53 percent compared with an expected 20 percent), and FT (45 percent compared with an expected 20 percent), disproportionately high rates of resistance in QS (53 percent compared with an expected 20 percent) and IM (34 percent compared with an expected 20 percent); and disproportionately low rates of resistance in FF (2 percent compared with an expected 20 percent) and FT (6 percent compared to an expected 20 percent); and disproportionately low rates of insistence in QS (8 percent compared with an expected 20 percent) and IM (3 percent compared with an expected 20 percent).

The fact that KCI results show a disproportionate rate in each of the insistences and resistances to the general population concurs with the unique characteristics in the engineering career description cited by the DOL.

Successful Electrical Engineers

Percent by Action Mode by Zone

	Initiate	Respond	Prevent
FF	53	45	2
FT	45	49	6
QS	8	39	53
IM	3	63	34

n=86

Pharmaceutical Scientists   In 1992, 29 successful pharmaceutical research and regulatory scientists employed by a national pharmaceutical manufacturer took the KCI to identify the conative energy distribution that is indicative of success in those professions. While the results indicated a strong insistence in FF for both groups, the specialization of the career paths caused a divergence in the other modes by specialty.

For example, based upon this study it can be inferred that in this company, regulatory scientists need to be accommodating in FT and

Successful Pharmaceutical Scientists
Percent by Specialty, Action Mode and Zone

	Initiate	Respond	Prevent
FF Reg.	83	17	0
FF Res.	65	35	0
FT Reg.	25	75	0
FT Res.	6	71	23
QS Reg.	25	25	50
QS Res.	12	47	41
IM Reg.	0	25	75
IM Res.	6	50	44

n=29

accommodating in QS, while the research scientists need to be accommodating in IM. This new information has caused the pharmaceutical firm to redesign its recruiting process to capitalize on the conative patterns identified for these specific jobs in the pharmaceutical sciences.

Marketing Managers   In 1988, 55 marketing managers attending the International Convention of Meeting Planners completed the KCI to identify the conative profile of a successful marketing manager. It was hypothesized that marketing managers would have higher levels of QS and FF than the general population due to their entrepreneurial and improvising talents. As expected, compared with the general population, the group was more insistent in FF, reflecting the need to research and gather data, and in QS, reflecting the conative need for risk taking.

Marketing Managers
Percent by Action Mode by Zone

	Initiate	Respond	Prevent
FF	31	55	14
FT	9	64	27
QS	45	44	11
IM	0	44	56

n=55

Accountants   In 1992, Dr. Alan Czyzewski, assistant professor of accounting at Indiana State University, and Dr. Harry Dickinson, assistant professor of accounting at Virginia Commonwealth University, reviewed the KCI results for 222 accountants working in U.S. offices of several large international accounting firms. The non-random sample contains 76 staff, 39 seniors, 87 managers, and 20 partners. The accountants could not be classified as audit, tax, or consulting. When comparing the general population's expected 20 percent insistent, 60 percent accommodating and 20 percent resistant in each mode to the KCI scores for CPAs at the four levels, the results proved convincing. As expected, CPAs were more insistent in Fact Finder than the general population (47 percent); only 3 percent of the sample were resistant to that mode. The pattern remains similar for the Follow Thru mode (32 percent insistent), with only 15 percent of the sample resistant to that mode. An equal number of CPAs were insistent in Quick Start as were resistant (approximately 29 percent).

The further CPAs progressed up the ladder, the more likely they were to be insistent in the Quick Start mode, reflecting the addition of new business development to the responsibilities of the more senior managers and partners. Thirty-six percent of the managers and 39 percent of the partners were insistent in Quick Start, compared with 18 percent of the staff and zero percent of the seniors. Fifty-one percent of CPAs were found to be resistant in the Implementor mode, with only 4 percent insistent, reflecting the abstract nature of their work, as opposed to the more tangible and concrete talents of the Implementor.

Public Accountants

Percent by Action Mode and Zone

	Initiate	Respond	Prevent
FF	47	50	3
FT	32	53	15
QS	29	42	29
IM	4	45	51

n=99

Health Care Staff The American Nursing Association states that health care professionals require the capability to manage, coordinate, and communicate with the entire team of health care providers as well as the patient. The KCI conative energy distribution for health care professionals suggests that this level of performance is most likely to occur when the health care provider is insistent in FF and accommodating in

FT and IM. This is confirmed in a 1992 study of 222 health care managers. Those who were in conative stress lacked the level of FT needed to adhere to the organizational demands of the health care system and its procedures.

Health Care Staff
Percent by Action Mode by Zone

	Initiate	Respond	Prevent
FF	46	46	8
FT	28	55	17
QS	20	35	45
IM	10	59	31

n=222

Lawyers The American Bar Association identifies a diverse set of abilities that attorneys need in order to be successful. Primary among these are the ability to gather and organize information, develop strategies and arguments, and carry through the process of litigation. It is essential that the lawyer have a fundamental understanding of rules and regulations concerning code and conduct. Central to all legal activity is the ability to improvise, generate ideas, and communicate both orally and in writing. Predicated upon this information, one could predict that a KCI profile of lawyers would find this professional population to be more insistent in FF and QS than the general population.

Lawyers
Percent by Action Mode by Zone

	Initiate	Respond	Prevent
FF	55	42	3
FT	11	60	29
QS	34	39	27
IM	4	45	51

n=146

Effects of Conative Stress

In addition to career development and selection, the KCI has proved to be an invaluable diagnostic tool for pinpointing organizational problems and opportunities. In combination with the KCI-B and KCI-C, it predicts absenteeism, turnover, and specific types of group productivity, including innovation and management of information systems. Identifying productivity roadblocks that cause conative stress and reorganizing tasks, talents, work groups, and organizational structures to achieve conative synergy are all areas where the KCI has proven valuable.

Absenteeism   As illustrated by the following research, when an individual employee is in a job that is a poor conative fit, she may experience a form of conative stress: strain due to unrealistic conative self-expectations, or tension due to the unrealistic conative requirements of others.

In a study conducted in 1992, 60 employees from a national marketing firm were studied. Half had the highest absenteeism in the company and half had the lowest absenteeism. Each employee completed an individual KCI and a KCI-B for his own position. Each employee's supervisor also completed a KCI-C for the employee's position. The results of the study indicated that 50 percent of the high-absenteeism group were experiencing conative stress, while only 20 percent of the low-absenteeism employees were experiencing similar stress. Years of employment and gender were analyzed to ensure that these factors were not influencing the outcome. The results indicated no differences in absenteeism between those who had been employed more than two years and those who had been employed fewer than two years, nor were there significant differences based on gender.

In another study, completed in 1992, 50 staff-level employees were selected by a national food processing company to study absenteeism. The employees were all rated on a three-point scale for absenteeism during the previous year. There were 16 percent of the employees in the medium to high range of absenteeism. Of that group, 62.5 percent were experiencing conative tension or strain. In contrast, *none* of the employees in the low absenteeism group were experiencing conative stress.

Reducing Turnover   Dr. Richard S. Deems, an independent Kolbe consultant, conducted a study in 1991 in which he used the KCI to predict branch manager turnover in a national financial services company. His study included all 483 branch manager trainees hired in 1991 who were divided into three approximately equal size groups:

1. a control group that was not given the KCI,
2. a study group of trainees given the KCI whose scores fell outside the recommended range but whose managers were

Conative Stress as a
Predictor of High Absenteeism

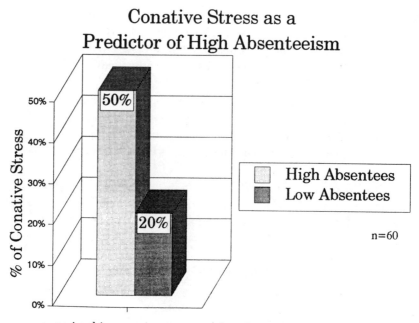

trained in conation to respond to the conative dissonance;
and

3. a study group of trainees whose scores fell within the
recommended range.

At the end of six months, 11.7 percent of the group that had not used
the KCI had left the company for job-related reasons; 5.5 percent of
those who were conatively mismatched but whose managers tried to
mitigate the conative dissonance by using the trainee's KCI results had
left for job-related reasons; and none of the conatively matched trainees
left for job-related reasons.

Identification of high potential employees and training managers on
use of the Kolbe Concept was effective in achieving significant improvements in retention. Total company turnover was reduced 12 to 15 percent below the lowest rate achieved in the past ten years. Dr. Deems
concluded, "Selection within the recommended KCI range resulted in
100 percent retention of the desired Branch Manager trainees."

The criteria used in the cited validation studies are job-related criteria
chosen by employers.[6] The studies cited rely on objective criteria (ab-

---

[6] Standard 1.12—All criterion measures should be described accurately, and the rationale of
choosing them as relevant criteria should be made explicit.

Use of KCI
Reduction of Turnover

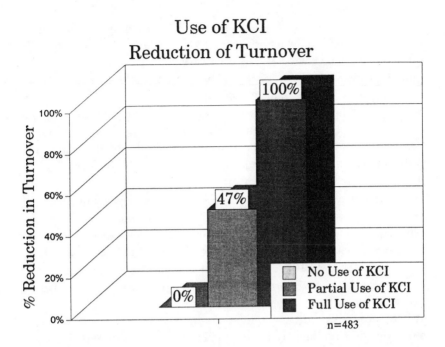

senteeism, attrition, sales volume) rather than subjective evaluations of supervisors or others. It is possible to utilize subjective criteria in validating the KCI in a particular job setting. However, employers are urged to review their criteria to ensure that such criteria actually reflect important measures of job-related success rather than affective assessments.

To ensure compliance with federal law, The Kolbe FairSelection System requires either a concurrent or predictive validation study to be performed any time the job is by its nature replicable, or where there are five or more employees hired or contemplated to be hired into the job within a five-year period.[7] A job is replicable by nature if (1) the job is primarily an independent-contributor position and five or more individuals perform essentially the same task within the organization, or (2) if the job is not primarily an independent-contributor position but ten or more individuals hold similar positions with similar tasks within the company.

In concurrent validity studies the conative characteristics of high and low performers presently performing in a job title are compared with the

---

[7] Standard 1.16—When adequate local validation evidence is not available, criterion-related evidence of validity for a specified test may be based on validity generalization from a set of prior studies, provided that the specified test-use situation can be considered to have been drawn from the same population of situations on which validity generalization was conducted.

conative expectations of supervisors (KCI-C) to identify selection standards for future employees. Such a study can be performed relatively quickly and inexpensively. The KCI tests instincts, not skills or acquired attributes, and the results have high test/retest reliability. These characteristics obviate major concerns regarding concurrent studies. Since individual conative criteria do not change with job experience, a conative concurrent validation study allows an applicant's conative makeup to be compared to the conative requirements of the position without concern about unfairly selecting against the applicant's potential for future change.

In predictive validation studies, new employees are conatively tested at the time of selection. Then their results are compared to their job-related performance after a period of time, typically six months or more. Conative ranges for future selection are developed by identifying those employees whose KCI results at the time of hire would have predicted high performance and correlating their KCI results with the conative expectations of their supervisors.

Concurrent or predictive validation studies are appropriate when an employer hires a relatively large number of employees into a single job category each year. However, many jobs are unique and are filled infrequently. To help an employer in such a circumstance, KolbeConcepts has developed a system for validity generalization of the KCI based on industry-accepted Bayesian techniques. This allows conative criteria for a unique job to be generalized from existing data for similar positions. If the conative characteristics identified by coworkers and supervisors are used with conative criteria identified through a conative job analysis, a conative range for selection can be identified that will predict high performance and enhance the conative strength of the employee group.

Bayes's theorem is a theory of probability. It is premised on the concept that the probability of an outcome is affected by subsequent knowledge. Bayes's theorem provides a way of translating instinctive response into a statement of increased probability. The theorem states that probability is equal to the initial or prior likelihood multiplied by the likelihood derived from subsequent experience.

When a large-scale conative validation on a replicable job is performed, it is possible to determine with a high level of confidence that the range of tolerance will not select anyone who is not well suited conatively for the job. For example, if a validation that included 70 KCIs were performed, there would be less than a 5 percent likelihood that a correlation of .23 would occur by chance. For a unique position, a validation study may include only five KCIs; the correlation would have to be .88 before you would have similar confidence that it had not occurred by chance. This difference is due to the large disparity between the sizes of the populations involved in the validation study.

When performing a validation for a unique position, a Bayesian algorithm is used to strengthen the statistical power of the identified correlations. For example, if the initial correlation for a unique position as a personal assistant was .45 for a FF range of 4 to 7, and the tested population, or n was 7, the statistical likelihood that such a correlation is a result of chance would be .5. If the likelihood that conative correlation for a unique position was modified by using likelihoods from conatively similar job families, then the predictive strength of the correlation might be significantly improved from .5 to .95.

Federal law requires employers to prove that their employment practices are (1) unbiased, meaning they create no "disparate impact" upon a protected minority group, or (2) that their biased practice(s) are good predictors of job success, and are the least discriminatory options available.[8]

Dr. Robert T. Keim of Arizona State University conducted an extensive study of bias of the KCI instrument in 1991, in which he examined 4,030 KCI results. These were divided into 17 groups reflecting common conative patterns similar to job-selection criteria.

Dr. Keim initially performed analyses of variance, treating each of the four conative instincts as dependent variables; and race, gender, and age as independent variables. In 65 of 68 analyses of variance (4 modes × 17 groups), the results showed that at the .05 level of significance, differences in scores on the KCI could not be attributed to the dependent variables of race, gender, or age. For the three values where the initial analysis of variance did not provide conclusive results, a chi square analysis was conducted by computing a chi square base-model value for each with gender, race and age. Subsequent analyses of variance and chi square values were computed, leaving out each of the independent variables. Comparisons between the base-model values and the subsequent values demonstrated that in no case do the independent variables of race, gender, or age explain differences in scores. Dr. Keim stated, "We

---

[8] Standard 1.20—Investigations of criterion-related validity for tests used in selection decisions should include, where feasible, a study of the magnitude of predictive bias due to differential prediction for those groups for which previous research has established a substantial prior probability of differential prediction for the particular kind of test in question.

can conclude that at the alpha = .05 level, the KCI is not biased by gender, age, or race."

In a 1992 selection bias study conducted by Dr. Ryan L. Thomas of Brigham Young University, 24,416 KCI results were cross-tabulated by each of 51 professions and 10 professional levels. In each profession and level in which there was an adequate minority sample (30 or more), the data were analyzed to determine whether the KCI would have selected any minority group (determined by the federally protected categories of race, gender, and age) less than 80 percent as often as the most frequently selected group (the criteria for adverse impact established by the EEOC). In no category in which there was an adequate minority sample would the KCI have adversely selected on minority status. There was no evidence that the KCI would have an adverse impact on any minority group if used as part of a properly designed selection process.

The KCI is free from bias both in general and as a selector for specific jobs. Consistent with the Civil Rights Act of 1991, there are not separate norms for any groups. Although the law does not allow evidence of an instrument's lack of bias to generally obviate the need for evidence of lack of bias in a specific job, the Kolbe FairSelection System ensures that, consistent with EEOC Guidelines, the KCI will not select any race, national origin, gender, age, or disability less than 80 percent as often as the most frequently selected group.

The following tables reflect the lack of bias in two typical conative job families:

Means by Mode and Minority Status
For Fact Finder Job Profile

	FF	FT	QS	IM
White	7.49	4.64	4.12	3.6
Non-White	7.41	4.64	3.96	3.67
Male	7.51	4.66	4.01	3.62
Female	7.42	4.59	4.26	3.58
Under 41	7.47	4.64	4.09	3.59
41+	7.49	4.64	4.16	3.56

n=24,416

There were no statistically significant differences between the means for selection purposes at the .05 level of significance.

Standard Deviations

Fact Finder Job Profile

	FF	FT	QS	IM
White	0.57	0.69	1.01	0.93
Non-white	0.57	0.59	0.93	0.93
Male	0.58	0.65	1.01	0.94
Female	0.55	0.69	0.97	0.91
Under 41	0.54	0.64	0.94	0.89
41+	0.67	0.72	1.13	0.95

n=24,416

Means by Mode and Minority Status
For Quick Start Job Profile

	FF	FT	QS	IM
White	4.07	3.51	8.08	3.71
Non-White	4.02	3.69	7.93	3.86
Male	4.14	3.45	8.05	3.78
Female	3.98	3.61	8.11	3.64
Under 41	4.09	3.57	7.96	3.83
41+	4.06	3.48	8.14	3.63

There were no statistically significant differences between the means for selection purposes at the .05 level of significance.

The Kolbe FairSelection program does not use cut scores; rather, it provides grades and ranks candidates using a range of success.[9] Use of the KCI in selection cannot obviate the effect of prior selection processes: including recruitment techniques, résumé screening, cognitive or affective testing, and/or interviewing. Any one of the other selection procedures may have the effect of limiting the number of applicants with a particular conative MO, and such limitations may result in a skew of the data in a validation study or may result in some skew on selection of applicants. In order to minimize the impact of such errors, the validation

---

[9] Standard 1.24—If specific cut scores are recommended for decision making (for example, in differential diagnosis), the user's guide should caution that rates of miscalculation will vary depending on the percentage of individuals tested who actually belong in each category.

Standard Deviations

Quick Start Job Profile

	FF	FT	QS	IM
White	0.87	1.07	0.83	0.91
Non-white	0.91	1.11	0.83	0.99
Male	0.83	1.04	0.81	1.11
Female	0.92	1.12	0.86	1.03
Under 41	0.87	1.04	0.75	1.09
41+	0.92	1.11	0.82	1.21

process relies not only on the KCI scores of successful and unsuccessful employees, but on independent identification of conative requirements through the Job KCI-B and the Job KCI-C.

RELIABILITY AND ERRORS OF MEASUREMENT[10]

IN A STUDY COMPLETED IN 1993, 125 EMPLOYEES FROM THREE COMPANIES (A "BIG Six" accounting firm, a public utility, and a manufacturing firm) participated in a test-retest reliability study. The retests occurred between six months and two years from the time of the original testings. The results were analyzed using paired T-tests and Pearson Product Moment Correlations for each Action Mode. Frequency tables and percentage distributions were also computed. This analysis showed that scores for the KCI do not change significantly over time.

The analysis of the frequency tables indicated that for the Fact Finder

---

[10] Standard 2.1—For each total score, subscore, or combination of scores that is reported, estimates of relevant reliabilities and standard errors of measurement should be provided in adequate detail to enable the test user to judge whether scores are sufficiently accurate for the intended use of the test.

Standard 2.2—The procedures that are used to obtain samples of individuals, groups, or observations for the purpose of estimating reliabilities and standard errors of measurement, as well as the nature of the populations involved, should be described. The numbers of individuals in each sample that are used to obtain the estimates, score means, and standard deviations should also be reported.

Standard 2.3—Each method of estimating a reliability that is reported should be defined clearly and expressed in terms of variance components, correlation coefficients, standard errors of measurement, percentages of correct decisions, or equivalent statistics. The conditions under which the reliability estimate was obtained and the situations to which it may be applicable should also be explained clearly.

mode, 94.4 percent of the subjects' retest scores remained consistent within a range of two units. Results for Follow Thru were 96.8 percent consistency, for Quick Start 92.0 percent consistency, and for Implementor 99.2 percent consistency.

The paired T-tests resulted in values that ranged from .87 to .50. These tests show no statistically significant difference in scores between the initial test and the retest at the .05 level. The Pearson Product Moment Correlation coefficients ranged between 0.67 and 0.88. These are well within the desired parameters for test reliability.

A study conducted in 1989 at a major educational institution demonstrated test-retest reliability of the KCI. Seventy-eight students completed the KCI and were not given the results of their tests. These students were then retested two weeks later. The results showed that the KCI had high temporal reliability. None of the 78 students had a variance of more than two in any one mode.

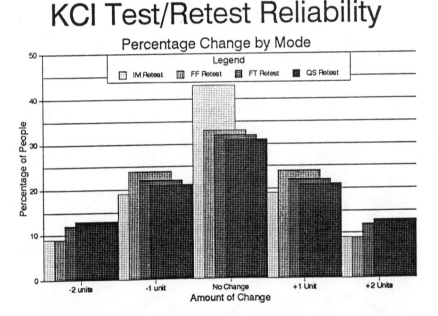

KCI Test/Retest Reliability
Percentage Change by Mode

To further test the reliability of the KCI, a 1992 study was done on a sample of 43 sets of test-retest results drawn from pooled KCI results. The results were compared to determine the frequency of change between zones (Resist, Accommodate, and Insist) from the initial test to the retest. Theoretically, movement between zones, even though it may be a change of only one unit, is less likely than a change of one unit within a zone. In over 96 percent of the cases, there was no change between zones from the test to the retest. This study has been replicated in numerous business environments with results within 2 percent of these figures in each mode.

The strong test-retest correlation and the comparatively small percentage of changes that fell beyond the standard error of measurement of the test are persuasive evidence that conative characteristics measured by the KCI are relatively constant over time and represent appropriate criteria for job-selection testing, which must not test criteria likely to change over time.

BIBLIOGRAPHY

Abel, D. C. *Freud on Instinct and Morality.* Albany: State University of New York Press, 1989.

Akert, K. T. *The Frontal Granular Cortex and Behavior.* New York: McGraw-Hill, 1964.

Anderson, J. R., and G. H. Bower. *Human Associative Memory.* Washington, DC: Hemisphere, 1974.

Anderson, J. R., P. J. Kline, and C. M. Beasley, Jr. "Complex Learning Process." In Vol. 2 of *Aptitude, Learning and Instruction: Cognitive Process Analysis of Learning and Problem Solving.* Hillsdale, NJ: Erlbaum, 1980.

Anderson, R. C., R. J. Spiro, and W. F. Montague. *Schooling and the Acquisition of Knowledge.* Hillsdale, NJ: Erlbaum, 1987.

Atkinson, J. W., and D. Birch. *The Dynamics of Action.* New York: Wiley, 1970.

Atkinson, J. W., and N. T. Feather. *A Theory of Achievement Motivation.* New York: Wiley, 1966.

Babson, R. W. *Instincts and Emotions, Should They Be Suppressed or Harnessed?* London: Faber & Faber, 1929.

Bakan, D. *On Method.* San Francisco: Jossey-Bass, 1967.

Bernard, L. L. *Instinct.* New York: Arno Press, 1979.

Birney, R. C. *Instinct, an Enduring Problem in Psychology: Selected Readings*, Robert C. Birney and Richard C. Teevan, eds. Princeton: Van Nostrand, 1961.

Bower, G. H. "Cognitive Psychology: An Introduction." In Vol. 1 of *Handbook of Learning and Cognitive Processes*. Hillsdale, NJ: Erlbaum, 1975.

Brimelow, P., and L. Spencer. "When Quotas Replace Merit, Everybody Suffers." *Forbes*, February 15, 1993, pp. 80–102.

Broadbent, D. E. *Decisions and Stress*. New York: Academic Press, 1971.

Bronowski, J. *The Ascent of Man*. Boston: Little, Brown, 1973.

Brown, J. W. "A Prelude to the Goldberg Variations on Motor Organization." *The Behavioral and Brain Sciences* 8 (1985): 588–89.

Brown, S. H. "Validity Generalization and Situational Moderation in the Life Insurance Industry." *Journal of Applied Psychology* 66 (1981): 664–70.

Brown, T. *Lectures on the Philosophy of the Human Mind*, Vol. I. Boston: Glazier & Co., 1828.

Brunswik, E. *Perception and the Representative Design of Psychological Experiments*. Berkeley: University of California Press, 1956.

Calfee, R. C. "Sources of Dependency in Cognitive Processes." In *Cognition and Instruction*. Hillsdale, NJ: Erlbaum, 1976.

Campbell, J. P. "Psychometric Theory." In *Handbook of Industrial and Organizational Psychology*. Chicago: Rand McNally, 1976, pp. 185–222.

Campbell, J. *The Power of Myth*. New York: Doubleday, 1988.

Carlyn, M. "An Assessment of the Myers-Briggs Type Indicator." *Journal of Personality Assessment* 41 (1977): 461–73.

Cattell, R. B. *Personality: A Systematic, Theoretical, and Factual Study*. New York: McGraw-Hill, 1950.

Cattell, R. B., and H. J. Butcher. *The Prediction of Achievement and Creativity*. Indianapolis: Bobbs-Merrill, 1968.

Chanin, M., and J. A. Schneer. "A Study of the Relationship between Jungian Personality Dimensions and Conflict-handling Behavior." *Human Relations* 37 (1984): 863–79.

Charlesworth, W. R. "Human Intelligence as Adaptation: An Ethological Approach." In *The Nature of Intelligence*. Hillsdale, NJ: Erlbaum, 1976.

Chopra, D. *Magical Mind, Magical Body*. Chicago: Nightingale Conant, 1990.

Conner, D. R. *Managing at the Speed of Change: How Resilient Managers Succeed and Prosper Where Others Fail.* New York: Villard, 1993.

Cook, M. *Personnel Selection and Productivity.* New York: Wiley, 1988.

Craig, R. L. *Training and Development Handbook: A Guide to Human Resource Development.* New York: McGraw-Hill, 1976.

Coan, R. W. "Critique of the Myers-Briggs Type Indicator." In Vol. 1 of *The Eighth Mental Measurement Yearbook.* Highland Park: Gryphon, 1978, pp. 973–75.

Cohen, M. D., and J. G. March. *Leadership and Ambiguity: The American College President.* New York: McGraw-Hill, 1974.

Cole, M., and S. Schribner. *Culture and Thought: A Psychological Introduction.* New York: Wiley, 1974.

Cooper, L. A. "Spatial Information Processing: Strategies for Research." In Vol. 1 of *Aptitude, Learning and Instruction: Cognitive Process Analysis of Aptitudes.* Hillsdale, NJ: Erlbaum, 1980.

Covey, S. R. *The Seven Habits of Highly Effective People.* New York: Simon and Schuster, 1989.

Crano, W. D. "Causal Analyses of the Effects of Socioeconomic Status and Initial Intellectual Endowment on Patterns of Cognitive Development and Academic Achievement." In *The Aptitude-Achievement Distinction.* Monterey: CTB/McGraw-Hill, 1974.

Cronbach, L. J., and R. E. Snow. *Aptitudes and Instructional Methods: A Handbook for Research on Interactions.* New York: Irvington, 1977.

Damasio, A. R. "Understanding the Mind's Will." *The Behavioral and Brain Sciences* 8 (1984): 589–90.

Davenport, T. H. *Process Innovation: Reengineering Work through Information Technology.* Boston: Harvard Business School Press, 1993.

Dibblee, G. B. *Instinct and Intuition: A Study in Mental Duality.* London: Faber & Faber, 1920.

Donagan, A. *Studies in Philosophical Psychology—Choice, the Essential Element in Human Action.* New York: Routledge & Kegan Paul, 1987.

Druckman, D., and R. A. Bjork. *In the Mind's Eye: Enhancing Human Performance.* Washington, DC: National Academy Press, 1991.

———. *Advances in Psychology—Volitional Action: Conation and Control.* New York: North-Holland, 1989.

Encyclopedia of Psychology, Vol. 2. New York: Wiley, 1984.

Ericsson, K. A., and H. A. Simon. "Verbal Reports as Data." *Psychological Review* 87 (1980): 215–51.

Estes, W. K. "An Associative Basis for Coding and Organization." In *Coding Processes in Human Memory*. Washington, DC: Winston, 1972.

Farber, L. H. *The Ways of the Will: Essay Toward a Psychology and Psychopathology of Will*. London: Constable, 1966.

Faris, R. E. L. "Reflections on the Ability Dimensions in Human Society." *American Sociological Review* 26 (1961): 835–43.

Ferguson, G. A. "On Learning and Human Ability." *Canadian Journal of Psychology* 8 (1954): 95–112.

Flaatten, P. O., D. J. McCubbrey, P. D. O'Riordan, and K. Burgess. *Foundations of Business Systems*. Hinsdale, IL: Dryden, 1992.

Fleishman, E. A. "Toward a Taxonomy of Human Performance." *American Psychologist* 8 (1975): 1127–49.

Fletcher, R. *Instinct in Man in the Light of Recent Work in Comparative Psychology*. London: Unwin University Books, 1968.

French, J. W. "The Relationship of Problem-Solving Styles to the Factor Composition of Tests." *Educational and Psychological Measurement* 25 (1965): 9–28.

Garcia, J., and R. Robertson. *The Evolution of Learning Mechanisms*. 1984.

Garfield, S L., and A. E. Bergin. *Handbook of Psychotherapy and Behavior Change: An Empirical Analysis*. New York: Wiley, 1978.

Gholar, C. R. "Wellness Begins When the Child Comes First: The Relationship Between the Conative Domain and the School Achievement Paradigm." Paper presented at the Annual Convention of the American Association for Counseling and Development, Reno, Nevada, 1991.

Gibson, J. J. *Army Air Force Aviation Psychology Program, Rep. No. 7: Motion Picture Testing and Research*. Washington, DC: U.S. Government Printing Office, 1947.

Goldberg, G. "Where There is a 'Will,' There Is a Way (to Understand It)." *The Behavioral and Brain Sciences* 8 (1985): 601–604.

Goodnow, J. J. "The Nature of Intelligent Behavior: Questions Raised by Cross-cultural Studies." In *The Psycholoy of Egon Brunswik*. New York: Holt, Rinehart & Winston, 1966.

Halisch, F., and J. Kuhl. *Motivation, Intention and Volition*. New York: Springer-Verlag, 1987.

Hamilton, Sir William. *Lectures on Metaphysics and Logic*, Vol. 2. Boston: Gould and Lincoln, 1860.

Hammer, M. "Reengineering Work: Don't Automate, Obliterate." *Harvard Business Review* 68 (1990): 104–12.

Hartigan, J. A., and A. K. Widgdor. *Fairness in Employment Testing: Validity Generalization, Minority Issues, and the General Aptitude Test Battery.* Washington, DC: National Academy Press, 1989.

Heckhausen, H., and J. Kuhl. "From Wishes to Action: The Dead Ends and Shortcuts on the Long Way to Action." In *Goal-Directed Behavior: Psychological Theory and Research on Action.* Hillsdale, NJ: Erlbaum, 1985, pp. 134–59.

Hellriegel, D., and J. W. Slocum. "Preferred Organizational Designs and Problem-Solving Styles: Interesting Companions." In *Human Systems Management* 7 (1980): 151–58.

Helson, H. *Adaption-Level Theory: An Experimental and Systematic Approach to Behavior.* New York: Harper & Row, 1964.

Henderson, J., and N. Venkatraman. "Strategic Alignment: A Model for Organizational Information Through Information Technology." In *Transforming Organizations.* New York: Oxford University Press, 1992.

Herschberger, W. A. *Volitional Control: Conation and Control.* Amsterdam: Elsevier Science, 1989.

Heuer, S. *Perspectives on Perception and Action.* Hillsdale, NJ: Erlbaum, 1987.

Hilgard, E. R. *Divided Consciousness: Multiple Controls in Human Thought and Action.* New York: Wiley, 1977.

————. "The Trilogy of the Mind: Cognition Affection and Conation." *Journal of the History of Behavioral Sciences* 16 (1980): 107–17.

Hinde, R. A. *Instinct and Intelligence.* London: Oxford University Press, 1976.

Hogan, J., and R. Hogan. *Business and Industry Testing: Current Practices and Test Reviews.* Austin: Pro-Ed, 1990.

Howard, G. S., and C. G. Conway. "Can There be an Empirical Science of Volitional Action?" *American Psychologist* 41 (1986): 1241–51.

Howard, G. S., and P. R. Myers. "Predicting Human Behavior: Comparing Idiographic, Nomothetic, and Agenetic Methodologies." *Journal of Counseling Psychology* 37 (1990): 227–33.

Hoy, F., and D. K. Hellriegel. "The Kilmann and Herden Model of Organizational Effectiveness Criteria for Small Business Managers." *Academy of Management Journal* 25 (1983): 308–22.

Huber, G. P. "Cognitive Style as a Basis for MIS and DSS Designs: Much Ado about Nothing." *Management Science* 29 (1983): 567–79.

Hunt, E. "Three Faces of Intelligence." Paper presented at NATO Conference on Intelligence and Learning, 1979.

Hyatt, C., and L. Gottlieb. *When Smart People Fail.* New York: Simon and Schuster, 1987.

James, W. *Principles of Psychology.* New York: Holt, 1890.

Johnston, C. "Cognition, Commitment. and Conation in Interdependent Team Leadership." Paper presented at the American Educational Research Association, Atlanta, Georgia, 1993.

Jung, C. G. *Psychological Types.* London: Routledge and Kegan, 1923.

Kant, I. *The Critique of Judgment.* Indianapolis: Hackett Publishing, 1987.

Kaufmann, W. *Discovering the Mind,* Vol. Two. New York: McGraw-Hill, 1980,

Keen, P. G. W. *Shaping the Future: Business Design through Information.* Boston: Harvard Business School Press, 1991.

Kemp, T. L. *Indications of Instinct.* London: Longman, Brown, Green and Longmans, 1854.

Kerin, R. A., and J. W. Slocum. "Decision-Making Style and Acquisition of Information: Further Exploration of the Myers-Briggs Type Indicator." *Psychological Reports* 29 (1981): 132–34.

Kilmann, R. A., and V. Taylor. "A Contingency Approach to Laboratory Learning: Psychological Types Versus Experimental Norms." *Human Relations* 21 (1974): 891–909.

Klahr, D. "Designing a Learner: Some Questions." In *Cognition and Instruction.* Hillsdale, NJ: Erlbaum, 1976.

Kolbe, K. *The Conative Connection.* Reading, MA: Addison-Wesley, 1990.

Kuhl, J. "Volitional Aspects of Achievement Motivation and Learned Helplessness: Toward a Comprehensive Theory of Action Control." In Vol. 12 of *Progress in Experimental Personality Research.* New York: Academic Press, 1984, pp. 99–170.

———. "Volitional Mediators of Cognition-Behavior Consistency: Self-Regulatory Processes and Action Versus State Orientation" In *Action Control: From Cognition to Behavior.* New York: Springer-Verlag, 1985, pp. 101–28.

———. "Motivation and Information-Processing: A New Look at Decision-Making, Dynamic Change, and Action Control." In *The Handbook of Motivation and Cognition: Foundation of Social Behavior.* New York: Guilford Press, 1986, pp. 404–34.

Lazarick, D. L., S. S. Fishbein, and M. A. Loiello. "Practical Investigations of Volition." *Journey of Counseling Psychology* 35 (1988): 15–26.

Lent, R. H., H. A. Aurbach, and L. S. Levin. "Predictors: Criteria and Significant Results." *Personnel Psychology* 24 (1971): 519–33.

Lewis, C. S. *The Problem of Pain*. New York: Macmillan, 1962.

Locke, E. A. "The Nature of Causes of Job Satisfaction." In *Handbook of Industrial and Organizational Psychology*. Chicago: Rand McNally, 1976, pp. 1297–1350.

Loevinger, J. "Objective Tests as Instruments of Psychological Theory." *Psychological Reports* 3 (1957): 635–94.

Loh, L., and N. Venkatraman. "Determinants of Information Technology Outsourcing: A Cross-sectional Analysis." *Journal of Management Information Systems* 9 (1992): 7–24.

Lohman, D. F. *Spatial Ability: A Review and Reanalysis of the Correlational Literature* (Technical Report No. 8). Stanford: Stanford University School of Education, Aptitude Research Project, 1979.

Lundholm, H. *Conation and Our Conscious Life*. Durham: Duke University Press, 1934.

Malone, M. *Psychetypes*. New York: Dutton, 1977.

Manz, C. C., and H. P. Sims, Jr. *Superleadership: The Art of Leading Others to Lead Themselves*. New York: Berkley, 1990.

March, J. G., and J. P. Olsen. *Ambiguity and Choice in Organizations*. Bergen: Universitetsforlaget, 1976.

Markowitsch, H. J. *Information Processing by the Brain*. Toronto: Hans Huber Publishers, 1988.

Martin, E. W., D. W. DeHayes, J. A. Hoffer, and W. C. Perkins. *Managing Information Technology*. New York: Macmillan, 1991.

Mason, R., and I. I. Mitroff. "A Program of Research on Management Information Systems." *Management Science* 19 (1973): 475–78.

May, G. G. *Will and Spirit: A Contemplative Psychology*. San Francisco: Harper & Row, 1983.

May, R. *The Courage to Create*. New York: Norton, 1975.

———. *Love and Will*. New York: Norton, 1969.

McDougall, W. *An Introduction to Social Psychology*. London: Methuen, 1908.

———. *Outline of Psychology*. New York: Scribner's, 1923.

Mearns, H. *Creative Power: The Education of Youth in the Creative Arts.* New York: Dover, 1958.

Mehrabian, A. *Analysis of Personality Theories.* Prentice-Hall, 1968.

Mehring, T. A. "Motivation and Mildly Handicapped Learners." *Focus on Exceptional Children* 22 (1991): 1–14.

Melden, A. I. *Free Action.* London: Humanities Press, 1961.

Mendelsohn, G. A. "Critique of the Myers-Briggs Type Indicator." In *The Sixth Mental Measurement Yearbook.* Highland Park: Gryphon, 1970, pp. 1126–27.

Mestrovic, S. G. "Rethinking the Will and Idea of Sociology in the Light of Schopenhauer's Philosophy." *The British Journal of Sociology* 40 (1989): 271–93.

Mitroff, I. I., and R. H. Kilmann. "Stories Managers Tell: A New Tool for Organizational Problem Solving." *Management Review* 64 (1975): 18–28.

Moran, R. T., and P. R. Harris. *The International Management Productivity Series: Managing Cultural Synergy.* Houston: Gulf Publishing Company, 1982.

Morgan, C. L. *Habit and Instinct.* New York: Arno Press, 1973.

Murray, P. T. *Studies in the History of Philosophy—Hegel's Philosophy of Mind and Will.* Lewiston, NY: E. Mellen Press, 1991.

Nagera, H. *Basic Psychoanalytic Concepts on the Theory of Instincts.* London: Allen & Unwin, 1970.

Neisser, U. *Cognition and Reality: Principle and Implications of Cognitive Psychology.* San Francisco: Freeman, 1976.

Newell, A., and H. A. Simon. *Human Problem Solving.* Englewood Cliffs: Prentice-Hall, 1972.

Payne, J. W., M. L. Braunstein, and J. S. Carroll. "Exploring Predecisional Behavior: An Alternative Approach to Decision Research." *Organizational Behavior and Human Performance* 22 (1978): 17–44.

Pear, T. H. *Are There Human Instincts?* Manchester, 1942.

Peters, T. *Thriving on Chaos: Handbook for a Management Revolution.* London: Pan Books, 1989.

Premier's Council Report: People and Skills in the New Global Economy. Ontario: Queen's Printer for Ontario, 1990.

Rank, O. *Complete Works of Dr. Otto Rank—Truth and Reality.* New York: Norton, 1978.

Riopelle, A. J. "Instinct." In *Animal Problem Solving: Selected Readings.* Baltimore: Penguin Books, 1967.

Rivers, W. H. *Instinct and the Unconscious.* Cambridge: University Press, 1920.

Robey, D., and W. Taggart. "Measuring Managers' Minds: The Assessment of Style in Human Information Processing." *Academy of Management Review* 6 (1981): 375–83.

Rosenthal, R. *Experimenter Effects in Behavioral Research.* New York: Appleton-Century-Crofts, 1966.

Russell, B. *The Analysis of Mind.* London: G. Allen & Unwin, 1921.

Scarr, S. "Heritability and Educational Policy: Genetic and Environmental Effects on I.Q., Aptitude and Achievement." In *Educational Psychologist,* September 1979.

Scarr, S., and R. A. Weinberg. "The Influence of 'Family Background' on Intellectual Attainment." *American Sociological Review* 43 (1978): 674–92.

Schoolland, J. B. *Are There Any Innate Behavior Tendencies?* n.p., 1942.

Schopenhauer, A. *On the Fourfold Root of the Principle of Sufficient Reason.* La Salle: Open Court, 1974

————. *On the Will in Nature: A Discussion of the Corroborations from the Empirical Sciences.* New York: St. Martin's, 1991.

Schweiger, D. M. "Is the Simultaneous Verbal Protocol a Viable Method for Studying Managerial Problem Solving and Decision Making?" *Academy of Management Journal* 26 (1983): 185–92.

Schweiger, D. M., and A. G. Jago. "Problem-Solving Styles and Participative Decision-Making." *Psychological Reports* 50 (1982): 1311–16.

Senchuk, D. M. *Against Instinct: From Biology to Philosophical/Psychology.* Philadelphia: Temple University Press, 1991.

Servan-Schreiber, J.-L. *The Art of Time.* Reading, MA: Addison-Wesley, 1989.

Shepherd, G. M. *The Synaptic Organization of the Brain—An Introduction.* London: Oxford, 1974.

Sieber, J. E., H. F. O'Neil Jr., and S. Tobias. *Anxiety, Learning and Instruction.* Hillsdale, NJ: Erlbaum, 1977.

Simon, H. A. "Identifying Basic Abilities Underlying Intelligent Performance of Complex Tasks." In *The Nature of Intelligence.* Hillsdale, NJ: Erlbaum, 1976.

Slocum, J. W. "Does Cognitive Style Affect Diagnosis and Intervention Strategies of Change Agents?" *Group and Organization Studies* 3 (1978): 199–210.

Snow, R. E. "Aptitude Processes." In *Aptitude, Learning and Instruction: Vol. 1, Cognitive Process Analysis of Aptitude.* Hillsdale, NJ: Erlbaum, 1980.

———. "Intelligence for the Year 2001." *Intelligence* 4 (1980): 185–99.

———. "Representative and Quasi-Representative Designs for Research on Teaching." In *Review of Research in Education*, Vol. 4. Itasca, IL: Peacock, 1977.

———. "Research on Aptitudes: A Progress Report." In *Review of Research in Education*, Vol. 4. Itasca, IL: Peacock, 1977.

———. "Theory and Method for Research on Aptitude Processes." *Intelligence* 2(1977): 225–78.

Steckroth, R., J. W. Slocum, and H. P. Sims. "Organizational Roles, Cognitive Roles and Problem-Solving Styles." *Journal of Experimental Learning and Stimulation* 2 (1980): 77–87.

Sternberg, R. J. *Beyond I.Q.: A Triarchic Theory of Human Intelligence.* Cambridge: Cambridge University Press, 1985.

———. *Intelligence, Information Processing and Analogical Reasoning: The Componential Analysis of Human Abilities.* Hillsdale, NJ: Erlbaum, 1977.

———. "Towards the Unified Componential Theory of Human Intelligence I: Fluid Abilities." Paper presented at NATO Conference on Intelligence and Learning, 1979.

Sundberg, N. D. "Critique of the Myers-Briggs Type Indicator." In *The Sixth Mental Measurement Yearbook.* Highland Park: Gryphon, 1970, 1127–30.

Svenson, O. "Process Descriptions of Decision Making." *Organizational Behavior and Human Performance* 23 (1979): 86-112.

Swann, W. B., and R. J. Ely. "A Battle of Wills: Self-Verification Versus Behavioral Confirmation." *Journal of Personality and Social Psychology* 46 (1984): 1287–1302.

Tanner, D. *You Just Don't Understand: Women and Men in Conversation.* New York: Ballantine, 1991.

Tate, J. J. "Identification of Individualized Self-Management Activities Emphasizing Achievement Motivation, Goal Setting, Conation, Attention Control and Locus of Control as Elements of Curriculum in a Stop

Smoking Program." In Vol. 47 (6-A) of *Dissertation Abstracts International*, 2037. Pittsburgh: Dissertation Abstracts International, 1986.

Taussig, F. W. *Inventors and Money-Makers*. New York: Macmillan, 1930.

Tead, O. *The Art of Leadership*. New York: McGraw-Hill, 1935.

Thayer, P. W. "Something Old. Something New." *Personnel Psychology* 30 (1977): 513–24.

Thompson, W. I. *The Time Falling Bodies Take to Light*. New York: St. Martin's, 1981.

Tinbergen, N. *The Study of Instinct*. New York: Oxford University Press, 1989.

Tolman, E. C. *Purposive Behavior in Animals and Men*. New York: Meredith, 1967.

Upham, T. C. *A Philosophical and Practical Treatise on the Will*. New York: Harper & Brothers, 1845.

Van Inwagen, P. *An Essay of Freewill*. Oxford: Clarendon Press, 1983.

Vessey, G. N. A. "Volition." *Philosophy* 64 (1964): 352–65.

Vitalari, N. P. "Knowledge as a Basis for Expertise in Systems Analysis: An Empirical Study." *MIS Quarterly* 9 (1985): 221–41.

Webb, N. M. *Learning in Individual and Small Group Settings* (Technical Report No. 7). Stanford: Stanford University School of Education Aptitude Research Project, 1977.

Wechsler, D. "Cognitive, Conative, and Non-Intellective Intelligence." *American Psychologist* 5 (1950): 78–83.

Weiner, B. *An Attributional Theory of Motivation and Emotion*. New York: Springer-Verlag, 1986.

Wertheimer, M. *Productive Thinking*. New York: Harper & Brothers, 1945.

White, F. C. *On Schopenhauer's Fourfold Root of the Principle of Sufficient Reason*. New York: E. J. Brill, 1992.

Woller, A. B. *Duns Scotus on the Will and Morality*. Washington, DC: Catholic University of America Press, 1986.

Ylvisker, P. N. "Teaching About a Human Instinct." *Liberal Education* 74 (1988): 26–36.

Zaleznik, A. "Managers and Leaders: Are They Different?" In *Harvard Business Review*, March–April, 1992, pp. 126–35.

ACKNOWLEDGMENTS

I feel as if I've spent the two years of writing this book in a constant battle to preserve my creative integrity. It's difficult enough to write a book—in this case to find the words to articulate a concept; it's even more difficult to do it within a system that betrays the very principles about which you are writing. The only way it has been possible to finally complete this imperfect effort has been with the amazing level of commitment of many good friends and cohorts. Several people have made great sacrifices of their own creative energies to help me.

Dr. Maren Mouritsen, the truest kind of friend, shared my frustrations and helped focus my energies. Dr. Ryan Thomas, Dr. Tammie Quick, Lynette Simmons, and Vally Sharpe believed so strongly in the project and contributed so much effort that they frequently renewed my faith in the purposes behind it. My daughter, Karen Kolbe, was a fine editor who gave helpful criticisms and sensitive support. Organizational expert Dr. Clyde Stutts' detailed comments on proposed chapters were insightful and thought-provoking. Maria Muto's expertise in training and team building provided clarifications and editorial assistance. Bruce Wexler's and Sheila Whalen's reviews of early versions of this work helped keep it alive. Diana Weistart, a friend and editor with uncompromising values, challenged me to fight for what I believed was needed in this manuscript. Gail Ross had the determination to find the right publisher and negotiate for the best product. Kenn Rapp, an experienced copy editor, kept his professionalism while reviewing his step-mom's manuscript. Alan and Amy Rapp supported my need to be me. David Kolbe used his legal mind to help me question, without judging my answers.

I'm indebted to the 410 people I interviewed for *Pure Instinct* and the Kolbe consultants who shared their professional experiences. While only a few could be included by name, all of their stories have added to the substance of this material and to my understanding of the implications of instinct on performance. The entire staff at KolbeConcepts, Inc., has been committed to the quality of the research and documentation of examples used here and I appreciate their high Level of Effort.

Sandy Wascher coordinated every aspect of this project, which involved literally thousands of phone calls and worldwide correspondence that fills three file cabinets. I value her loyalty and the fact that she has handled many difficult situations with gumption. She and my husband, Will Rapp, have shown great patience and understanding. Will's expertise in the Kolbe Concept has made him the one person I could depend upon to be sure I was saying what I meant to say.

INDEX

COMPLETING THE KOLBE CONATIVE INDEX

The KCI is available on page 349. You may complete it by cutting out the Response Form on page 355 and filling in the circles that correspond to the questions on the previous pages. You do not have to mark on the KCI or cut it out of the book.

You may choose to have your KCI result sent as a part of the Kolbe Catalyst™ program or separately.

Option 1:

Kolbe Catalyst includes:
Prescriptions for professional and career development.

a.   Your KCI result with eight pages of prescriptions for using your talents, avoiding stress, communicating effectively, and maximizing available time.

b.   A Natural Advantage tape cassette on which I provide information regarding your MO and how you can benefit from it.

c.   A KCI-B, which will be sent to you with the above items. After you complete and return it to my office, I will send you three pages interpreting your self-expectations in a job situation.

d.   An Analysis of Stress Factors, which provides information on pressures you may have by working against
your own grain and recommendations for reducing such
stress.

e.   Career advice pamphlet with recommendations suited to
your KCI result.

Kolbe Catalyst = U.S. $150

Option 2:

MO of Success includes:
KCI result
Natural Advantage tape

MO of Success = U.S. $68

KCI results will be sent only to the person completing the MO of Success
or to a certified Kolbe Consultant. It is inappropriate to use this information to make management decisions without a trained expert available
to analyze the implications. For information on certification as an in-
house expert or external consultant, please contact KolbeConcepts, Inc.,
at our Phoenix address.

For information on the KCI-A, B, and C in Spanish, please inquire at our
office.

Send Order Form and KCI Response Form with payment to:

KolbeConcepts, Inc.
3421 North 44th Street
Phoenix, Arizona 85018

Because the results of the Kolbe Conative Index are computer generated,
it is important to carefully cut the Response Form from the book. The
Response Form can only be duplicated after it is removed, in order to
ensure the accuracy of the scoring process. I realize that cutting a page
from a book is an abhorrent act to many people, but this form was
inserted for the sole purpose of being removed.

There are two responses for each of the 36 questions—MOST (M) and LEAST (L). Mark the ONE response that best describes how you would MOST likely act and the ONE response that best describes how you would LEAST likely approach the same situation. The Response Form has one column for each of the four pages of questions. Match the number in the response box with the question number. Fill in the circles completely with a soft lead pencil and be sure to erase any changes.

Please complete the information on the back of the Response Form and mail to the address above. We will process your KCI and return it within three weeks.

Example

1. If I were solving a difficult problem, I would rely most heavily on my:
    skill
    research
    ability to structure
    experimentation

RIGHT

WRONG

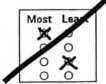

WRONG

1   **If I were solving a difficult problem, I would rely on my:**
skill
research
ability to structure
experimentation

2   **If I believed something important could be made to help humanity, I would:**
investigate it
design it
sell or promote it
build it

3   **If I were told to hurry finishing a project, I would:**
skip to the bottom line
decide what could be done properly
work diligently until time was up
consider craftsmanship most important

4   **If I were trying to get off the hook for something, my arguments would be:**
consistent
unique
detailed
technical

5   **If I were to win a contest, it would be for:**
craftsmanship
neatness
originality
being the most realistic

6   **If a task required my best work, I would:**
double check results
practice it
take it on as a challenge
do adequate research

7   **If I got into trouble, it would be because I:**
was bored
couldn't keep my hands off things
resisted change
wanted to know too much

8   **If I were deciding whether to use a new method, I would consider its:**
practicality
clarity
impact
durability

9   **If I were working as a member of a group, I would:**
tackle physical tasks
have lots of ideas
be efficient
outline goals and objectives

10   **If I had my choice, I would work for:**
security
upgraded equipment
commissions
a significant title

11   **If I can, I avoid:**
guessing
discussions
machinery
interruptions

12   **If I won a prize for artistic effort, it would be for:**
neatness and interesting patterns
realism, perspective or good detail
good use of color
model building, sculpture

13   **If I were teased about a characteristic, it would be:**
touchiness
impulsiveness
preciseness
predictability

14   **If I were demonstrating my talents, it would be with:**
writing and data
diagrams
speaking
models

15   **If I were in charge of a project, I would:**
meet specifications
use quality materials
be cost effective
add my own ideas

16   **If I were working to my greatest potential, my activities would be:**
varied
structured
researched
demonstrated

17   **If I were setting standards, I would find it important that they be:**
visible
uniform
flexible
measurable

18   **If I were criticized, it would be for being too:**
impatient
literal
structured
argumentative

19 **If I were assigned one task, I would begin by:**
probing
constructing
innovating
planning

20 **If I were exploring a new object, I would:**
check how it was made
approach it systematically
examine it in detail
have a strong first impression

21 **If I were explaining an idea, I would be :**
spontaneous
methodical
technical
thorough

22 **If communicating an idea, I would:**
provide written proof
use props
use imagination
use charts and graphs

23 **If gathering information, I would:**
put it in a clear format
get thorough background material
seek a variety of unusual sources
explore physically

24 **If I were describing a place I had visited, I would mention:**
location or placement
specifics and details
quality of equipment and materials
the general atmosphere

25 **If I earned recognition, it would probably be for:**
speed and cleverness
strength and endurance
dependability and design
judgment and accuracy

26 **If I were choosing my own work situation, I would:**
do the work myself
have others available for brainstorming
be able to delegate
have the work flow to me smoothly

27 **If free to be myself, I would get things done by:**
establishing priorities
planning ahead
quality craftmanship
taking on challenges

28 **If I were concentrating on a single effort, I would be:**
efficient
intuitive
skillful
thorough

29 **If I were working on a puzzle, I would try:**
working against a deadline
putting physical pieces together
using my memory for facts
organizing the options

30 **If I were asked to prove my point, I would:**
show it in some form
explain my method
explain the pros and cons
explain the benefits

31 **If I could do things my way, they would get done:**
realistically
physically
rapidly
cautiously

32 **If I were setting up a display, I would:**
do it in an orderly way
try clever, unique ways to do it
find what worked in the past
set it up personally

33 **If something in the system didn't work, I would:**
work around it
repair it
find out why
report it

34 **If I were trying something new, I would learn by:**
taking chances
practicing
reading about it
following examples

35 **If I were sharing results, my method would be:**
durable
exacting
coordinated
spontaneous

36 **If I ran a business, I would:**
provide steady performance
define realistic objectives
develop new products, or services
give high quality workmanship

Pg. xxx   Pg. xxx   Pg. xxx   Pg. xxx
M L   M L   M L   M L

Kolbe Conative Index®

RESPONSE FORM

Last Name

First Name

OFFICE USE ONLY

1 O O O O O
2 O O O O O
3 O O O O O
4 O O O O O
5 O O O O O
6 O O O O O
7 O O O O O
8 O O O O O
9 O O O O O
0 O O O O O

1   10   19   28
2   11   20   29
3   12   21   30
4   13   22   31
5   14   23   32
6   15   24   33
7   16   25   34
8   17   26   35
9   18   27   36

1337

Pure Instinct Order Form

Last Name:_____ First:_____ Initial:___ Sex: M

Street:_____

City:_____ State:_____ Zip:_____

Phone H:(_____)_____-_____ W:(_____)_____-_____

Fax Number:(_____)_____-_____

Please assist our Research by answering the following questions:

Employer:_____ Job Title:_____

# of Employees:_____ Years in Position:_____ Years with Company:_____

Circle one in each category:

Job Type:	Managerial	Professional Services	Unskilled	Skilled
	Educational	Admin/Clerical	Technical	Sales
	Public Safety	Job Applicant	Housewife	Studen

Education: Grade School   High School   Trade School

Jr. College   College (4 yr)   Post Graduate

Age: Under 20   21-30   31-40   41-50   51-60   61-70   Ove

Race: Hispanic   African Amer/Black   Asian/Pacific Islander

White/Caucasian   Native Amer/Amer Indian   Other _____

Annual Compensation (in thousands--US dollars): 0-10   11-20   21-30

31-40   41-50   51-60   61-70   71-80   81-90   91-100   over 100

ORDER FORM

_____ Option 1: Catalyst Program $150   *OR*   _____ Option 2: MO of Success $

Mastercard or VISA No._____

Name as it appears on card _____

Signature _____ Exp. Date _____

If paying by check: No. _____

Mail to: KolbeConcepts, Inc.   3421 North 44th Street   Phoenix, Arizona 85
PHONE: 1-800-642-2822